Rethinking the Education Improvement Agenda

Also available from Continuum

British Labour and Higher Education 1945 to 2000, Richard Taylor and
   Tom Steele
Philosophy of Education: An Introduction, edited by Richard Bailey
The Philosophy of Education, Richard Pring
Quality in Education, Denis Lawton, Jo Cairns and Roy Gardner

Rethinking the Education Improvement Agenda

A Critical Philosophical Approach

Kevin J. Flint and Nick Peim

continuum

Continuum International Publishing Group

The Tower Building   80 Maiden Lane
11 York Road   Suite 704
London SE1 7NX   New York NY 10038

www.continuumbooks.com

British Library Cataloguing-in-Publication Data
A catalogue record for this book is available from the British Library.

ISBN: 978-1-4411-2973-4 (paperback)
       978-1-4411-6189-5 (hardcover)

Library of Congress Cataloging-in-Publication Data
A catalog record for this book is available from the Library of Congress.

Typeset by Newgen Imaging Systems Pvt Ltd, Chennai, India
Printed and bound in Great Britain

Contents

Introduction

The inspiration for this book arose from our earlier paper, 'Testing Times', written for a specialist audience of educational philosophers (Peim and Flint, 2009). It had been concerned with the pervasive ethic of assessment and its relationship with strenuous ongoing efforts on an international scale to improve formal systems of education at all levels of practice. When a reviewer suggested we should develop our ideas about 'techno-logical enframing' – or simply 'the enframing' – into a book, the remark crystallized for us the need to address a social phenomenon that hardly seems to warrant a mention outside specialist philosophical discourses, including educational philosophy. This project brings with it the chal-lenge of connecting educational and philosophical discourses to develop a language for fresh and critical thinking about educational improve-ment. Paradoxically, our original paper – a critique of pervasive forms of educational practice and thinking identified with improvement – was already cut off from mainstream practices as a consequence of the his-torical unfolding of the enframing in education it had sought to question. The challenge became to develop a new language for educational improvement that connects more directly with educational practices and opens the possibility of radically rethinking practices, institutions and ingrained modes of understanding the 'world' of education.

Our main purpose in writing this book, therefore, is simple: we want to explore and encourage a new language to define educational improve-ment within the contemporary configuration of education. In this book, educational improvement is seen as a form of technology, not in the conventional sense, but as a particular way of revealing the world. We present this perhaps counter-intuitive argument by showing how it applies to educational discourses and their associated practices in a number of their obvious guises. Prominent in our thinking is the devel-opment of what we see as a new language for what has remained for many years a silent, powerful force in the world of education: the enframing.

Education has come to be occupied by enframing, we contend, in a double sense. First, we consider how in formal systems around the globe, technologies of schooling have come to significantly define 'education'. Although rarely explicitly, these technologies shape the world of education, ensuring that practices and people are transformed. Both individuals and populations are domesticated into becoming – in Foucault's sense – 'docile bodies', to be known, defined and rendered optimally viable within social, cultural and economic systems. Historically, schooling as a technology continues to function as the key means of transforming people into politically and culturally active citizens. We question the mechanisms and effects of those transformative apparatuses and processes. Chapter 8 brings into sharp relief the 'principle of assessment' as the primary shaper of educational practices in formal systems of schooling. Schooling has come to be based almost entirely on assessment as *the* defining measure of what counts as education. In this book, we take issue with that standpoint.

Secondly, education has also assumed the position of an ontological principle upon which any possible development of our societies is based. Just about every area of practice in the workplace has incorporated 'education and training' as the principle of development. Similarly, 'education and training' have become watchwords in any forms of management and leadership that want to be taken seriously throughout the developed world. In the academic world, 'education' has just about always constituted the grounds for the development of disciplined inquiry and practice and for achieving the highest levels of understanding. That function is now enmeshed in systems of regulation and control, involving benchmarks and quality assurance procedures, designed to render higher education useful and relevant. The stratification of qualifications in higher education follows the pattern of norm-related stratified levels of attainment in the nursery, at school and in Further Education, FE. All forms of learning in formal learning contexts, then, seem to have been gathered within the aegis of quantification.

Is it not also the case – and questionably so – that, given the contemporary significance of educational credentials and the impact education has on our sense of who and what we are, education more broadly defines our identity as well as our possibilities for becoming? We want to question the assumptions in that strong correlation of education with being.[1] Part of our questioning also aims to ask how education has come to function as a governmental apparatus within modern societies, that is, an apparatus primarily concerned with the 'conduct of conduct'. We wish to open questions about the possible foundation and application of education as an ontological principle inscribed in forms of 'governmentality', or mentalities of government mediating particular historical and cultural settings.

In writing this book we recognize that each one of us is already situated within our own particular historical and cultural settings. Kevin Flint is a senior lecturer in education at Nottingham Trent University who began his work there in teacher training and has now moved into research as one of the leaders of their professional doctoral programme. In that particular role over the past two years, Kevin has been concerned with understanding and finding ways of constituting meaningful spaces in the language of research in which individuals can be encouraged to develop their studies. Outside his professional work, Kevin has a strong background in mountaineering and rock-climbing.

Nick Peim is a senior lecturer in education at the University of Birmingham. He began working there as a tutor for the Post-Graduate Certificate of Education, PGCE, programme and migrated into teaching undergraduate educational studies, post-graduate research philosophy and doctoral supervision. Nick has published extensively in educational theory and philosophy in writings concerned with the nature of the school, the institutional history of state-sponsored education, the politics of the curriculum, and theories and philosophies of education. Much of this work has been dedicated to rethinking fundamental ideas about education and its role in the contemporary world, especially questioning its pretensions to social salvation.

Kevin writes:

> I can trace my own understanding of the enframing in language mediating practices back through my life in mountaineering. Although I was unaware of it at the time, my former obsession to climb harder routes, reach higher peaks and take on ever greater risks was essentially my very being in thrall to what I now see as the enframing. At the same time, I also recognized

---

1 'Being is that on the basis of which beings' or entities in the world 'are already understood' (Dreyfus, 1991: ix).

the way technological enframing opened up possibilities in life that were hitherto not possible without it. In rock-climbing and mountaineering I have always found a powerful motivator for keeping fit and healthy in a form of aesthetic engagement with the natural world. I understand this in the sense used by Spinoza in which nature is everything; it is all inclusive. Similarly, in technologies of modern medicine I have a particular appreciation of penicillin and other antibiotic agents, in their many different varieties, without which as a young child, like so many young people in earlier times, I would have almost certainly died (in my case, of pleurisy).

I now see us all variously caught up in, and continually adapting to, various forms of language mediating our lives. Language is our essential home. When combined with my many years experience as a science teacher and manager in secondary education, where I felt pushed – paradoxically – to take fewer risks, there seemed to be something similar at work to the enframing I found in the language of climbing and mountaineering.

The experience of my doctoral thesis and the opportunity to discover the works of leading European, post-modern thinkers, notably Heidegger, Derrida and many of their descendents, was pivotal in developing an understanding of the enframing in language that is common to my earlier domains of experience in both education and mountaineering. It also opened the possibility of further exploration that makes connections between philosophical discourse, educational practice and the way such practices mediate our understandings of what it means to be human in this post-modern age.

Much of my work at Nottingham Trent has been directed towards new ways of thinking and understanding the educational world we inhabit. After writing several papers and journal articles seeking, through scholarship, to challenge educational discourse, this book represents a significant milestone in the development of what I believe to be a complex, but highly relevant discussion about educational practice. Our primary approach in this entire book reflects Bertolt Brecht's technique of 'making strange the familiar' (Willett, 1971: 91). Our objective is to open a language for rethinking educational improvement in a number of its obvious and dominant forms.

Nick writes:

As an English graduate, embarking on a PGCE in 1975, influenced by F. R. Leavis and entranced by the new vision of social order that comprehensive education seemed to promise, I taught English in a large comprehensive school in a dynamic department that believed its duty was to convey real culture to the masses, including teaching Turgenev and Eliot with Certificate of Secondary Education (CSE), year 10 and encouraging all our charges to think of themselves as authentic creative writers. In spite of all our good intentions, patterns of examination success and failure followed the usual class-based pattern. In the late 1970s, when a colleague seconded to do educational research came back from time to time with news of alternative ways of understanding the cultural project of education, Althusser, Bourdieu and Gramsci helped to explain the apparently ingrained class bias in examination systems. At the same time, a new wave of ideas was confronting subject identity. English was being probed and problematized by the incursion of 'theory' – 'literary theory' in the first instance – but the impetus for this had been developments in philosophy in the history of ideas and in psychoanalysis. A new generation of resources for thinking about education, culture and schooling appeared. Foucault, Derrida and Lacan, often then represented as the vanguard of 'post-structuralism' in France, crossed the Channel in paperback and became readily available in direct form furnishing dynamic ideas on history, discourse, language, writing, thinking and subjectivity.

During the 1980s, as head of another large department in another large, comprehensive upper school, the extremely liberal examinations that had come with General Certificate of Secondary Education, GCSE, suggested that a new world order was on the horizon for English teachers. With local and national groups of like-minded colleagues, the work of transforming subject identity was under way at both 16+ and 18+ examination levels. We seriously considered the idea that the traditional subject's days were numbered and that the strange and arbitrary traditional configuration of language and textuality that had been English would inevitably be displaced by something closer to cultural studies. The range of theory now impinging on the main concerns of English was extensive and carried far-reaching implications. Or so it seemed.

Sociolinguistics, psychoanalysis, philosophy, the history of ideas, cultural studies, media studies: all provided ways of looking at and understanding the field of language and textuality quite beyond the ken of English. But the national curriculum, instituted by the 1988 Education Reform Act, put paid to the idea of an imminent school curriculum revolution. Some of the more hard-headed accounts of education history that were emerging out of the work of Michel Foucault now gathered force. Such histories problematized the very possibility of liberating education via changes to subject practices. What they taught essentially was that schooling had arisen as – and remained – a regime of 'governmentality'. This founding identity could not be shaken off by the desires or intentions of would-be reformers. The sociologists of education had to be taken seriously. Inspection regimes contributed to an increasing sense that schooling wasn't a free space of action and wasn't the natural ground of liberal – or any other kind – of reform. A new wave of bureaucracy within education put everyone and everything under increasing scrutiny. Life became more heavily norm related than ever: tables of attainment, benchmark statements for degree subjects and competences for teachers in training regulated professional life.

This process put reform into question and darkened the prospects of 'improvement' in the sense of liberation. In my own case, the interest in theory that had come through English had awoken a long-standing interest in philosophy. Long ago I'd read Wittgenstein. Theory in the work of Derrida, Foucault and Lacan was philosophical in character and strongly influenced by Heidegger, I discovered and read on. The European philosophical tradition, including Spinoza, Kant, Hegel and Nietzsche, seemed to have a great deal to offer in terms of understanding both the tradition of thinking that had informed the rise of the schooled society and the means for thinking beyond or outside it.

So my interest in education remained intense, a focus for all my other intellectual interests. The ground had shifted. The ontological perspective I'd been drawn to prompted a series of fundamental questions: What is education? What is the school? Why is the world today so strongly pervaded by the idea of education and the institutions of schooling? I remain actively interested in the rise of the schooled society and the history of education, its architecture and its social and temporal organization. I remain fascinated by the idea that the school is essentially, and in many positive ways, the key instrument of government in our kind of society. I am also interested in the way that the school works upon the very substance of the person – and therefore of the people – cultivating competences and tendencies within us, inviting us constantly to see ourselves as a project for improvement and development and encouraging us to be ever vigilantly working on ourselves. Working now in higher education, I am interested in parallels between school and university – intrigued, if often wearily beset by, the increasing bureaucratic controls conducted in the name of quality assurance and the current drive towards tangible, immediate and measurable 'impact'.

I remain fascinated by language issues in education and in social life generally, fed by an awareness of systemic functional linguistics, by modern British sociolinguistics and especially by philosophy of language. The twentieth century's obsession with language continues to provide productive ways of doing philosophy and, above all, exploring the relations between symbolic systems, history, identity and what gets all too easily described as reality. At the same time, reading Heidegger had stirred a sense of the big and disturbing question – 'the question of questions' – that opened the potential to call into question all our favourite assumptions and ways of thinking about the world. Derrida's deconstruction of Western metaphysics, opening up deconstruction and critique of historically sedimented systems of ideas; Lacan's elaboration of the role of the Symbolic Order as a complex patterning of the 'real'; and Foucault's development and application of 'discipline' in relation to modern institutions and forms of life – all seemed to offer a strong purchase on contemporary civil society. From these perspectives, the comfortable assumptions about education, progress and social transformation that I had entertained, that continued in a general if vague way to inform much educational thinking, had to be set against other ways of knowing our world.

In the context of our own settings it is perhaps not particularly surprising that in each of the chapters that follow, we have chosen to explore the various ways practitioners are positioned in the enframing in a number of discourses and practices. Each chapter, therefore, provides an occasion to explore what Michel Foucault called 'regimes of truth' that structure the instrumental rationality of the enframing. In so doing, each chapter opens reflection on the forces that are shaping discourses and colonizing their associated practices in the name of improvement. It is hoped that by developing a language that opens thinking in this way the book will contribute to a different form of debate about educational improvement, one which we hope will draw upon and bring closer philosophical discourse and practice.

Chapter 1, centring on the complex interrelationship between education, the school and the state, begins with a case study of Saltaire as an example of nineteenth-century philanthropy. It considers the school as a pivotal structure in the formation of the modern state and the rise of Foucault's bio-power and the development of technologies of the self as mechanisms in the governance of populations. The chapter traces the history of the school to its present formation under the rhetorics of improvement and lifelong learning.

Chapter 2 questions the ethic of improvement and the identities constituted in the play of difference in such language. It puts a spotlight on the ways in which discourses of improvement as regimes of truth define the nature of things in education, and how schools and other associated educational institutions function as governmental apparatuses. The various narrative structures and the metaphors they each reveal in the world of education are deconstructed. They each serve to illuminate the issue of professionality and how the practitioner is variously positioned within such discourses. In fact, two case studies of exemplary research projects provide examples of how even the most experienced researchers can still become locked within the contradictory ethic of improvement.

In Chapter 3, we examine the intensification of governmentality and its relationship with childhood. The argument draws on Foucault's concept of pastoral discipline that dominates modern regimes of care. We examine age stratification as a metonym for a technological world order that seeks to define and rank all that falls within its compass. The chapter raises concerns about the practices of person management and norms of development, which we see as intimately connected with the invention of 'childhood' and the grand epistemic change that occurred in the nineteenth century. The increasingly close association of state apparatus and the child is illuminated in and through various movements of transformation, not least the massification of higher education, the emergence of lifelong learning, the overarching framework of 'Every Child Matters' and various associated policy initiatives.

The subject of Chapter 4, educational research, has for many years set itself apart as a special and specific domain. Within this field, the principle of improvement has remained not only sovereign, but, we argue, it has become a production juggernaut that Giddens (1991) has seen as one of the consequences of modernity. We see the standard operative formula for research in the field as a perfect and self-enclosed hermeneutic circle. At the same time we also see that professional identity and attachment to knowledge in this field is grounded in the ethic of improvement. It is our contention that such an ethic constitutes the enframing, in which what counts as professional knowledge and practice is significantly delimited and constrained. We conclude this chapter highlighting resources that are available for thinking and acting otherwise.

At issue in Chapter 5 are those fundamental social technologies, schools and schooling, which are shown to be of considerable significance in governmental apparatuses. This chapter re-examines the history of the school as a governmental instrument, creating the context for explicating the key features of the contemporary complex institution, the school that exists under the sway of the techno-scientific ethic of improvement. It is our position that this ineluctable social phenomenon has been dominated by an empiricist enframing in which schooling and the curriculum continues to unfold and develop. The effects of an almost universal ethic of testing we connect with contemporary curriculum structures, pedagogic modalities and institutional priorities. We also consider the scandalous possibility that inequality is a systemic product of institutions of improvement. Finally, we consider the ways in which practitioners have become variously positioned within such discourses and their associated practices.

In our consideration of teacher education in Chapter 6, we begin by reminding readers that in England there has been a change of focus from professional development to practice in the wake of government legislation to introduce the national curriculum. We weigh the benefits of the emphasis on practice with the diminution of other kinds of knowledge. In the context of developing practice, we demonstrate how such developments and the policies informing them operate within a general ethos of performativity. The chapter offers historical insight taken from Kay-Shuttleworth's nineteenth-century vision of the 'coming' teacher, opening questions concerning the fundamental requirements of teacher identity at the inception of state-sponsored education. Reflecting on a number of contemporary strictures to professional identity, we explore several of Derrida's proposals for resistance, drawing on 'reform pedagogies', including Montessori, Freinet, the Dalton plan and the Greek concept of *paitheia*. In examining the mythology of teacher identity found in popular culture, we conclude this chapter by exploring the various ways in which the episteme of teacher identity colonizes particular practices in the mode of instrumental rationality.

Chapter 7, on leadership and management, focuses on the remaking of the welfare state. The literature of democratic participation is critically reviewed in relation to educational leadership and management. We examine the impact of democratic participation on practice and demonstrate how practitioners are positioned in relation to dominant discourses of educational change. The chapter analyses threats of competition and promises of social progress as allied means of effecting the realignment of the professional environment. The questionable concept of improvement as an organic discourse of change is subjected to ontological critique to illuminate the character of the manager. We also examine school performance management relative to social stratification and its assumption built into the management of performance of the role of education in the social order. In fact, we seek to show that the hierarchies of educational organizations are homologous with systematic social distinctions as opposed to offering a potential to enact social equality. In concluding this chapter we adopt a Lacanian perspective, which connects desire with the development of professional identity, rhetoric, aspirations and practices.

In Chapter 8, we explore the managerial relation between education and population in reference to lifelong learning. We illuminate how such discourses and practices begin when conception becomes public knowledge. The managerial relation between education and population through lifelong learning is shown to create a symbiosis between policy discourses, academic-professional discourses and emerging practices reflecting the enframing. Turning to consider the ethic of self improvement through learning, we see self development as the outward manifestation of enframing. In practice, the enframing that reveals lifelong learning is seen as a way of assuaging anxieties of the self caught up in the liquid modern world and a pedagogized society. A case study drawn from the Children's Fund examines the governmental significance of lifelong learning, addressing problematic identities at the level of the individual, the family and the community. The case study illuminates the positioning and repositioning of the self within such discourses as a product of technology enacted through a regime of care and improvement. The argument demonstrates how the multi-agency practitioner is the new invention of this regime of practice.

In concluding this book, Chapter 9 returns to the question of being and its relation to the field of education. At issue in this chapter is the questionable presupposition of a direct correspondence between numbers and how things *are*. The chapter takes a historical look at the authority of statistical data and its claims to demonstrate the reality of things in the field of education. It shows how the internal logic of numerical data appears to offer a stringent account of things, while it is already dislocated from the reality it purports to represent. It indicates how a mathematical logic holds sway within its own circular movement and that, outside that movement, the logic has no necessary purchase. Examples taken from discourses that draw upon statistical data are deconstructed to show how advocates use numeric data in seeking a purity of knowledge in the ghostly Platonic ideal of truth. The historical privileging of empiricism in the English cultural tradition is examined as a 'natural' grounding for numerical, statistically validated modalities of knowledge. We consider an alternative view whereby empirical reality is already compromised by the presence of a regime of truth. On this view, numerical distractions – that is, statistics – can be seen as a means for avoiding any confrontation with the issue of representation and its relation to being.

In returning to the question of being, the chapter concludes with a brief reflection on the various ways of thinking that the book as a whole has explored. While we are not attempting to provide any easy or ready-made solutions to the issues raised by the enframing, we hope that the arguments developed in each of the chapters will open further debate and the possibility of rethinking educational improvement in ways that develop the philosophical discourse about educational practice that Heidegger and Derrida inspired. Whether such hope is warranted is, perhaps, a matter of the hospitality given to the ideas explored in this book and any language that this discussion may have inspired in attempting to further develop the practice of ideas.

This book is the product of endless dialogue between the authors. It was closely planned and agreed. The labour of writing was then divided for the main chapters. Kevin J. Flint largely composed Chapters 2, 6, 7, 8 and 9. Nick Peim largely composed Chapters 1, 3, 4 and 5.

Kevin Flint and Nick Peim, July 2011.

Education, the School and the State

School and state: An ontological perspective

When educationists complain of too much state interference in education, they are making a powerful, and perhaps questionable, assumption. The assumption is that the state and education are, essentially, separate operations, areas or departments of existence, from a 'purely' educational point of view, therefore state interference in education is inappropriate; such interference transgresses a natural boundary and offends against the proprieties of identity for both education and state.

This chapter will explore this opposition between education and the state, especially in the light of the modern development of education in the United Kingdom, an exemplary case for 'the West'. One of the things we will explore is the rise of the schooled society and its recent (post-1988) intensification. Rather than arguing, as some educationalists do, for more separation between state and education, we will consider the coming together of state and education as a fact of a particular and unprecedented history. We will suggest that over the last 150 years or so, the growth of education has represented both a transformation of the state and a vast extension of state power (Wardle, 1974; Hunter, 1994). All attempts to recover a 'pure' educational space or practice or essence at the heart of this history, we will argue, are only possible by denying the ontological conditions grounding the 'modern' rise and proliferation of educational discourses, practices and institutions.

We will demonstrate the increasing convergence of state and education. We will further consider the possibly scandalous proposition, for educationists at least, that education has become the dominant modality of state power, exceeding in scope and significance the usual organs of state power, such as church, military and other explicitly government bodies. We will also consider that, beyond the walls of formal institutions of education, contemporary social life is characterized more and more as a 'pedagogized society', in the words of the educational sociologist Basil Bernstein, suggesting that teaching and learning relations dominate social relations and the distribution of recognized forms of knowledge is supremely important in social interactions in all spheres (Bernstein, 2000).

This chapter, then, will consider the rise of state schooling and its impact on populations from a less than usual perspective. We will describe this 'social technology' in terms of the characteristic features and functions of schooling seen through a specific philosophical perspective. We realize we are giving a very unconventional account of what the school is in the modern period. We will also seek to explain why the school takes this particular form in this particular era. In this account we will be partly following and transposing the general logic of the argument Foucault presents in *Discipline and Punish* concerning the transformation of social space, time and institutions in the modern period. We will note Foucault's account of a general and momentous transition from one dominant form of power – sovereign power – to another form of dominant power – capillary, or dispersed, 'bio-power'. In this transformation we will track the transformation of the state from a more centralized and visible apparatus of power to a dispersed state embodied and distributed in institutions, ideas and practices (Foucault, 1977, 2007). This new form of society – 'a pedagogized society' – is characterized by the proliferation and ubiquity of the school as a key instrument of its modus operandi.

As the state changed its nature – especially during the latter part of the eighteenth century and all through the nineteenth – so the practices and accoutrements of the state were extended and transformed. In the rise of schooling as a manifestation of state power, we can see huge changes in the very nature of politics and in the relations between politics, knowledge, learning and social identity. Once again, the school had a central role in this transformation, becoming the site par excellence of a new form of politics, a new kind of political practice and a new arena for the political.

One of the tasks of philosophy is to examine closely the everyday assumptions that construct our sense of how things are in the world. These assumptions, on the whole, are easy to summon and confer authority on what we say or claim. They usually take the form of common sense statements that are beyond question, that have a taken-for-granted status and seem to shape daily reality.

Our approach to philosophy is primarily ontological. We begin from the premise that things are the way they are partly – and very significantly – because of our historical understanding of them, and the historical processes that have made them what they are. We believe that this is especially true in the social world where key entities – the state, the people, government, power – do not exist in some pre-given form but in relation to the historical shaping that defines them. Essentially, we take this to be a dynamic way of looking at the order and the nature of things: it opens things to the possibility of being different. But the ontological dimension also demands that we work hard to understand, from every point of view possible, the 'given' nature of things. This frequently means – and this is the very essence of philosophy for some – that we are called upon to interrogate the dominant assumptions about the order and nature of things and to put their apparently independent existence into question. We are committed, then, to asking such questions as: What is 'given' about the 'nature' of things? What is the role of our symbolism, our current forms of representation in producing ideas about how things are – as well as ways of engaging with them and working on them? Ultimately, such questions lead to what Heidegger refers to as 'the question of questions', that is, the question of being (Heidegger, 2000). In other words, within what large, overarching framework of understanding feeling and thinking do we live? There is no doubt, from an ontological point of view, that even our most simple statements betray assumptions about grand matters, even though we are often unaware of the necessary commerce between the everyday and the transcendental.

Childhood: Governing the condition of the population

One very important aspect of the transition – in the so-called West, at least – from one form of power to another is the attention that is given, in the new dispensation, to childhood and children (Aries, 1962). From a contemporary perspective, a remarkable thing about the nineteenth century was the gradual rise of legislation concerning the welfare of children. This was a slow process that came to life primarily in the latter part of the century. It was as though it only very gradually dawned on government that the well-being and general condition of children should be of any interest to formal state power. The slow and uneven rise of concern for the well-being of working children was accompanied by a question concerning what was and should be the child's appropriate condition. This transformation can be seen as partly a philosophical matter – or at least a matter of thought. Gradually, the identity of childhood changed so that it became unthinkable for children to begin their working lives as young as 3 years old in some cases, going on by age 7 to work 18-hour days in cotton mills potteries or coal mines or struggling to earn a basic living as crossing sweepers, doing piecework straw-plaiting or even working in prostitution in large, newly industrialized urban centres (Bédarida, 1979; Thompson, 1990; Horn, 1994; Cody, 2010).

A new imagery of childhood coincided with a new concern for the well-being of the population as a whole – as a definable entity, in fact. While ideas about 'station' were strongly embedded in the general consciousness, so too were ideas about the protection, welfare and rights of children. This mostly benign concern was partnered by an equally powerful but perhaps more ambiguous concern with the condition of the people, a concern that came to the fore most dramatically in the mobilization for war. This concern was symptomatic of the emerging sense that the nation's productivity and competence depended on the health and hygiene of its population, the population that would be mobilized for industrial and military action. It's worth recalling here that the very idea of 'the population' as we know it was the product of a history of emergence (Foucault, 2007). 'Population,' however, was not simply an idea: its emergence as an idea was accompanied by a range of practices and concerns, including census development and the accumulation of knowledge and statistics, mechanisms for defining class strata and a slowly growing discourse of welfare relating to both philanthropic concern for well-being and bureaucratic–managerial concern for efficiency and productivity (Hunter, 1988; Donald, 1992).

Saltaire: Education for labour

Something of the early stage of that concern with population and the management of population can be seen in some of the great philanthropic schemes instigated by nineteenth-century industrialists, men (invariably) of wealth who expressed a strong commitment to the well-being of their workers, seeking in some cases to provide them and their families with a complete and ideal living environment. In these schemes, we can see a strong desire to liberate labour from industrializations' worst effects, or at least to compensate for those conditions with the construction of home and community facilities. But these schemes also sought to provide a stable, supportive and even spiritually rich environment for workers throughout their lives. Any lifelong learning envisioned here was to go along with lifelong labour. Relations between owners and workers were not to be disturbed (Owen, 1824; Donnachie and Hewitt, 1999).

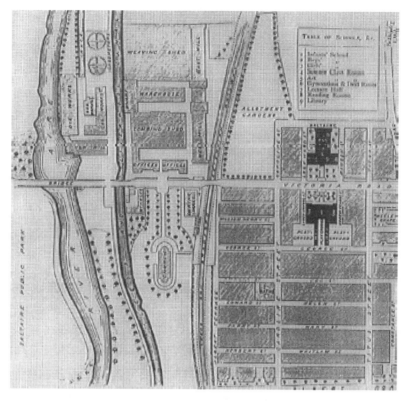

Seaborne, M. and Lowe, R. (1997) *The English School: Its Architecture and Organization*, Volume II, 1870–1970, London: Routledge & Kegan Paul. Reproduced with permission.

In the second half of the nineteenth century, Titus Salt built the model village of Saltaire, with its massive industrial installations and architecture, by the river Aire in Yorkshire. The town, planned and built on a grand scale, included all the provisions needed for the life of its workers – and the vision was for no mean, impoverished lifestyle. The neat and well-appointed workers' cottages were eloquently constructed; the nearby church was both Italianate and grand. The estate included washhouses with running water, bathhouses, a hospital, an 'institute for recreation and education', a library with a reading room and a concert hall. The village also provided almshouses, allotments, a park and a boathouse. The new social order envisaged by Salt's expensive construction was to cover all conceivable aspects of life, a carefully crafted milieu where all the material, aesthetic and spiritual needs of workers and their families would be catered to. The school was positioned at the very centre of this new world (Lowe and Seaborne, 1977; Jackson et al., 2010).

This was not a vision, however, projecting the school as a means towards social advancement or improvement of status. Social mobility was not on the agenda. It's interesting to note that the school – founded in 1853, well before the Forster Act of 1870 – was considered central to the well-furnished social landscape. The social ecology here is benign, beneficent even, but it does not at all include the idea of social mobility through education. If mass urban working-class populations were to be schooled, schooling would at this stage take on a particular and particularly powerful governmental form. That form, corresponding closely with Foucault's account of the rise of bio-power, put major emphasis on training dispositions and ultimately producing a self-managing, basically literate and numerate populace in tune with dominant national values. There is abundant evidence of this disciplinary–pastoral school regime, vividly captured in photographs of Victorian and Edwardian schools and school children (Horn, 1989).

One of the tasks of contemporary educational theory, we believe, is to understand this formative concept – and its attendant technologies – that shaped early schooling. It is our strong conviction that this early, limited vision of working-class school and schooling persists in the contemporary scene where the significance attached to education has both changed and intensified. While schooling has become – in the present era – strongly associated with social mobility, in discourses of school improvement, for significant segments of the population, schooling still takes on a predominantly governmental character, inculcating personal management skills, offering some publicly valued forms of knowledge and fostering dispositions and goals – but by no means insisting on anything more aspirational.

Of course, few of the new elementary schools constructed after 1870 were as luxuriously endowed as Saltaire. Nevertheless, many of the thousands of schools constructed in the period before the First World War were relatively grand structures, representing a significant investment in the new project of universal education. Conan Doyle famously made reference to them in the Sherlock Holmes story as 'light-houses' reflecting a spirit of optimism, 'capsules with hundreds of bright little seeds in each, out of which will spring the wise, better England of the future'. While in some cases the schools borrowed form from the local industrial architecture, in many instances they were clearly an expression of civic pride and were constructed with a certain grandeur of scale designed no doubt to reflect a corresponding grandeur of purpose. The better England Sherlock Holmes envisioned was not necessarily a more socially equal England. It was certainly an England with a more ordered, managed and instructed population.

The idea of mass education

One perhaps obvious effect of universal schooling was that children, en masse, became subject to a new regime of surveillance. The whereabouts of children came under a policed scrutiny, a change that represented a significant shift in the labour market and the politics of childhood. That children should not be subjected to industrial, commercial or agricultural labour was not automatically accepted as a truth universally acknowledged. There were fears – from both traditionalists and radicals (chartists, for example) – of the potential dangers of education for the masses. Some feared that the working classes might lose sight of their proper station and get ideas above themselves. Others feared that the state would inevitably seek to imbue the working classes with a capitalist ideology. Education by the state would prevent the working classes from educating and thereby potentially liberating themselves. Clearly, from the beginning of the process that led to universal state schooling there were deep divisions of opinion on its validity as well as its proper function and likely effects.

> I have no doubt that the right honourable member (Michael Sadler) is actuated by the best intentions and motives, but I think that the course which he pursues will fail in attaining the object which he has in view. Undoubtedly the system which is pursued in these manufactories relating to the working of young children is a great evil; but it appears to me that the remedy which the honourable gentleman proposes to apply is worse than the disease. There appears to me to be only a choice of evils – the children must either work or starve. If the manufacturer is prevented working his mill for more than a certain number of hours together, he will often be unable to execute the orders which he may receive, and

consequently, the purchaser must go to foreign countries for a supply. The result will be that you will drive the English capitalist to foreign countries, where there is no restrictions upon the employment of labour and capital. (William James, speech, House of Commons, 16 March 1832)

Bertrand Russell wrote:

The industrial revolution caused unspeakable misery both in England and in America . . . In the Lancashire cotton mills (from which Marx and Engels derived their livelihood), children worked from 12 to 16 hours a day; they often began working at the age of six or seven. Children had to be beaten to keep them from falling asleep while at work; in spite of this, many failed to keep awake and were mutilated or killed. Parents had to submit to the infliction of these atrocities upon their children, because they themselves were in a desperate plight. Craftsmen had been thrown out of work by the machines; rural labourers were compelled to migrate to the towns by the Enclosure Acts, which used Parliament to make landowners richer by making peasants destitute; trade unions were illegal until 1824; the government employed *agents provocateurs* to try to get revolutionary sentiments out of wage-earners, who were then deported or hanged. Such was the first effect of machinery in England. (Russell, 1998: 31)

If children are not suitable subjects for labour, what should they be and do? While some form of education may have been a norm for segments of the population, it was utterly unthinkable in the early industrial era that education should be not only available but compulsory for all children. Gradually, however, a number of forces and ideas conspired to promote the idea of universal state-sponsored education as a viable proposition. It is important to stress here that education used in this sense is not education used in the broadly contemporary sense.

By 1870, when Forster's Education Act was passed, universal compulsory state-sponsored schooling in England and Wales was no longer unthinkable but had become a subject of heated debate. By 1900, the process was largely complete, with some exceptions for older children who were allowed to attend school half-time while also working. This was particularly true for children working in cotton mills, then considered a major component of British industrial and commercial effort.

Mass schooling was not only a matter for public political debate. It was also a question of technique: a contingent and practical problem. If children were to be schooled, what form should this schooling take and within what kind of institution? It's not as if there were ready-made institutions that could easily cope with the new influx. Wealthy schools were places of privilege, often built at great cost as showpieces of wealth, clearly marking social superiority. The kinds of training and learning they may have offered were not applicable to a mass constituency. Grammar schools were sparsely scattered, catered to the already-accomplished middle classes and accommodated a small student population (Jones, 1977).

Pioneer bureaucrats

A new form of school had been imported from India at the end of the eighteenth century and had proven very successful. This was the monitorial school, also known as the Madras system or the Bell and Lancaster system. Characterized as 'an experiment in education', Bell's scheme was supported by the National Society for the Education of the Poor backed by the Church of England (Bell, 1808). It was the proud boast of such schools that they could accommodate and teach up to one thousand children at a time and drill them effectively in literacy and numeracy. But by the time the Forster Act had been through parliament, though, the Madras system had fallen out of favour and a more subtle, more dynamic and far-reaching idea of a school and a teaching process had taken root (Donald, 1992). A significant figure in the emergence and rise of this new conception was the well-travelled James Kay-Shuttleworth (1804–1877), a 'pioneer bureaucrat' who had developed strong ideas about the nature of the new state-sponsored education, about the nature of the institution most suited to that system and about the kind of teaching force that would be required to run it (Hunter, 1988).

Kay-Shuttleworth had been educated and trained as a medical doctor and had witnessed social distress on a large scale among the newly urbanized industrial working poor in Lancashire mill towns. Imbued with a strong pastoral ethic and with a concern for the well-being of such populations, Kay-Shuttleworth began to see schooling as a mechanism for inducing good habits as well as providing social training and the skills required to manage the new urban environment. Kay-Shuttleworth's vision of schooling – while never entirely paternalistic – was nevertheless a far cry from any modern conception of education as access to a potentially unlimited set of social goods for the individual, including economic wealth and personal fulfilment. Drawing on David Stow's earlier experimental urban school in Glasgow and on Stow's model of teacher training, Kay-Shuttleworth conceived of the new state-sponsored school to come as providing a pastoral and disciplinary social technology that would train and enable the working classes in living skills, provide basic levels of literacy and shape the moral 'quality of the people'. The product of this vision was not simply a population that would be governed by schooling; much more importantly, it would be a self-managing population that would be fit to engage in more complex – and more literacy-oriented – industrial environment.

Stow was a founding member of the Glasgow Educational Society. Kay-Shuttleworth, a passionate advocate of mass education, knew that the model school system he sought would require a well-developed socio-bureaucratic process and found in Stow's 'training system' an instructive model. Stow's model was designed to help the newly conglomerated urban populations – poor and potentially wayward – to achieve a state of moral and practical self-management (Stow, 1850). The self-governing pupil was the ideal product of this concept of education, a concept that, now overlaid with generations of further purposes, still holds sway in contemporary schooling. As F. J. Gladman, another influential figure in the development of the new mass school system, realized, Stow's 'training system' aspired to cultivate the whole 'nature' of the child. Its mission extended beyond mere learning into matters of conduct and disposition (Gladman, 1886).

The form of the 'modern' school took shape and proliferated post-1870 and became the model of all subsequent schools, including all the 'experimental' (usually moderately so) schools that later became a feature of state-funded schooling. This school shared a number of durable and decisive features, including:

- organized, supervised play spaces
- classrooms for dividing the school population into manageable units and enabling 'relations of proximity' between teacher and pupils
- a space for collective, frequently moral messages to be conveyed, rehearsed and illustrated
- a teaching staff relatively close to its charges in terms of social identity
- age stratification

- spaces for the conduct of physical exercises
- provision for the learning of literacy and numeracy
- an ethos of disciplined self-management

The classic architecture of the modern school – including playground, classroom and hall – enables pursuit of the intended goals. The playground operates as the space where pupil culture meets the gaze of the official culture and values system; the hall acts as an arena where the collective body of pupils can be adjured to participate in acts and discourses of collective identity and to assent – or at least be offered the opportunity to assent – to explicit rules for conduct; the classroom is the space where pupils are subjected to a more intimate technology of the self that seeks to produce a mode of self-governing subjectivity (Peim, 2001).

Foucault's discipline

The organization of space and time are decisive features in Foucault's account of the transition from sovereign to capillary power. According to this general process – a process without a centre or guiding consciousness – techniques for training subjects in required accomplishments initially depended on training the body, accompanied by constant efforts to train the 'disposition'. Foucault indicates something of the nature of this change by claiming that, before a certain period, a given physique and disposition lent itself to the 'soldier type'. After decisive changes in the social order, however, the soldier could be made.

Discipline was the key to this achievement. Clearly, the potential for moulding forms of subjectivity was considerable and had far-reaching consequences for the deployment of labour. Foucault's *Discipline and Punish*, ostensibly an account of the 'birth' of the prison, describes the historical process whereby a range of techniques became inscribed in practices that became institutionalized – practices that conspired to work on the condition of various segments of the population.

It is in this period, which ushered in the modern industrialized era, that the school took shape in the hands of a range of practitioners, including Stow, Kay-Shuttleworth and Gladman. In public discourses during this period, the condition of the people became an object of interest. Concern was expressed for diet, hygiene and health care in general. Early nineteenth-century schools in urban centres in England, for instance, were places where local authorities could ensure that poor children could receive carefully controlled diets to meet their basic nutritional needs. By the 1950s, state schools in England and Wales were visited by medics, dentists and the nit nurse, whose collective presence expressed a more than casual interest in the health and hygiene of the people. Physical training was well established and the moral quality of the people was being formed through minute practices of self-control and coordination – from handwriting exercises to behaviour management through supervised play.

For Foucault, the thinker most strongly associated with a far-reaching redescription of modernity, 'the rise of the schooled society' corresponds with the gradual arrival of the dispersed system of governance referred to as 'discipline'. Foucault's history of institutions and practices identifies how gradual but convergent transformations in the government of space and time change the social topography. According to Foucault, this process involves the enclosure, separation and coding of spaces as 'functional sites'. Such places enact identity and rank and get deployed for productive purposes (Foucault, 1977: 144–6). Barracks, factories, schools, hospitals and prisons are key examples. One key form of organization for space in this regime is the cellular. The cell, or enclosed space divided from similar enclosed spaces, is concerned with the management of bodies. Bodies can, in the first place at least, be managed in small units. As units of management get larger, the political dimension becomes clearer. The 'tableaux vivants' of organized spaces works as a kind of choreography of potentially confused, useless or dangerous 'multitudes' into 'ordered multiplicities' (Foucault, 1977: 148). Growing, urban and potentially wayward populations are rendered predictable, productive and efficient in their activity.

Another key element in the process of discipline is tabulation, an administrative principle designed to organize people and things with the same cellular but collective emphasis. Tabulation is manifest in timetables as well as in educational norms, and is as visible in early versions of schooling as in contemporary versions. The grids of assessment in national curriculum specifications or teacher-training grids of competence are the apotheosis of this 'micro-physics' of 'cellular' power' (Foucault, 1977: 149).

One key function of such instruments of order is the management, if not the transformation, of time itself. In the period of the rise of discipline, there was a concern – economic, moral, governmental – about the quality of time used in various institutional settings. Unregulated time is transformed into disciplinary time, programmed to ensure 'the elaboration of the act itself' in myriad practices, including many that owe their existence entirely to their disciplinary role (Foucault, 1977: 152). Time now regulates the individual, 'penetrates the body and with it all the meticulous controls of power' and maximizes the productivity of both the individual and the collective body (Foucault, 1977: 152). Disciplinary practices from late seventeenth century onwards exhort 'exhaustive use', working to produce 'a positive economy' (Foucault, 1977: 154). Time must be pressed to the maximum, 'getting as much out of it as possible', 'taking charge of the time of individual existences' (Foucault, 1977: 157).

Similarly, detailed elaborations of the purposeful correlation of body and gesture appeared in terms of 'the correct use of the body'. The school, increasingly the key instrument of personal formation, is the context for instigating disciplinary procedures for the body: 'A well-disciplined body forms the operational context of the slightest gesture. Good handwriting, for example. Codes invest the body in its entirety' (Foucault, 1977: 152). Innumerable photographs of early schooling demonstrate this bodily training (Horn, 1989). The body gets worked on in relation to a series of objects: 'Discipline defines each of the relations that the body must have with the object that it manipulates' (Foucault, 1977: 153). From handwriting to operating a rifle, for example, 'the instrumental coding of the body' prepares for body–tool and body–machine relations (Foucault, 1977: 153). In this the rise of techniques for the training of bodies, extensive apparatuses of person–production can be seen as a shift in the relations between government and population (Foucault, 2007).

Discipline operates through the genesis, dissemination and reproduction of techniques and institutions. The school divides pupils into age-stratified classes, designating time periods for activities and affirming norms for performance and competence. The school exemplifies the process of norm-related person–formation crowned by the examination. The purpose of examination is threefold: to ensure the level of competence achieved, to ensure parity of training and to differentiate the abilities of individuals (Foucault, 1977: 158). Schools became the institutions par excellence for this specific organization of time, 'disciplinary time . . . that was gradually imposed on the pedagogical practice' gets transposed into an array of settings that share the same technologies of organization (Foucault, 1977: 159).

Foucault brings Marx's 'analogy between the problems of the division of labour and those of military tactics' to bear on the development of the pervasive social technology used in population production and organization manifest in the modern school (Foucault, 1977: 163). 'Discipline is no longer simply an art of distributing bodies, of extracting time from them and accumulating . . . but of composing forces in order to obtain an efficient machine' (Foucault, 1977: 164). The demand for efficacy transforms both the individual and collective body within an organization designed towards purposeful ends: 'The body is constituted as a part of a multi-segmentary machine' (Foucault, 1977: 164). The development of the individual is organized according to a series designed to differentiate purpose and function. To implement this, a precise system of command is required for the 'carefully measured combination of forces' (Foucault, 1977: 164; Lowe and Seaborne, 1977).

Care and self-regulation

Discipline operates also through and with its more subtle companion, care. The pastoral dimension is the means for discipline to inhere in the self, even as that self is in process of formation. A threefold spatial organization effects the complex form of governmentality that operates through the specific topography of the school. Essentially this subtle, varied form of governmentality addresses the self via distinct but linked technologies of person–formation (Hunter, 1988; Peim, 2001).

Through age stratification; through prescription of norms of development; through proscription of cultural forms, identities and social modalities, the school effects a systematic management of identity, accrediting the normative attainments of the dominant culture. These include specific knowledge and competences, but are also matters of conduct and disposition. The school operates a *pastoral* regime, designed to provide both care and an ethic of self-care, self-direction and self-government. Through innumerable practices and an array of relations, the school coaxes the pupil to increasingly take charge of his or her own conduct, own performance, even own assessment – and to give an account of oneself, one's development and one's future. Such pastoral practices serve to ensure that the exterior practices of discipline are properly internalized. The most effective form of government, after all, is the carefully crafted and norm-driven self-management of the population (Hunter, 1994; Foucault, 2007).

The school stands in a special relation to government. Occupying a near universal constituency, geographically dispersed throughout the territory, historically so deeply embedded in general consciousness, it is difficult to envisage a world without schools. Sherlock Holmes's overworked reference to 'beacons of the future' now signifies an entity so well established, so much a feature of the social landscape that any future this overpowering institution does not manage is foreclosed (Donald, 1992: 17). The future is thus rendered predictable, programmed and constrained (Derrida and Ferraris, 2001). Schooled, in short. Governing body and soul are the tasks of this ubiquitous institution.

If the history of state-funded schooling in the United Kingdom begins formally with the Forster Education Act, it has a prehistory that includes the various Factory Acts restricting working times for children and insisting that employers provide instruction. The bureaucracy that would shape the school system had been instigated in the late 1830s and had developed with successive moves to account for, chart and audit school provision. When 1870 arrived, things gradually were put in place for the formation of a coherent provision. Schools were originally to be set up by local boards that would govern them and levy rates for their provision and upkeep. By 1902, school governance was handed over to local authorities and the shape of the curriculum for secondary schools was being centrally defined. Secondary schools were provided sporadically and did not mesh with the provision of elementary schools.

The pattern of provision varied across Europe and in the United States, although it could be said that the idea of universal and state-sponsored education had taken root by the end of the nineteenth century (even if not fully achieved). Before the unification of Germany, the Prussian state had provided schooling since the eighteenth century. After World War I, the newly independent Poland had a state school system. In France, during the 1880s, the 'Jules Ferry Laws' (named after the Minister for Public Instruction) had wrested control of schooling from the clergy and installed a mandatory regime of 'public instruction' requiring all children under 15 to attend, thus founding the idea of the 'ecole Republicaine'.

Schooling, a social technology

The contemporary form of schooling is not at all accidental; it is fundamental. It is constitutionally and genetically at odds with any democratic modes of order. Its mode of pastoral discipline exists within an essentially feudal hierarchy of being. To imagine that the school can be refunctioned to serve the liberal dream of equality or to become a vehicle for democracy is to fail to understand the role schooling plays in the social division of labour. The everyday social practices of the school and its characteristic structuring include the enactment of specific social relations and the technological organization of space and time. In order to explore the idea of the school as a specific and powerful social technology, the following section will briefly examine how new technologies have been grafted onto a historically relatively deep-seated human technology in the bureaucratic-pedagogical interface of the school.

New technologies that promised to displace conventional pedagogic relations have not had that effect. While enthusiasts may proclaim a brave new world of decentralized, active and essentially self-directed learning, sceptics may doubt the viability of the Information Communication Technology (ICT) revolution to fulfil any utopian deschooling mission. In fact, a powerful bureaucratic management system has entered schools under the guise of new technology. The technology in question most commonly in the United Kingdom goes under the brand name 'Bromcom', though there are other versions. It provides various functions as an internal data system. It provides an electronic register, but then links the classroom with the administrative centre of the school and presents a communications system for the different locations of school practices. This style of data system also has the potential (realized in some US versions) to link institutions and central management centres – providing a complex nodal system.

> It started out essentially as an 'Electronic Attendance Registration System' and has become increasingly an integrated system for administrative data

management. The Bromcom company and Schools proudly boast of the flexibility and scope of the system:

> Each teacher in a school has their own wNET folder in which they can enter data across a wide range of fields, including attendance, behaviour and grades. All the folders are linked by a radio network to the school's central administration computer. This means data can be quickly sent and received to and from the central database, without staff having to visit the school office. Data can also be prepared at home, stored on the folder and then transmitted to the school's computer the next day. wNET provides staff with unprecedented access to data, and also allows for the rapid generation of reports, letters and analysis. (Bromcom, 2002)

This institutionally centralized radio technology enhances the pastoral-disciplinary role of the teacher in quite specific ways. Pupil profiles are automatically produced and are constantly under construction and redefinition in relation to the managerial trinity of attendance, behaviour and curriculum performance level – a constant work of profiling keeping pace with daily developments. Its nodal nature (each teacher has one) means that an enormous quantity of disparate bits of information can be accumulated, processed, stored and represented. Its centralized nature also means that all the information can be brought within a unifying system. Any nodal point can access information provided by all other nodes.

Information can be keyed in for every lesson. The attendance profile of any pupil at any given time and across any time span can be rapidly tracked. The measurement of absence then becomes a mark of the efficiency of the institution, as does the speed of detection: 'Beauchamp's Bromcom registration system is set up to record absence very precisely. We record absence from registration and at every lesson', writes one school proudly in its Christmas message to parents (Bromcom, 2002).

The system has now passed through several generations. Each successive generation not only promises greater efficiency, but provides a more complex and sophisticated data system. Ongoing grades for individual pieces of work, as well as general assessments of achievement and progress, are tracked, as is information concerning behaviour. For every pupil, then, behaviour and attainment profiles can be accessed and worked on. As all this information is fed into the system on an ongoing basis, the system can, theoretically at least, provide a more or less complete and up-to-date profile of the pupil's attainment and conduct at any time to any person authorized to access it. As the capability of the system expands, the data it holds and processes and the way it processes data become more extensive and sophisticated. A miscreant pupil can be checked against records, for instance, that indicate special knowledge concerning the pupil's current recorded profile – information about family, for instance, or problems of disposition, recent conduct, medical details and so on.

Technology of efficiency in the logic of improvement

In the promise of such technological systems we can see an invest-ment in a logic of efficiency that stands within the dominant ethic of school improvement. The contemporary school deploys more sophisti-cated technologies of control in the name of efficiency in fulfilling the national educational agenda within the unrelenting logic of improve-ment. Electronic registration systems represent an advance but must also be seen as an intensification of the school's historical function of disciplinary care.

This is clearly evident in the emphasis given to charting attendance and absence. The demand for pupils to be present is a powerful indicator of the essential social function of the school in promoting social cohesion and social efficiency through the development of specific personal accom-plishments, attributes and dispositions. Absence or truancy from school has been valued highly in any improvement agenda. Absence puts sub-jects out of reach, outside the domain of surveillance. As schools increas-ingly become expected to operate their own regimes of self-surveillance, it is hardly surprising that schools should feel impelled to deploy hi-tech systems for tracking the absence of pupils. The coming together of the disciplinary and the pastoral through the combined operation of a 'new' communications technology and an existing and persistent social tech-nology has been organized around such nodal lexical items as 'efficiency', 'improvement', 'inclusion' – all of them ultimately related to ideas about national efficiency and general social well-being (Hopkins, 2004): in short, to what Foucault might have referred to as 'bio-power'. (Foucault, 1988b)

Attendance is the most fundamental condition of the realization of governmental function of the school. It is the potentially wayward elements of the population that are likely to slip through the schooling net and become the social problems of the future. Anxieties about truancy arise from concerns for the ability of the school to perform its governmental, citizen-forming role (Cohen, 2002).

Attendance at school has a manifold significance:

- the social, 'police' significance of being subject(ed) to the logic of pastoral discipline
- the personal benefit to be gained from acquiring education conceived of as a good in itself
- the instrumental (technologico-Benthamite) distribution and regulation of capacities and dispositions in relation to the social division of labour

All three may be supplemented by various different senses of a sociocultural mission: for instance, to provide alternative modes of being from a commodified culture, to provide an awareness of ethical conduct, to provide fair and equal access to social goods, to realize the productive potential of the population, to impart significant knowledge and or social skills and to cultivate good character and proper attitudes.

As Foucault has suggested, much of the work of modern education systems is based in disciplinary practices that produce subjects of a particular kind, differentiate populations according to the attribution of dispositions, and individualize and work to transform (and, in many cases, reform) the subject. The school has long deployed systems for gathering and storing information. These discourses of information 'capture' the pupil within a network of calculations and statistics that characterizes identities within relations of difference that are normatively defined and charted – as with levels of attainment, for instance. Monitoring and testing practices – along with age stratification, 'simultaneous instruction', the segmentation of the curriculum, the systematic attribution of character facets and pedagogical relations – define and confer identities on the organized population of the school. The bureaucratic machinery of the institution, with its forms and techniques and modalities of language, combines to grant positions and ascribe characteristics. Contemporary CAT1 scores provide a good, if rather sinister, example of how the school produces information concerning the pupil – in the case of the CAT score about the pupil's general level of competence (CAT, 2011). The information is then used to chart the pupil's progress and to monitor the performance of the school or any of its operations or personnel in relation to that score (Foucault, 1977).

The school operates primarily, at a fundamental level, as a social technology. Realized through an array of techniques, 'a regulative ensemble' – a synthesis of relations and practices (Aglietta, 1979: 101), this social technology is supplemented by a bureaucracy, including technologies of information directed at the pupil. The key function of this general technology is the production of self-managing, self-regulating subjects/ citizens. Such governmentality deploys bureaucratic, technological resources to monitor and manage its populations and institutions and their operations. Contemporary governmentality realized in the school cannot suffer any but the smallest minority to escape its reach. Its social practices, including its 'moral' and managerial technologies, have been adapted to operate at both an intimate and mass scale (Hunter, 1988, 1994; Rose, 1990; Donald, 1992).

The *personalized* environment of the classroom is where the gaze of the teacher meets and charts the dispositions of the pupil in a relation of trenchant and unremitting scrutiny. This scrutiny is all the more powerful and pervasive for its pastoral inflection: We care. We are watching you.

A complex, many-sided technology effects this work of scrutiny. It consists of an architecture; practices of teaching and learning (including conceptions of literacy, for example); a discourse or series of discourses on conduct, on the self, on culture and on values; and – at the same time, and not to be forgotten – a bureaucracy, a set of procedures that will detail and enhance the processes of scrutiny and surveillance that this specific life–world requires. The process of productive governance enacted by the school requires its own specialized topography that organizes the social spaces of the institution and defines their relations of difference. The teleological end point of this process of governance through education can be perhaps best be seen in contemporary discourses of lifelong learning, where pedagogic relations, with their emphasis on the development and cultivation of the social self, pervade both laterally across social domains and longitudinally through the entire trajectory of life itself. This is the double triumph – if triumph it be – of the governmental technology of education (Harvey, 1991; Bauman, 2000).

Personalization: Technology of the self

A key component in the production of citizens is the *construction* of the person, who must be granted a form and a content. In this view, the process of personalization – rather than being a simple liberation of individual free expression – entails charting qualities and features that are subject to description and definition within a normative regime of personal identity. This personalization takes different forms: it can be seen in the various measurements children have undergone, in the various invitations for self-expression that the school enacts – through literacy practices, for instance – and through the frequent invitation to pupils to define and in effect become themselves. Personalization must not be taken here as the release of the inner self, as it were, or some Rousseauesque idea of the person's proper being – acknowledged and realized in and through this form of person-oriented social practice. The substance of the person is always being worked on and is subjected to the kinds of definitions that may be charted according to the terms of the discourse. This personalization is (positively, we might be tempted to say) constructed according to normative discourses of value; these in turn are both charted and hierarchized according to a formal system of accounting – which may take the form of a discursive definition (as in reports and self-evaluations) or a precise calculation of attendance, conduct and level of performance against a strictly formalized chart of achievement.

The National Record of Achievement (NRA), deployed for many years in the United Kingdom, offers an exemplary case of the use of self-descriptions and self-assessments to produce a thoroughly institutionalized identity. It was being proposed in the 1980s as a profiling system, a textual record of all the pupil has done, been and achieved. More than a scholastic record of knowledge or skills, the National Record of Achievement aims to provide a full portrait of the individualized self, ideally through an individual's own words. We all know, of course, after Bakhtin, that a word is always at least half someone else's and that the social self is discursively produced within a setting where certain forms of expression signify a typology of identity (Crespi, 1992).

> The National Record of Achievement, launched in 1991, was designed as a lifelong record of achievement to support self-development for all throughout life.
>
> Although not an award in itself – when owned, compiled and updated by the individual it can:
>
> - encompass academic, vocational and personal achievements and experiences
> - help plan learning and set targets for future achievement
> - contain evidence of achievements, for example photographs and certificates
> - motivate further achievement through acknowledging existing skills.
>
> The NRA supports a cycle of review, reflection and planning, and enables individuals to record all achievements of formal qualifications (including those in progress or partially completed) and informal experiences and achievements. (www.dfes.gov.uk/nra/bkg.cfm, accessed October 2003)

The NRA's function is clearly not simply realized in the end product, the final document that provides as full as possible an account of the pupil's 'achievements and experiences'. In the process of producing self-generated data, the subject takes responsibility for their own development and realization (DfES, 2003b).

Discourses and practices of personalization also impinge on the figure of the teacher. Clearly the person of the teacher is one focus of identification for the emergent self of the pupil. At the same time, formal and informal discourses categorize the performance and identity of the teacher. Clearly this is a different process, but there is significance in a certain proximity between pupil and teacher within the social and topographic space of the classroom. Such a condition for possible, although constrained, intimacy enables the relative closeness of the social relations between teacher with pupils to act as a governmental force (Kay-Shuttleworth, 1862; Jones, 1990). The presence of the teacher figure enables a certain relation of care to come into being between teacher and pupils. This relation of care is also, fundamentally and simultaneously, a relation of discipline: hence, the magic formula 'pastoral-discipline', which characterizes the modus operandi of the modern school. The teacher's care for the pupil – for well-being and progress, but also for conduct and the development of general disposition – can be transferred by a process of interpellation whereby the teacher, as representative of the institution and its values invites the pupil to see him or herself in a certain way. Above all, it is important that the pupil begin to see him or herself as the legitimate focus for the discourse of self-production and self-transformation that the governmental role of school enacts (Althusser, 1977).

For the pupil, the practice of self-production is caught up in the ongoing operations of the classroom. The pupil's personality is reflected in writing; the pupil expresses self in choosing books and activities (often at a very young age); the pupil is encouraged to explore self through identification with a series of others who have the very function of reflecting back on the emergent self. In fact, this reflecting is the technique deployed for the production of this reflective self.

In the classic activity of the liberal classroom, the formation of this person is achieved through and complemented by the construction of the autobiography (frequently composed at different stages of scholastic life). The autobiography is only possible given the audience of the receptive and sensitive teacher. This teacher will teach you to read, what to read, to sing, to sew and cook, to put together a project on badgers, to play football or cricket and to climb a rope, but will also teach you to keep your desk neat and tidy, to take care of your pens and pencils and to dress appropriately. What's more, the teacher will teach you, through her own person, to be the reflective, self-directing, self-managing subject – author of yourself, as it were (Bauman, 2000; 2004).

Of course teachers, like pupils, are increasingly required to produce themselves as norm-regulated persons within a regime of competence, attainment and aspiration. Teachers are themselves subject to profile, analysis and critique. Teachers and schools are required to promote and set goals for themselves, identify their positive attributes and target their areas for development. Teacher appraisals, 'threshold dossiers' and masters degree journals replicate much of what the NRA set out to achieve for pupils. All constitute practices of self-production. A plethora of materials, occasions and discourses of reflection now exist whereby the professional self is brought into a problematic, or at least developmental, relation with itself. The confessional mode of practices of self-revelation serve to underscore the cultivation of the person in the professional context. This constitutes another powerful ritual of interpellation, realized through pedagogical relations of professional development and practices of self-appraisal: the entire social technology of the self that pervades professional life in the 'medicare' world, and that is ultimately informed by the overriding ethic of improvement. Bureaucratic operations of performativity that carry a personalized dimension grip the scrutinized professional self all the more tightly (Ball, 1999).

The personalization of the pupil, then, is mirrored in a double logic with the personalization of the teacher. This too constitutes a regulatory mechanism. In and through the person of the teacher, the pupil is interpellated to realize the development of the social self – through a range of accomplishments (drawing, woodwork, making things with straw, reading silently on one's own), but also a range of relevant conducts (sitting up straight, talking quietly while working, answering the register politely and clearly) and attitudes (respect for others, the ability and desire to ask questions, sharing, competing, etc.). In and through these accomplishments, conducts and attitudes, the pupil is being taught – not necessarily consciously – to configure the self as a person, to adopt a social identity and a social profile. Should the pupil fall outside the regime of the school – through delinquency or the broad range of mishaps that fall under the name of social exclusion –a new cartel of services and expert managers, including the police, psychological services, social workers, youth workers and charitable institutions will supplement the work of the school to redirect the individual's trajectory within the borders of social inclusion. Clearly, government is being enacted through this array of care.

This model of governance – that seeks to transform the subject – is not to be confused with a purely ideological project (although there will inevitably be ideological work done in the process). The vital mechanism at work here however can be understood in terms of the *production of subjectivity*, the process of interpellation. Interpellation is the ongoing 'hailing' of the social subject, a key mechanism for identity formation. Conventional accounts of subjectivity (metaphysical, logocentric) define the subject in terms of qualities that may pre-exist the social being of the subject. Althusser's expansion on Marx's formula (being determines consciousness) presents a radical re-reading of identity. The act of interpellation brings the social subject into being. This can be seen at the most fundamental level in the process of naming. In different cultural contexts, the name will signify different aspects and elements of identity. The name will attach the subject to the process of hailing. The name will also confer identity upon the social subject, enmeshing them in a symbolic network that organizes the stuff of their world (Althusser,

1984). As Judith Butler puts it, 'The act of recognition becomes an act of constitution: the address animates the subject into existence' (1997: 25). The act of recognition – in the process of interpellation – is an *ongoing* and necessarily complex process whereby the social self is hailed in relation to those elements of identity that are deemed significant (as defined in the national curriculum, for instance) or that are more loosely, but nevertheless powerfully, inscribed in the general social milieu or culture. The primary mode for this process is in the exchange between self and 'Other', where – in the case of the school – the other is most positively identified with the figure of the teacher. Hence the emphasis in teaching manuals on the importance of establishing proper relations of proximity and distance with pupils in order to more effectively engage them both cognitively and performatively. The logic of interpellation is clearly the fundamental strategy deployed in this scenario.

The ideal pupil is interpellated as a self-governing individual who adopts the mores of the classroom and the school in terms of its social and work orientation. Both teachers and pupils are required to produce the mode of self-description and self-analysis that falls within the practices of self-evaluation. The pupils are frequently asked to give account of their feelings, their thoughts and their orientations – cultivations of the person. In producing such accounts, subjects are not simply giving an account of themselves in terms required; they are identifying themselves with the symbolic order that requires this of them (Lacan, 2006). The discourses of the self demanded by the logic of personalization enact the process of becoming a subject. Now, through newly formulated discourses (in England, at least) of citizenship, teaching and learning methods are being devised to make this self-consciousness a ritual component of the national curriculum. Citizenship as thus conceived is not simply a matter of learning about national institutions, laws and mores; it is an orientation, a modus vivendi, a self-critical and self-regarding comportment.

But what is technology? Technology and 'we contemporaries'

At this point we can consider relations between the apparently hard, electronic technologies of surveillance, the formal social technology housed and symbolized in the architecture of the school and the more intimate technology of the self.

It should be clear that technologies of bureaucracy are not an alien intrusion onto the warmly personal traditions of classroom interaction, as some teachers surveyed have claimed, nor do they interrupt the pastoral business of the school. The warmly personal traditions of classroom interaction – 'relations of proximity' in Kay-Shuttleworth's conception – were already a form of bureaucratic technology, a social technology of the person. The 'high-tech' Bromcom information system, by its production of the individual as a locus of data, serves the personalizing agenda of the school. The discourses of personalization are well established in practices that form the mundane social technology of the school: modes of addressing pupils and modes of pedagogic relation. The mundane formal and bureaucratic procedures of the school – age and 'ability' stratification, report-writing, file keeping, profiling – complement them. The regime of surveillance is one with the regime of care. Both are essential to the productive mode of the school as a technology. Schools themselves, under recent modifications of inspection, are required to be self-organizing, self-managing and self-monitoring systems of being; in this we witness an increasing homology. Schools, teachers and pupils are requested to partake in the definition of the self. It's an offer that simply can't be refused. This working on the self indicates that older, and what some might regard as warmer, human technologies are not inimical to new, hi-tech, electronic, digital, data technologies. They operate in symbiosis in the school.

Digital technologies have sped up and intensified the administrative, pastoral and managerial practices enacted habitually through the school. The promise of this data management – whether realized, realizable or not – is in accord with the dominant logic of performativity that requires an ever-increasing record of efficiency. 'School improvement' can thus be seen as, to borrow Heidegger's terms, 'the essence of technology' (Heidegger, 1993b). Indeed, Heidegger's idea of 'technological enframing' is useful in this context, although it can only be very briefly outlined here. For Heidegger there is a consistency in modernity's engagement with the world that is characterized in technology. Technology, for Heidegger, turns out, after a careful and complex analysis, to be a way of revealing and a way of inhabiting the world (the essence of technology is not something technological). In the school's (post-1870) characteristic modes of production, concerns with norms, rigorous organization of time and space, segmentation of knowledge and classifications of identity, as well as its more recent addiction to a logic of performativity – in all this we can discern the coming together of techniques and mechanisms. This changing array of social and instrumental technologies belongs to a particular way of ordering the world and of producing subjects. This ensemble is consistent with what Heidegger identifies as *das Gestell* (the enframing), a particular way of projecting the world that belongs to modern technology. For Heidegger, modern technology is linked to a particular mode of conceiving our relation to the world through a process of objectification, a 'productionist metaphysics' that is consistent with Heidegger's critique of 'Western metaphysics' and the 'technological enframing' that constitutes the contemporary modality of being (which is at the same time a forgetting of the being of beings).

It seems that Foucault both draws on and transforms Heidegger's position in his own account of technology. In *Technologies of the Self*, Foucault focuses on historically specific 'ontologies' or ways of being through which the subject is created and creates itself (1988b). Rejecting any idea of an essential self or pre-given subject, Foucault emphasizes modes of 'subjectification' as the way that human beings become or are formed as subjects. He sees these processes as historical, and he locates power at the centre of his enquiry. Power here is positive, productive and capillary – and is engaged with the will to knowledge and truth.

In our contemporary world in the so-called West, state-sponsored subjectivication – both formal and informal – occurs from the cradle to the grave. The nursery, the school, the university and, in many cases, the workplace, are infused with discourses, curricula and practices that work upon the substance of the self. The self is presented essentially as a developmental project, within established norms that are more and more specified and publically circulated, endorsed and enforced.

These norms frequently appear through processes that are hard to trace back. They are often the outcome of bureaucratic processes. As such, though they may insistently address the personal dimension, they are impersonal in their origin and in their power. They cannot be attributed to an individual person or institution. They operate with the authority of 'common sense' under a logic of necessity. No one controls them. They can only be managed and they cannot be evaded. It is easy to think of any number of procedures in the workplace that follow this general ontology: quality assurance procedures, staff development (including self- and peer-evaluations), institutional audits, annual reviews. All contribute to 'technological enframing' in our 'pedagogized society' (Heidegger, 1993b; Bernstein, 2000).

Heidegger's idea of 'technological enframing' and Foucault's description of 'discipline' usefully conjoin to explain the impersonal forces that appear to operate outside of the usual logic of agency and intention as the characteristic order of the contemporary. It may also be useful, or at least instructive, to consider how much of the embedded social technology of improvement has a structure of nihilism that Nietzsche and others have defined as the necessary outcome of an instrumental, means–end rationality. Of course, in the operations of the modern, state-sponsored school we can see much that unquestionably improves upon the conditions of life over pre-school times when, for example, working-class children were included in the labour market and often lived in insanitary poverty (Reports, 1842; 1867). But the contemporary condition of the school as a highly regulated, norm-dominated space, colonized by centrally managed discourses of improvement and their attendant bureaucratic practices In that space are constructs regimes of truth that regulate discourses and practices for the sake of regulation, according to a very limited agenda that privileges testing. Consequently, the ascription of identities 'o'erflows the measure' delimiting the world of practice, positioning practitioners and organizing identities in its own restricted image while making promises of reform that cannot be delivered.

One problem with this present deconstructive reading of the modern school is that it threatens the very existence of academic discourses of education that remain strongly predicated on a misplaced ethic of improvement or an unaccountable faith in reform (Peim and Flint, 2009). In modern and contemporary educational discourses there is a frequently expressed assumption of progress. Either education is inevitably progressing towards more effective and more egalitarian forms and practices, perhaps helped along by the work of the improvement, or education naturally resists egalitarian reform and self-improvement, requiring constant vigilance by the vanguard of educational thinking.

Thus, against all evidence, education will be forced to improve itself in the directions both of efficiency and equality.

Within both the political and the academic fields, the idea that education is both essential to the well-being of the nation and the path to a more socially just society remains overwhelmingly powerful. While it is a strange compact, it is a very persistent one. The persistence of the idea of necessary progress that dominates educational thinking, against all the accumulated evidence, itself partly indicates a failure of reform. Shifting political priorities can use incomplete conditions to sustain the various rhetorics that the politics of education engenders. But might there not be some serious, albeit sobering, merit in considering the possibility that questions concerning education have been dominated by reform and improvement, even while reform and improvement have been elusive?

2

Education, the Language of Improvement and Governmentality: The Enframing in Practice

Practitioners' reflections on practice

'I was almost refused permission to take my group on a field trip the other day. We had been studying "Kes" and I had found a local centre where they could see hawks, and even handle them, themselves. It's one of my own ways of trying to improve what I do to help my students learn new things. I really think that these students might have the chance of engaging in "deep learning" on the basis of their experience. But, senior managers kept on asking me to justify the time taken against what the children might learn that would help them in their examinations.

When I meet with my students, now, the emphasis is always on raising their achievement. That's not a bad thing in itself, they need to be challenged. I know that I've got to keep on trying to find ways of helping them achieve beyond what they, their families and the communities might expect. But, with this whole emphasis on assessment, I often feel that I am trying to work against the grain of the system with my students. I only want to find ways of listening to them, so that I can try and understand their worlds. For me, teaching is about getting close to your students and finding out what makes them tick: helping them to widen their own horizons. I used to love the way we would all start laughing over something; that spontaneity and their bubbly expressions of joy now seem much rarer occurrences. My work is forever foregrounded by "monitoring" students' "progress" against official "benchmarks" and I'm eternally involved in "levelling" students, which takes me away from what is important.'

This is Alex Love's contemporary recollections of his teaching in a secondary school in northern England. The discourse is taken from conversations the authors had with teachers over the past few years in all sectors of formal education. Though this excerpt appears far removed from government, in exploring just how Alex's conduct and the locus of actions and freedoms he enjoys is shaped by a body of knowledge in the form of discourses of improvement, this whole chapter concerns itself with the issue of governmentality, particular rationalities of government and care of the self (Chapter 1). In being concerned with actions and freedoms within discourses of improvement and how the whole institution of improvement functions as governmental apparatus, this chapter opens questions concerning identity (Dean, 2010: 24).

It is clear that the countervailing and sometimes contradictory social forces in the education system continually shape Alex's identity. What is dear to Alex is the possibility of getting close to his students and listening to them. He is concerned that listening to them amounts to grasping what they say as an 'object' that can be used at some later stage in discussion with colleagues, including Office for Standards in Education (OfSTED) inspectors and other professional visitors to the school. For Alex, listening to the students amounts to opening his own world to the possibility of meeting with people who have different world views than his own.

The language of school improvement

Alex was already immersed in the 'liberal humanist parlance that education is actually about more than assessment'. In regarding the language of improvement, some may protest that education is grounded in far more than the assessment of pupil progress. Ubiquitous to public concerns regarding formal education systems is the injunction, 'Education should be about more than exams', and a lament, 'If only we could liberate education from the tyranny of exams and recover a sense of its true purpose' (Peim and Flint, 2009: 343).

In these examples and the discourse in which they are situated 'education is thought of as properly belonging to an enlightenment ideal of complete development': Alex's activities are always already shaped by extant forms of language (Peim and Flint, 2009: 343).

In contrast, so many neoliberal discourses of education assume that agencies and agents are at the centre of concerns about improving education. These discourses appear to be based on convictions that greatly improved education systems will result from systemic perfection, mastery and control. In accord with this *trompe-l'oeil* of certainty, improvement continues to remain a matter of the now familiar mantra of continuous professional development and training; of leadership; of building capacities for change; of focusing, coupling and energizing top-down and bottom-up approaches to change; and of targeting resources upon teaching and learning within schools and their associated organizations and infrastructures.

Whelan (2009) noted that 'England has implemented more of the policies that would be expected to improve performance in a school system than any other country in the world'. However, he also observed that in terms of international comparisons of examination results for young people 'its overall performance at age 15 is little above the average for developed countries'. This contradiction could be the result of the selectivity allowed in determining who becomes a teacher. According to Whelan, the English school system has 'fewer than 1.2 applicants for every position in teacher-training', compared to 'school systems which have made teaching an attractive career choice and are selective about who becomes a teacher', which tend 'to outperform those which are not'. Whelan notes that 'Finland, South Korea, Cuba, and some parts of Canada all have at least five applicants for every teacher training position' (Whelan, 2009: 58). But, this would seem to place undue emphasis upon empirically determined teacher applicant ratios; nor does it consider the high value particular societies attribute to education.

In this much cited text regarding school improvement policy, even Whelan (2009), like so many in the field of improvement, does not take account of the language where policy and practice are situated. In rethinking school improvement, this chapter questions the grounding assumptions of improvement and the powerfully egregious illusions of mastery and control that these discourses serve to engender.

Rather than the *agent* (for example, the child, student, teacher, principal, governor and others) along with the *agency* (including the school, college, network, community and the whole education system), this chapter opens further debate about improvement from the perspective that such gatherings are always thrown in language. In exposing us to the endless flux of time Heidegger (1962) talks about Dasein[1] – and indeed all entities including language – being in the 'throw'. We are using the term 'Dasein' as an indication of our work being premised on assumptions drawn from post-humanist discourse, in which human beings are no longer placed at the centre of the world, but are regarded as 'decentred' and in the throw of existence. It is our position that this language is inscribed by forms of governmentality which has been in place from the start of mass education. This book seeks to explore some of the implications of this particular standpoint.

While Alex's language of improvement refers to what many would regard as somewhat worn out and clichéd metaphors of place, space, time and understanding being, they have significance for him and his students far beyond their lowly status as terms used in language. In containing their own ambiguities of meaning, these clichés of horizons of being – 'making them tick', 'broadening their horizons' – attempt to understand what is involved in his teaching beyond the classroom. They reflect everyday understandings of the world that easily make sense to people from all walks of life. Through metaphors, Alex lifts himself beyond the immediate confines of the classroom, in order to reach out to a far wider community.

---

1 In the eighteenth century, 'Dasein' connoted 'existence' and Heidegger (1962) uses it to mean 'the being of humans' and 'the entity or person who has this being' (Inwood, 1999: 42).

In using these metaphors, Alex structures the natural rhythm of his teaching by the continual 'play of difference'. This notion of difference arises whenever we attempt to make sense of something and give it an identity. We tend to define the new in terms of what we already know. To do this, we use a variety of signs including, for example, words, icons, pictures, sketches, ideas, thoughts and bodily expressions, that each point to something else. In this way, difference is necessarily always fluid and in play in the ongoing construction of identity. For example, in Alex's clichéd metaphors there is at the very least the difference in play between the metaphorical expressions and the ambiguities in the pictures they each create. This 'play' is not at all confined to the subject manipulating 'objects'. It is the continual play of difference among that vast array of signs mediating our world; the play of difference does not occupy a subordinate role; rather, it foregrounds Alex – and indeed everyone – in ever making any sense of the ethic of improvement (Flint, 2009).

But, how are Alex's 'enlightenment ideals of complete development' played out in practice? (Peim and Flint, 2009). In England, for example, despite major reforms of the education system it would seem that little space remains for people beyond the boundaries of economic activity (Fielding, 2001), following the implementation of the national curriculum. In the enframing, ranking and sorting is about maintaining a certain order in the world that belongs to a number of dimensions of existence outside the ordinary confines of economic activity. In Fielding's words, the reforms

> seemed to have no place for either the language or the experience of joy, of spontaneity, of life lived in ways that are vibrant and fulfilling rather than watchfully earnest, focussed and productive of economic activity. (Fielding, 2001: 9)

There is something ironic here, given that in England there has been much trumpeting of the Every Child Matters (ECM) agenda as a rallying call for partnerships of engagement that mobilize the entire system (Fullan, 2007: 227, 246). After much consultation with the public, educators and even children themselves, formal education policy has been formulated around five basic goals closing down the identities of young people in what is re-presented as the 'well-being' of children in terms of: (1) being healthy, (2) staying safe, (3) enjoying and achieving, (4) making a positive contribution and (5) economic well-being. What is evident from the language of this policy agenda is that the discourse funnels down upon five specific goals to concentrate efforts on developing services for children (DfES, 2003a; Fullan, 2007: 10–11, 47, 227).

ECM is one example of a large-scale improvement agenda. But what exactly these policies mean for Alex and thousands of other teachers, young people and others involved in formal education is a matter of our relationship with institutional forms of language.

Means–ends logic in the language of improvement

Educational discourse containing the sometimes 'absent presence' of the 'means' constitutes the grounds for ordering people. In his discourse, Alex drew upon resources in order to assess his own students' performances. These means ordered Alex's world according to a predetermined logic connecting with his own performance as a teacher. At the level of education systems we have also encountered another form of means that, in its ordering of systems, serves to concentrate professionals' work on the delivery of particular services for people.

In making connections between practice and educational discourses it is apparent that practice is structured in terms of our being-with-others as Dasein in a much wider horizon of the 'play of difference'. The latter, of course, includes the possibility of more narrowly conceived means–ends, subject–object relationship, which continually arrests any possible play. In the play of language and in contrasting the natural impulsiveness of young people in learning new things with the logic of productive economic activity, Fielding (2001) further reinforces the point that Alex's concerns are shared more widely.

As Heidegger (1998: 242) also suggests, the 'quiet power of the possible' at play in Alex's concerns is a mark of Dasein's ever unfolding relationship with being, which foregrounds much great literature and philosophy. William Wordsworth, for example, in exploring his relationship with nature and the nature of things, in *Lines Written a Few Miles Above Tintern Abbey* in 1798 wrote:

> I have felt
> A presence that disturbs me with joy
> Of elevated thoughts; a sense sublime

> Of something more deeply interfused
>
> . . .
>
> Well pleased to recognise
> In nature and the language of sense,
> The anchor of my purest thoughts, the nurse,
> The guide, the guardian of my heart, and soul
> Of all my moral being'

(Wordsworth, 2000: 134).

The lack of any calculus here is palpable, for Wordsworth a 'presence' of the 'nature' of things, and an 'anchor' to secure his thoughts arises from what he calls his 'soul'. In some ways Alex's economy was also one that stood outside the calculus of 'objectives', and of objective measures of improvement.

Alex was drawing upon a discourse that does not readily fit with the hegemonic discourses and practices of school improvement.[2] His narrative echoes contemporary forms of feminist discourse, opening consideration of listening to, and being sensitive to, the other and interacting with each other as active subjects, rather than in the traditional grammar of subject–object relations – challenging any moves towards the illusion of mastery (Irigaray, 2002; 2008).

Alex's reflections had been concerned with the very *means* of enacting an economic system, namely, the monitoring of progress against 'benchmarks for success', the continual levelling of students, the emphasis placed upon assessment and the privileging of interest in forms of learning, thought to lead to some measurable outcome in examination results. The 'value added' in Alex's teaching is that the children learned things they would not have learned without his help, enabling them to exceed expectations.

The logic at work in these systems of education is, of course, a means–ends logic; the very means are identified of making improvements in the outcomes of formal education – means including, for example:

- instituting the principle of assessment as grounds for all formal systems of education so that what counts as education can be measured on the basis of assessment

---

2 Including, for example, Fullan and Hargreaves, 1988; Louis and Miles, 1990; Burridge and Ribbins, 1994; Hargreaves, 1994, 2003; Hopkins et al., 1994; Hopkins, 1997, 2001, 2005; Fullan, 1999, 2003, 2007; Joyce et al., 1999; Hopkins and Reynolds, 2001; Hargreaves and Fink, 2006; Hargreaves and Shirley, 2009; Creemers and Kyriakides, L. 2011.

- implementing a state system of accountability in education (in the England, for
  example, OfSTED) that provides the basis for the measurement of educational
  performance
- ensuring that the management and leadership in schools and colleges is directed
  towards goals for performance identified within the state apparatus
- continually raising the bar for 'standards' in education as determined by quantitative metrics of educational performance
- revising recurrently the training of teachers in a bid to ensure that current standards are surpassed in the future.

Improvement becomes a rallying cry for these causes to be served – the targets or ends to be reached through formal education – not least, raising examination performance levels.

While Alex's approach to guiding his students does not fit readily into the foregoing logic of improvement, it is never disregarded by anyone working in educational practices, as long as the ends are shown to be improvements in what has been learned on the basis of official measures.

The system in which Alex is situated has a seemingly voracious appetite for improvement. In fact, the teleology of the ends is almost always confounded. Particular endpoints in the system – for example, the end of each key stage in the English system – are almost invariably used by teachers, classroom assistants, students, headteachers, managers and other stakeholders to justify the means of improving the outcomes of learning, as measured largely by examination results.

The signifier – 'the means' – has already come to signify something quite different in Alex's preamble to the discourse of improvement in which Alex is now situated. There is no essential truth about the means. As a sign on the page or spoken in conversation, 'the means' only makes sense within a differential network of signs that each point to something other than themselves. And, in making sense of signs mediating identity, the individual has recourse to memory. But, as Derrida (2004) reminds us, in coming to be signs, including the means, what we are left with is only a trace of being. He talked of 'a fabric of traces referring endlessly to something other than itself, to other differential traces' (Derrida, 2004: 69).

Derrida spent much of his life opening questions about the context of identity that surfaces in our memory. For him memory is always a catastrophe: it carries with it 'the wild desire to preserve everything and to gather everything together in its idiom' (Derrida and Ferraris, 2002: 41).

The 'trace' in Derrida's discourse points to the 'possibility of any identity is simultaneously its impossibility' (Dooley and Kavanagh, 2007: 4). In other words, because everything that Alex says has a context and a history which are impossible to recount fully, there can be no such thing as Alex's pure identity. In making sense of Alex and what he says by comparison with our own experiences, the understandings revealed in this way are always mediated by the play of signs. His identity unfolds in the endless 'play of difference', where we are left only with traces. The traces carry with them their own testament of 'passion and desire always to do more', always to strive to remember more that was lost. It is the force of passion and desire that in part lies behind the ongoing drive for the improvement of education (Derrida and Ferraris, 2002: 41; Dooley and Kavanagh, 2007: 6, 10).

Alex's approach encourages many possible outcomes, including a love of learning, a sense of delight and pleasure from learning, a respect for the dignity of others and continual attempts to make sense of Dasein. But none of these possible outcomes are causally related to inputs by the teacher, and none lend themselves readily to measurable outcomes. While they have all been recognized within discourses of school improvement, they tend to be covered over by the privileging of examination results as the officially recognized, so-called objective measures that mark the ideological telos of the system. The ideological telos tends to reduce the play of difference in the dominant official language of education.

There are other ways, too, of 'playing on the play within language' that Miller (2004: 188) indicates we draw upon in the process of 'deconstruction'. In being deconstructive regarding the outcomes of the system, it is not the education system, per se, that elides possibilities identified by Alex; it is a structurally inescapable aspect of the means–ends logic grounding the system itself that creates the elision. As Reiff (1975: 2) has acutely noted, 'Weber's ends, the causes there to be served, are the means of acting; they cannot escape service to power'. The 'capillarity' of power is not something possessed by the individual, but works as an 'absent presence', as Clarke and Newman (1997: xiii) observed, permeating differential networks of signs that we call discourses (Foucault, 1980a).

In not being reducible to 'objects', love, spontaneity, joy, dignity, respect and other 'traces' of distinctly human qualities are not easily transformed into commodities. One possible difficulty in each case is that these signs do not readily mirror, or stand in mimetic relation to an empirically verifiable 'object'.

Here also the tradition of metaphysics has always sought to provide the philosophical grounds for an object. Derrida wanted to challenge thinking: the identity of these signs, including these ideological 'objects' and all signs more generally, is derived from repetition: 'identity is proportionate to repetition' (Caputo, 1987: 123). In fact, taking account of the incomplete contexts, incomplete histories and multiplicity of possible meanings that continually unfold from the play of difference, he also explored the language of reiteration, a repetition repeating differently. 'Systemic' forms of improvement are driven by the desire to reduce down any reiteration to a faithful repetition of the same (Derrida, 1972: 52; 1982: 26; Caputo, 1987: 123).

In our societies, because the foregoing gathering of signs does not lend itself to commodification within any economic system, it tends to be undervalued in relation to productivity and the value added of employees. Our dominant discourses of economic activity give license to productivity before human qualities.

The scope for improvement is almost without limits. In its rhetoric it also proves to be the most seductive discourse; its very aspiration towards progress in raising the levels of achievement for young people renders counter-critique difficult. After all, who could possibly argue against the improvement of education? Developed and developing countries around the globe continue to become ever more focused upon raising student achievement levels over and above expectations by the time they reach the conclusion of formal secondary education (Fullan, 2003a; 2007).

What has already become clear is that in looking for the meaning of text concerning improvement, we have found nothing but the play of signs that have deposited other traces. As Dreyfus and Rabinow (1982: 107) suggested, 'the more one interprets the more one finds not the fixed meaning' of improvement 'or of the world' of education that continually unfolds in this regime, 'but only other interpretations'.

The language of the enframing

Accordingly, given the number of interpretations possible, why has the education system not been brought to its knees in chaos? For one possible answer to this particular conundrum we will need to continue to look beyond discourses of education. From this perspective the logic of means–ends structures is not confined to the field of education; the logic embodies what Heidegger (1977b), called 'technological enframing'. It is the precondition for commodification that forms the basis of our economies of formal education.

For Heidegger, discourses structured in the enframing are rooted in philosophical discourses of metaphysics that defer to the writings of Plato. In Caputo's (1987) reading of Heidegger and Derrida's works, language changes, evolves and develops through 're-iteration', that is, we all repeat language slightly differently. This has to be the case; the context of what is said is itself partial, incomplete, continually changing and never fully defined.

It should be no surprise, therefore, that the form of discourses that have been developed in the name of improvement in accordance with means–ends logic in 'technological enframing', or simply the 'enframing', match those found in other domains of the economy. For Dasein, there is always the danger that the means–ends logic reduces us, constituting just one way among many of revealing the world. The very ubiquity of 'enframing' has meant that it has simply unfolded over time as hegemony. What, after all, could be more obvious than 'change'? Here we are concerned with the deployment of change in the construction of specific social projects creating a sense of order within the field of education.

In fact, although Clarke and Newman, in their critical examination of the political forces at work in 'the remaking of social welfare' in England, have already identified five distinct 'narrative structures' carrying the imperative for 'change' (1997: 40), their study falls short of uncovering 'the enframing' itself.

Of interest is that much larger story that goes beyond questions of social welfare and formal education to issues of the very ordering of human existence. Is this also not a matter of education? Here, interest will be confined to Clarke and Newman's five particular forms of narrative, found to be currently shaping discourses of improvement. These narratives are conceived as essentially the dominant technological means of ordering and shaping human existence and revealing what is deemed to be reality within formal education systems. Such revealing is a mark of the temporal unfolding in the enframing in these narratives – it is always in danger of reducing our world down to being revealed only on the basis of the principle of reason, or its off-spring in education, the principle of

assessment. Such technological enframing as one way of revealing, therefore, colonizes an ordering of the world. This is the new reality of what
Foucault (1991) had called 'governmentality'. In our deconstruction, it
has been uncovered as being constituted within at least five narratives of
change within the field of improvement – each narrative unfolding in different ways in response to the dominant governmental agenda of 'raising
standards' in education. What is deemed by the government to be real in
formal education is then determined almost exclusively by one of these
dominant narratives of change. On this reading improvement discourses
constitute both governmental apparatus and the very means of raising
standards within formal systems of education. But, as a dominant and
dispersed modality of bio-power inscribed by the state in the enframing,
the new reality of governmentality has retained an almost uncanny silence
in the literature on improvement. We ask is 'enframing' in improvement
made real in terms of five complementary narratives of change:

- change as natural
- change as hopeful struggle
- transformative change
- change as uncertainty and turbulence
- change as re-engineering (Clarke and Newman, 1997: 40–6, adapted from the original)

Each of these narratives forms a new 'object' of government – improvement – where 'subjects, and the forces and capacities of living individuals, as members of a population', are constituted as available resources
readily fostered and optimized within formal systems of education.

We have re-named the second narrative 'change as hopeful struggle', reflecting the contrasting emphasis placed within the field of education. At issue is how these particular hegemonic narratives shape,
order, delimit and constitute a ready-made language of improvement
for the entire domain of formal education. It is in the nature of the
hegemony of change that the roots of these narratives tap into the very
hearts of all teachers and educationalists more generally. The hegemony connects directly with the common 'ethic of care' that Alex displayed at the start of this chapter (Hargreaves, 1994: 173). Is there not
also a danger that our very human qualities adapt to the dominant
machine-like logic in 'the enframing'?

When the feminist critic, Haraway (2003: 429), created her political mythology, 'the cyborg', 'a hybrid of machine and organism, a creature of social reality as well as a creature of fiction', it was supposed to have been ironic. Is it not perhaps doubly ironic that some of our education systems are now in danger, inadvertently, of encouraging the adaptation of Dasein into cyborgs – cybernetic creatures for whom the spontaneity and vibrancy of play and laughter is no longer valued, who are 'watchfully earnest' and 'focussed' and – above all – encultured into the privileging of productive economic activity? Hopefully readers will be shocked by even the possibility of this question. But let us for the moment keep this possibility in mind in considering the narrative structures where so many practitioners have been thrown, carrying with them the moral imperative for change.

The language of 'being thrown' might appear a little misplaced to some readers. After all, is it not the case that, as agents, we always have the possibility of shaping and creating particular forms of language for ourselves? Being thrown does not deny the possibility of agency. But it does point to the fact that language is always present, mediating our activities; thus, to some extent it has a claim on any agency involved.

Narratives at work

What follows is a brief account of how narratives work before further exploring what lies concealed within the five dominant narrative structures of improvement.

Narratives re-present or present again our lived experiences in various ways. In this way our experiences become 'pedagogized' (Bernstein, 2000), that is, 'recontextualised' in comparison to the setting in which they had originally unfolded. Narratives of change tend to colonize agents around particular ways of understanding 'change' in education. By creating the illusion of being grounded in research from the classroom and other environments for formal learning, narratives of change purport to create causal connections between the 'evidence base' and moral imperatives for agents to act in particular ways. With the dominant focus in narratives of educational change upon 'empirical evidence', only a relative minority of researchers have ever examined the possibility that it is the always broken circular repetition of language itself that attempts to create the ground for connections (Stronach, 2000, 2006; MacLure, 2003, 2006a, 2006b).

Narratives of change and improvement in education order time in a conveniently neat chronological system of beginning, middle and end phases. By means of this retrospective gaze, many of these narratives overlook the hidden lacuna, chaos, confusion, disorder, fragmentation, discontinuity and ambiguity that many have experienced in their efforts to change particular organizations and institutions. Indeed, we will also explore one particular narrative structure in which particular forms of chaos, themselves provide yet another rationale and motivation for a particular approach to change (Fullan, 2003a).

Each narrative of change produces its own vehicle, which highlights particular connections. In Bruner's words:

> Every telling is an arbitrary imposition of meaning on the flow of memory in which we highlight some causes and discount others. (1990: 7)

Viewed through the lens of Derrida's discourse, Bruner's standpoint is in fact quite impossible. For Derrida, power is at play in all our narratives, constituting simplified dominant plots that take precedence over other possible plots and imprison our lived experience. As Derrida puts it, narrative becomes 'a violent instrument of torture'. This is his way of saying that 'we are always already caught up in a tradition or a circular economy; we are always already claimed by forces, including language and the law, which precede us and determine our beliefs and practices' (Derrida, 2004: 78; Dooley and Kavanagh, 2007: 122).

The absent present language of means

Even in this short preamble, there is already a risk of becoming immersed in a discourse that may be interpreted as establishing the 'obviousness of change'. This is characteristic of the 'change as natural' narrative. We seek to illuminate the structure of similar narratives found in remaking and improving formal systems of education in schools. It is also important to foreground the absent presence of the means of improvement.

Means, in their various guises as powerful narrative structures telling the story of school improvement, order the world of education (Clarke and Newman, 1997: 40–1).

It is our claim that these very means gather together researchers, teachers, students and other educational professionals into particular forms of action in the name of improvement. These very means, which we are about to uncover in the form of five interrelated narratives of improvement, determine and delimit to some extent what can be said and thought about improvement. Therefore, we reflect again on the identities of teachers, who tend to become immersed in governmental apparatuses.

In moving beyond Clarke and Newman's (1997) sociological thesis, this chapter opens further consideration and debate regarding the moral force of this narrative of 'change as natural'. We have called the ordering of our world in the name of improvement 'the enframing', taking Heidegger's (1977b) discourse on the essence of technology beyond his original understanding. Ordering is already tangible in the metaphoric language of 'change as natural'. It invites us to see everything in terms of change and positions us in our world as if change could be controlled and mastered – almost a matter of tending plants in the greenhouse (Peim and Flint, 2009).

The means of improvement: Change as natural

In the early development of the language of *School Improvement in an Era of Change* (1994), Hopkins et al. invite us to believe that the very roots of improvement lie within this all-pervading natural phenomenon of 'change' in the modern world. Although their language makes typological distinctions between incremental, planned, internal and external forms of change, they do not give the reader any resources to question what might be concealed behind the language. The narrative is locked in its own circular economy of signs.

Indeed, in the references made in this form of narrative, there is almost an invocation to an 'evolutionary framework' and to the idiom of 'building an evolutionary school', suggesting that innovative improvements in formal education are simply a matter of 'adaptation to the environment'. But how do human cultures of improvement connect with what some might regard as an outdated Darwinian worldview? These questions are never addressed. What tends to be privileged is the imagery of 'living in a state of learning' arising from the 'embedding of staff development', where the use of the present continuous tense suggests that 'improvement' is an integral part of our lives and will continue to be so. The imagery simply obfuscates the continual drive for learning about 'objects' of the economy, which are always themselves rendered as traces of being (Dalin, 1993: 5; Burridge and Ribbins, 1994: 191; Joyce et al., 1999: 113).

In practice, Alex now finds himself having to use the currently fashionable metaphor of 'learning muscles' (Claxton, 2006) and to absorb the new idiom of young people as 'learners'. It is revealing that the enframing in improvement discourses, in which this metaphor and its associated idiom tends to inculcate the belief that learning is a natural function; the mind lends itself to training, just as an athlete trains in order to reach higher levels of performance. Paradoxically, the metaphor of 'learning muscles' might be seen as essentially 'dumbing down' the discourse of education. Is its uptake and acceptance by professionals a mark of the way people tend to be 'docile bodies' in accepting of the language of improvement? Within the circular economy of this language it tends to engender a calculus of correlation between what are re-presented as 'objective' measures of 'what has been learned' and performance rather than, as Alex has suggested at the start of this chapter, the possibilities of learning and human well-being.

Linguistically, 'The Past, Present and Future of School Improvement' pragmatically separates clock time into a linear sequence of events. This narrative has 'completely killed off' the possibility of the complex interplay of Alex's and other teachers' senses of their own temporality. But, in the everydayness of education, where time and temporality tend to be conflated, this narrative cleverly situates the ideological figure of the 'educationalist' on a developmental platform ready for the departure of a 'third phase of change'. In this context the imagery of 'the third age' pictures an entirely natural and inescapable global phenomenon (Hopkins and Reynolds, 2001).

The means of improvement: Change as hopeful struggle

The symbolism of 'What's Worth Fighting for Out There' might suggest the distinct possibility of a battle within discourses of improvement. But, the metaphors used in this particular narrative are much less about fighting a possible enemy than campaigning 'to do the right things well . . . and to keep the momentum and impact going'. It is the continual struggle for professional identity. We might include in the metaphors the imagery of objectives, targets, strategies and goals, represented within narratives that emphasize a 'hopeful struggle against the odds of drift, despair and despondency' (Fullan and Hargreaves, 1998: 3).

The story line in this form of narrative is more proactive, requiring teachers and their leaders to take command of improvement. For example, in support of the work of the individual teacher, the language of 'the strategic use of special teaching and learning models' is seen as grounds for enhancing student achievement. Etymologically, the term *strategic* still carries with it echoes of the Greek *strategia*, connoting the office or command of a general. Again, the language of differential strategies is used to provide a focus for support involving failing, moderately effective and effective schools. While the imagery of strategy in this form of narrative positions agencies in command of improving aspects of their organizations, the imagery of targets and objectives in the narrative purports to give a sense of direction. Similarly, the imagery of 'The New Strategic Direction' positions 'school leaders' in command of the 'strategic flow' from analysis through to 'school strategy' and the 'development of the school' (Joyce et al., 1999: 142; Davies and Ellison, 2003; Hopkins, 2005: 16).

Paradoxically, the multiplicity of ideological objects uncovered from the science of improvement in this discourse – each themselves traces of being, and remnants of reality constitute, as we will see shortly, the very locus of desire for improvement.

The means of improvement: 'Transformative change'

In positioning key agents as upbeat in terms of improvement, in this more expansive discourse the signs point to nothing less than organizational and social transformation. For example, West et al., (1997) detailed the outcomes of 'The Moving Schools' project, which attempted to understand and connect leadership with transformations in schools (West et al., 2002: 38). The symbolism of the moving school suggests that this ideological object is being re-presented as both dynamic in the organizational process of school improvement and effective in terms of the outcomes. Indeed, more than a decade later, Fullan's (2007) injunction, 'The New Meaning of Educational Change', as the re-presentation and exploration of a new social order of improvement in formal education extending around the globe, incorporates the language of the 'parent and community' as part of its concerns regarding the 'systemic' improvement of education. The ideological language of the 'system', from the Greek *systema*, indicates a network of signs gathering together agencies and resources in the name of transforming and improving formal education. We now have the language of 'Improving Communities' (Hopkins et al., 1994: 91; Cotton and Mann, 2003).

The subtext of the command and control imputed by strategic forms of improvement efforts has been re-presented pragmatically, for example, in terms of 'sustainable leadership'. Its language makes recourse to seven principles that purport to open a new doctrine of leadership reflecting the newly emergent zeitgeist of sustainability from the turn of the millennium. In drawing directly from corporate and environmental literatures on 'sustainability' and 'sustainable development' (Hargreaves and Fink, 2006), the narrative has aligned itself with a progressive social force in modern society. In grounding itself upon 'seven principles in educational change and leadership' (Hargreaves and Fink, 2006: 18–20) the narrative constitutes itself almost as a law of social transformation. These principles situate the educationalist within the lawlike moral foundations of a seven-part doctrine for leadership of educational change that makes the claim to sustainability (Hargreaves and Fink, 2006: 18).

Other versions of this transformational narrative of change work from a vision of what is claimed to be 'new'. For example, 'the vision' narrated by Hopkins (1997: 138) in his inaugural lecture as a professor at the University of Nottingham was 'of students engaged in compelling learning situations, created by skilful teachers in school settings designed to promote learning for both groups of people'. Again the discourse connected this vision with six principles grounding the capacity for successful improvement.

Paradoxically, within this particular circular economy of signs – which in leaving its trace provides an essential driver for improvement – this narrative has become a powerful hegemony *for* change. The narrative positions educational agencies with visions of how reconceptualized forms of leadership can become part of a framework for enhancing every aspect of learning. The narrative even appears to incorporate those aspects of Alex's teaching that so often are lost through the emphasis on assessment. The powerful social forces at work take the reader away completely from any questions regarding what might lie behind this language.

The means of improvement: Change as uncertainty and turbulence

Narratives of change as uncertainty and turbulence have unfolded in Fullan's (1993; 1999; 2003a) discourses. The circular economy of signs, which in every case is always already broken, makes strong connections with the foregoing narratives. In the field of education, the metaphors of discontinuity, instability, fluidity and chaos serve to identify some of the limitations of planned change. This language also provides a rationale for different ways of thinking about the means of bringing to fruition systemic forms of improvement. The imagery of transformation conveys a more 'expansive view' of improvement (Clarke and Newman, 1997: 42).

The narrative structure conflates the language of 'complexity theory' with discourse exploring 'evolutionary theory' (Fullan 1993:4–10). It makes connections between what Louis and Miles (1990: 201) call 'an evolutionary planning process' and Senge's (1990) discourse *The Fifth Discipline*. In these contexts, the narrative of change as uncertainty and turbulence positions agencies within much wider evolutionary systems. The outward manifestations of the narrative, symbolized by turbulence, chaos, discontinuity and fluidity, were once used to provide a rationale for '*productive change*' as an ideological '*process of mobilization and positive contagion*' (Fullan with Steiglebauer, 1991: 31; emphasis as in the original). More recently the discourse has changed: the 'need to know more' about the 'dynamics' of 'change' has become important for Fullan (2007: 117).

In fact, readings of complexity theory concerning the possibility of order emerging from chaos are expropriated to provide an ideological rationale for situating 'change agents'. Agents are re-presented in the flux where 'moral purpose and complexity' (Fullan, 1999: 10) play themselves out in the relationship between education and democracy. The hegemony not only sells educators the very idea of change itself, it also represents itself as a rational basis for the management of all forms of educational agency. The discourses of improvement, re-presented with élan and beautifully crafted with rhetoric and symbolism, provide the educationalist with ready-made understandings of improvement, which tend to appeal directly to average everyday experiences of forms of organization.

Some of the language used in narratives of change as uncertainty and turbulence has a distinctly evangelical and theological tone to it. For example, according to this hegemony, 'moral purpose is the antidote to the march of folly' (Fullan, 1991). Moral purpose is represented as reconciling 'powerful new forces for growth and development' (Fullan, 1991). Educators are about to receive no less than 'eight basic lessons of the new paradigm of change' from their readings of some of Fullan's work (1991; 1999), and a further eight new lessons in the final book in this series (Fullan, 2003a). Without even a hint of double irony the discourse legitimates what is re-presented as the 'new' management of formal education involving so-called learning organizations. There is certainly no hint of the enframing that has unfolded over the past two millennia.

Here is a prime example of what Foucault (1984: 132) called a 'regime of truth'. It is truth understood and witnessed as a system of ordered procedures within the field of improvement 'for the production, regulation, distribution, circulation and operation of statements', here concerning educational improvement. Truth, revealed also in these discourses 'is linked in a circular fashion' with the enframing – the system of power which it induces and which extend it – a 'regime' of truth (Foucault, 1984: 132) as *the* way of revealing the world.

But, the particular regimes of truth, constituted as narratives of school improvement, contain their own paradox. Each of the circular economies re-presented in these narratives, which are always broken, leaves only its remnants, the trace of these economies of improvement, constituting the very locus of improvement efforts. Put another way: *paradoxically, in producing scientific narratives of improvement, the apparatus used to construct this science is in fact the very locus driving improvement efforts.*

The means of improvement: Change as re-engineering

As grounding and as the means of improvement efforts, this narrative ideology represents itself as opening a 'much sharper curtailment' of selected 'old realities and practices' (Clarke and Newman, 1997: 44).

This narrative structure first came into fashion in the early 1980s in the world of business following a number of publications (Juran, 1979; Deming, 1986; Peters and Waterman, 2004). But it was Hammer and Champy's (1993) much-quoted exploration of 'Business Process Re-engineering' that proved the guiding light in further shaping this particular discourse. Ideologically, and once more without even a hint of irony, this process is re-presented as 'a fundamental rethinking and radical redesign of business processes to achieve dramatic improvements in contemporary measures of performance' (Hammer and Champy, 1993: 32; Clarke and Newman, 1997: 44). Again the dissimulation of 'enframing' is almost comprehensive.

Caldwell's (1997) paper provides a similar case. Although the logic of enframing is there in the title, this particular discourse plays down the possibilities of causality. Caldwell, who contributed to three books on this subject, has pictured 'three tracks' involving the re-engineering of school education (1997: 202). The metaphoric language of 'tracks' immediately places the reader on one of three parallel journeys, each with their own definite structure and direction.

To continue the metaphor, the places where tracks have been already laid, according to Caldwell's claims, are in Australia, New Zealand and England. At issue here is the language that unfolds in 'track 3'. In track 3 in Caldwell's metaphorical schema, involving the 're-engineering of a gestalt or vision for school education', experiences mediating learning are re-presented in terms of 'excited live involvement' in 'electronic networking' (1997: 214). It is in this discourse that the enframing is made real in terms of the possibilities opened by technologies, not least in terms of re-engineering the very fabric of the workplace of the school and of the school curriculum on a global stage (Caldwell, 1997: 213–4). However, the structure of the narrative, which emphasizes the radical rethinking at the heart of re-engineering, never opens the shutters for readers to breathe new air into their thinking about our complex relationship with technology (Peim and Flint, 2009; Flint, 2010a, b, c; 2011a, b).

The re-invention of 'fractal' government presented in Barber's (1997) discourse makes clever use of metonymy to make tacit connections with complexity and turbulence once more. The narrative makes claims to 'fundamental, radical and dramatic reassessments of the role of the state and the means of delivery of public services' (Barber, 1997: 44). At the very point of a complete change of administration in England, in Barber's words, 'the (education) minister's chief responsibility is not to tinker with Whitehall, but to promote successful change in every classroom' (1997: 189). In practice, the new administration was marked by a deluge of new policies for schools and England.

Reflections upon the discursive means of improvement

What has been uncovered in these five distinct narratives of change is the enframing. The enframing in the complex interplay of these narratives signifies the continual ordering of the world of education, in accord with hidden means–ends logic. In official terms the world of education is then reduced to being only revealed in one way in accordance with the grammatical logic of subject connecting with object on grounds of the principle of reason. In nearly all formal systems of education, this logic accords with the 'principle of assessment': nothing of educational value (measured in accordance with laws inscribed by professional protocols) is without assessment (Heidegger, 1977b; Peim and Flint, 2009).

Caught up in its own regime of truth, academic discourse within the field of improvement tends to reinforce improvement as the one true path and to create a particular synergy between education, practice and research. This regime opens only one way of revealing the world and does not see the paradox of its own standpoint. In other words, the attempts to elevate school improvement to a science have failed to see that the form of science is the precise locus of its own improvement efforts (Flint, 2011b).

Regarding Alex's professionality, and the professional identity of teachers more generally, the foregoing deconstruction has revealed a number of the countervailing and contradictory historically shifting discursive and practical possibilities that both shape and are shaped by professional identity in a number of regimes of truth called school improvement, spreading in all of the developed – and many developing – economies throughout the world.

Enacting critique of education

Research provides a number of avenues of critique of aspects of education that avoid recourse to the language of improvement. What follows are two short case studies from leading researchers. The deconstruction will illuminate the contradictory logic of the selected research. It will show that in their critique of modern systems of education grounded in the ethic of improvement, these researchers' arguments remain locked within the very same language of improvement (Peim and Flint, 2009).

Both Gorard and Gillborn have been selected because they both have pre-eminent track records as researchers within the field of education. Moreover, neither are strongly associated with the extant fields of school improvement and school effectiveness.

Gorard is now professor of education research at the University of Birmingham in England. As a leading quantitative researcher in the field of education, his list of publications from research conducted between 2001 and 2008, published on his website, extends over eighteen pages. He is regarded as a major authority in the field.

We present our readings from three of Gorard's papers in two steps as follows. In the first step, we provide a critical reading of two of his recent papers, that project the world of improvement as the reality in education. Secondly, we examine a paper published chronologically between the two papers considered in the first step – a paper that makes no mention of improvement in any form whatsoever.

The first step involves a critical reading of Gorard's (2006) re-analysis of official 'value-added figures' published for schools in England by the DfES in 2004. This indicator purports to provide a measure of the value added by a school in raising a student's learning above that predicted on the basis of performance measured when the student was younger. Gorard's re-analysis of the 2004 value-added figures sought to show that these figures turn out to be a proxy measure of the overall attainment of the school and are almost entirely independent of student progress.

Gorard suggests that 'improvement policies, at least in the narrow sense' of policies designed to enhance performance in examinations and other test scores, 'are likely to be ineffective' (2004: 6). However, in examining the basis for improvement policy, his argument contradicts itself by presupposing the extant order of improvement within the field of education that it has sought to appraise. For Gorard, an improvement in test scores that cannot be explained by a change in the nature of the school intake must be established in order to show that a school has improved. Otherwise, school effectiveness and school improvement (SESI) is a 'sleight of hand' (2006: 5; emphasis as in the original). He fails see the contradiction of using the paradigm of school improvement to evaluate improvement efforts.

His next paper was published two years later and seeks to assess 'the rates of social mobility in Britain'. Gorard's paper attempts to show that an earlier study of declining social mobility in Britain 'appeared to have had an impact on policy makers out of all proportion to its scale and rigour' (Gorard, 2008: 317). The overriding concern in this more recent paper is that of the quality of research presented in one paper by Blanden et al. that had made two claims regarding the 'decrease in mobility over time and poor international standing of Britain' (2005: 318). For Gorard, the impact of their paper had been made significant by powerful advocates in the government of Britain adopting its findings. Ruth Kelly, the secretary of state for education, and her successor Alan Johnson had both put social mobility at the top of their agenda on the basis of the research. However, Gorard's own re-analysis of the figures was entirely consonant with a study by Jantti et al. concluding that 'the United Kingdom bears a closer resemblance to the Nordic countries than to the United States of America' (2006: 5) in terms of 'social mobility'.

It is ironic that Gorard should preface his own work by stating that 'one lever that is more fully under the control of researchers is the quality of research' (2008: 317). Because, in critiquing 'the rates of social mobility' and seeking to reposition Britain's standing on a global stage in terms of its policy of enhancing social mobility, he remains contradictorily aligned to *the* only apparent reality of education projected as the world of improvement – which his paper is in part seeking to critique.

The second step in these critical readings of excerpts from Gorard's recent work is to take an example that makes no reference to improvement. His critique is structured in response to the question: 'What does an index of school segregation measure?' (Gorard, 2007: 669). His re-analysis centres upon a research paper by Allen and Vignoles (2007). It shows that there was a subsequent rise in segregation after 1997 that is hardly congruent with any notion of school improvement. At one level, the paper presented deals with this inconsistency by simply exorcising any reference to the improvement ethic. But, here authoritatively and symbolically, in proceeding as if the discourse of school improvement does not exist, Gorard directly contradicts two former papers.

There is, of course, an alternative explanation. This leading authority within the field of education, who colonizes ideological 'objects' and identities through the symbolic authority invested in his research, projects the world of improvement as *the* reality of education. The research we have briefly identified in the second step could then be seen as his way of removing his research from reality. But, in fact, the reality – that of the enframing – is branded in its very language.

Gorard's papers identified in this brief case study of our critical readings all feature a fundamental contradiction. There is also a second source of contradiction. These texts exhibit further incongruity, magnified by the authority currently invested in his research.

The final stage of this case study involves a further critical reading of excerpts of research from Gillborn. As professor of critical race studies at the Institute of Education in London, Gillborn is another leading figure in the field of educational research. His website reveals that he has twice won the 'Best Book in the Field of Education Studies' from the Society for Educational Studies (SES) on the basis of two leading publications (Gillborn and Youdell, 2000; Gillborn, 2008a).

Gillborn's book provides 'detailed research accounts of systematic and deep rooted institutional racism' and argues 'that race inequality should be placed centre-stage as a fundamental axis of operation' of racism' (2008: 1). Although his research is mostly based in England, he suggests that the 'analyses are just as applicable to education systems in the US, Canada, Europe and Australasia' (2008: 1).

The studies presented as a whole constitute for Gillborn a 'damning critique of the racist nature' of the English education system, highlighting the institutional racism within the system. This system is seen to 'feed off' and to be 'reinforced by' a very public 'conspiracy', namely, a 'concert of action for common purpose', serving to maintain the domination of whites through 'the dialectical relationship' between the wider structures and individual agency (Gillborn, 2008b: 230). However, in enacting his critique of racism within the education system, symbolically recognized as being based upon continuous improvement, Gillborn contradicts himself. He uses the same benchmark of improvement of education as a measure of the success that all ethnic groups 'have enjoyed' over the past fifteen years. However, he does recognize that 'significant problems persist' (Gillborn, 2008a: 1, 60, 192, 194).

In fact – ironically, given the extant dominance of Caucasians – his critique projects and gives further license to the world of school improvement, authoritatively symbolized as *the reality* of education. His claim, 'It takes a nation of millions (and a particular kind of education system) to hold us back', grounds itself in the same contradiction, centring itself upon examination reforms and the 'disproportionate number of Black pupils to achieve the best grades in their GCSEs'. In applying 'critical race theory' once more to uncover 'education policy as an act of white supremacy', Gillborn remains stubbornly wedded to the same incongruity (Gillborn, 2005; 2005b: 89).

This is contradictory because the performative constitution of ethnic identities remains dominated by the multiplicity of means of improvement. Are these very means not implicated in Gillborn's (2008a) 'conspiracy'? Certainly, within these narratives of improvement, beyond grounding assumptions concerning the law of equal opportunities, there is very little direct engagement within the SESI literature that either recognizes or addresses 'institutional racism'.

Reflections

These two cases and the chapter illuminate the complexities and the powers of the enframing in the name of educational improvement. The writing has put a spotlight on the ways discourses of improvement as regimes of truth both define the nature of things in education and how agents and educational agencies have become structured and driven in their activities within the governmental apparatus of the state. It renders Dasein as resources that are available for use to be optimized within systemic forms of schooling.

It has been possible also to recognize other forms of language and pedagogies standing outside the enframing. It is tempting to suggest that these and other radicalized pedagogies might provide an alternate way out of an aporia, but the means–ends logic would itself constitute yet another incongruity of the highest order. In our increasingly ped-agogized society – witnessed here in the five narratives – is there not a danger that the object of pedagogical systems is always constituted as a remnant, fuelling our seemingly voracious desire for improvement? Have not our pedagogies lost sight of our relationship with the pos-sibilities of being constituted as networks of traces? (Bernstein, 1996: 41–63; Irigaray, 2002, 2007; Irigaray with Green, 2008).

Where is the future that is continually tending to be lost in the aporia of a programmable tomorrow? In opening *Of Grammatology*, Derrida declares that 'the future', signifying in this context the play of language that – as we have witnessed – is always beyond our capacity to con-trol, 'can only be anticipated in the form of an absolute danger. It is that breaking absolutely with constituted normality and can only be pro-claimed present as a sort of monstrosity' (1974: 5).

The French word *arrivant*, in the phrase the 'monstrous *arrivant*', indicates what comes to shore, but Derrida was concerned to think of the monstrous *arrivant* not as something that arrives, but as 'subject' – in this case the subject of the almost absolute illusion of 'objects' in our world, rather than the traces left behind by being. The monstrous *arriv-ant* in question for educational improvement, for the desire of the gift, for the need to make good performatives necessarily inhabited by the ghost of their own failure, opens questions about our relationship with the horizon of being. It is a questioning directed towards the horizon of being for education that currently remains circumscribed and delim-ited by both the principle of assessment and particular rationalities of government. Whether questioning education challenges us to open-ness – indeed, to a certain hospitality, given to the subject in this case – remains an open question.

Governing Childhood 3

Enframing and the rise of childhood

In Chapter 1 we claimed that children became the object of an intense and growing interest of government and the systems of governance, including the educational institutions that came with industrialization. Some have argued that this interest in children was the product of a new and quite different 'episteme' of childhood (Aries, 1962). Often in the name of protection, often in the name of moral hygiene and the future efficiency of national production, successive acts of parliament in the United Kingdom brought children's activity within the remit of government. This occurred at the juridical level, initially, with Factory Acts, such as that of 1833 delimiting children's working hours. It also happened at a more governmental, capillary level with the development of the elementary school.

By the end of the nineteenth century, a state apparatus enframing the lives of children had come into being, constituting what we might reasonably refer to as a social technology of childhood. Universal schooling was the key instrument in this transformation. Developments in the history of governance have intensified this concern: 'childhood' and 'the child' remain key foci for legislation and for social practices that manage children against specific norms of development expressed in the nursery curriculum and in citizenship specifications in schools.

The child is an abstraction, a spectral figure taking different forms. A specific concern attaches to the child as a potential source of social dysfunction, and this special, remediable figure is the focus of part of this chapter. As the potentially dangerous expression of social exclusion, the wayward child represents an affront to the dominant regime of normative development. Child welfare systems that emerged out of nineteenth-century concerns have taken special interest in defining children according to their own category systems. Some groups of children get treated according to an often negative identity: immigrant children, socially excluded children, traveller children and even, in the not so distant past, 'backward' children (Copeland, 1999).

Recent emphasis on the child implies an autonomous unit of address: increasing recognition of the 'self' of the child as target of social action – in a move that works on the agency of the individual. Acts of parliament concerning child welfare in 1889 (Prevention of Cruelty to Children Act) and 1908 (Children Act) to more recent Children Acts bear witness to the force of Hannah Arendt's dictum that education serves 'to protect the child against the world, the world against the child' (Arendt, 1993: 192).

According to Foucault, disciplinary practices produce subjects against a normative grid. Discipline operates with a repertoire of types, to individualize subjects to socially differentiate them. Another function of discipline is to reform the potential delinquent, to police the borders of social identity. To redirect the disoriented subjectivity of the wayward child, state regulation seeks to identify individuals, families, even 'communities' in need of remedial provision. Through the presence and application of 'services' – in the present jargon – 'service users' can be brought back within the ambit of the disciplinary mechanisms that operate through the nursery, the sure-start centre, the school, the police and child-protection services. Child-protection services, initiated in the United Kingdom between 1880 and 1910, provides access to children and families, diagnoses inadequate childrearing and care, prevents or at least hinders the movement of recalcitrant families and produces a 'scientific' knowledge of child abuse. All these forms of knowledge are embedded in practices that contribute to the business of managing liminal 'communities', social identities ill-attuned to the proliferating norms of progress and development. As childhood became a condition of dependence attended by powerlessness, it signified openness to malign influence demanding care, attention, discipline and rigorous management (Steedman, 1995).

Child protection is an element of the governance of childhood and, according to Durkheim's account of social symbolic processes, provides a range of objects and subjects with a domain of activity. This activity around children and childhood is structured as a symbolic domain of identity and action (Lacan, 2006). Its work is not socially neutral. The shaping of social space–time of this symbolic ordering interpellates subjects affectively, producing specific identities for children and for those who work within the governmental domain of childhood: nursery care workers, teachers, social workers, police, psychologists, educational administrators – all inhabit the world of the child within a complex social formation.

In philosophical terms we might see this array of identities and the activities and ways of being they give rise to as a particular enframing of childhood, one that has become inescapable in modernity and beyond. This regime of disciplinary care constitutes an ontology of childhood, and it is this ontology that we wish to explore here, examining some of its effects and attempting to 'see' it from a perspective outside of itself. It is not that we wish to question the value of this important condition of modernity. Child protection remains an absolutely vital, if as yet incomplete, triumph of what Giddens has referred to as 'reflexive modernity' (Giddens, 1984).

What we want to emphasize is how the modern and contemporary 'world' of childhood produces specific modes of being within a set of beliefs and practices arising from a version of reality that remains open to interrogation (Heidegger, 1962). As the figure of the child becomes the focus for a range of social concerns, this variously constructed image acquires special significances for discourses about the relations between society and nature, industrialization and urbanization. Images of poor, swarming children haunt nineteenth-century consciousness (Walvin, 1982: 117). This mindset, in the West, begins to see itself impelled by moral force to construct a new kind of future in answer to Blake's urgent question:

> Is this a holy thing to see,
> In a rich and fruitful land,
> Babes reduc'd to misery,
> Fed with cold and usurous hand? (Blake, 1971 {1794})

Social redemption focuses on childhood and children. Later, the idea that pedagogy can redeem the uncivilized and often abandoned child emerges. This realization demands a new order of responsibility and a new apparatus.

The case of the 'wild boy of Aveyron', captured in the Lacaune region of France in 1800, seemed to haunt the western European imagination, disturbing its consciousness of its capacity to put scientific knowledge to redemptive use. Civilization had abandoned the wild boy, who had probably been the victim of a murder attempt in infancy. He survived but did not acquire language and appeared in a animalistic guise beyond the pale of the symbolic order (Lane, 1979). All the pastoral and socio-medical efforts of well-intentioned, philanthropic carers could not redeem the wild boy – perhaps explaining why this figure remains an intractable symbolic knot in Western thinking. One relatively recent ruse, to assuage the problem this historical occurrence presents, has been to retrospectively diagnose the problem as a specifically medical issue. Autism provides a culturally 'useful' explanation for the wild boy's intractability to civilization (Bettelheim, 1967: 371–2). Alternatively, it is possible that the story of the wild boy refers to a fear of the untutored child, a fear of the 'nature within' that may signify a kernel of resistance to the project of civilization.

There is no doubt that the Enlightenment seems to have given rise, against its confident assumption of rationality and progress, to feelings of abandonment and loss. Childhood appears as such a condition in much of William Wordsworth's writings, for example. Wordsworth's 'Ode on Intimation of Immortality' presents the untutored child as a figure attuned to the natural world (Coveney, 1967: 80). Loss of innocence and the interventions of culture in that natural bond carry a powerful and difficult question of responsibility. In what manner and under what regime of truth should such a critical and fundamental process be managed?

In modernity, childhood becomes a complex 'thing' shaped in myriad practices, representations, ideas and discourses. Some claim childhood as an 'invention' of modernity, insisting that any 'common sense' perception of childhood as clearly differing from adulthood is the product of recent social and cultural change (Aries, 1962; Cunningham, 2006; Bray, 2009).

Ontology and other worlds of childhood

A significant factor in determining the identity of a thing – as we have claimed – is the framework of thinking it arises from as nameable and knowable. It is not just that other historical periods, peoples and cultures have configured childhood differently. If the very idea of childhood is specific to a recent period in Western history – a recent set of representations, dispositions and practices – then what is childhood? For present purposes, we should perhaps ask: What is the significance of the contemporary governmental obsession with childhood? Why is childhood as we now know it such an intensely scrutinized and regulated domain?

The ontological position we have adopted here, influenced by Heidegger and Derrida, encourages thinking in terms of the historical, discursive identity of things being always subject to a movement – temporal or otherwise – of difference. This materialist position understands the nature of things to be dependent on the material practices that enfold their being, including the discourses and activities that frame them. A vital consideration in this kind of ontology is the question or issue of 'world'. The identity of things, or of any specific thing, is very much a matter of understanding the nature of the world it inhabits. In 'The Origin of the Work of Art', Heidegger (1993a) explores how the Greek temple belongs to the Greek 'world', how its existence as itself is intricately entwined with that world. Its meaning derives from its being within a specifically Greek ontology or understanding of being and things. Realization of the relation between objects, identities and the 'world' doesn't pertain only to works of art. The dynamic relation objects and identities have with their world – shaped by and shaping – is in fact evident in just about everything. Our 'world' is an agglomerate of the objects and identities that inhabit it and of all the practices that position us and enable us to make sense of things, to ask questions and to reach beyond our immediate understandings and knowledge (Gadamer, 1989; 1994).

One way of understanding our own idea of childhood is to consider an example or two from radically different understandings. The ancient Inca practice of *capacocha* has only relatively recently been discovered and explored. It is known that the Inca practiced child sacrifice of a particularly elaborate, chilling kind. It is now believed that children and their families were honoured to be selected for the rite, which involved lengthy preparations. Such children were invariably of high social status. They were feted and often presented to the emperor. Once selected for sacrifice they were treated with special reverence. Eventually taken on an enormous journey to some of the highest peaks in the Andes, they were sacrificed on sacred, elevated sites. Their frozen remains were left *in situ* with an array of accoutrements, rare objects of material and symbolic value (Ceruti, 2004). It is difficult from a contemporary perspective to understand these rituals or to feel empathy towards the people who perpetrated them. Is not their world very remote from ours – to the point of mutual incomprehension? And yet archaeological evidence and extant narratives suggest that the sacrificed children, both sons and daughters of the socially elevated, were highly prized.

Capacocha, the rituals associated with critical events in the life of the Inca emperor, was not the only form of child sacrifice practiced at this time. Children were exchanged for sacrifice in processes of treaty ratification, apparently. During the same period, the Aztecs in central Mexico also practiced ritual child sacrifice, carried out in public places. These events were freighted with immense religious significance and regarded as vital for the continuity of life itself. A variety of theories exist about the meaning of these practices: associations between children and play, and children and purity, rendering them suitable partners for the gods. Sacrifice apparently signified a renewal of a bond with nature, restoring a relation between the people and their world. These violent practices were highly regulated and rule-bound and occurred entirely within the legal framework, in both codified and less formal symbolic senses.

A description of the Aztec example indicates something of the ritual weight attached to this practice:

The children were kept by the priests for some weeks before their deaths (those kindergartens of doomed infants are difficult to contemplate). Then, as the appropriate festivals arrived, they were magnificently dressed, paraded in litters, and, as they wept, their throats were slit: gifted to Tlaloc the Rain God as 'bloodied flowers of maize'. (They were thought then to enter the gentle paradise of Tlaloc, which may have assuaged the parents' grief.) The pathos of their fate as they were paraded moved their watchers to tears, while their own tears were thought to augur rain. (Clendinnen, 1991: 98–9)

Such events transgress our ontological coordinates, although we are familiar with cases of child abuse and systematic murder in modern European history. Our knowledge of such things is characterized by our horror that they could happen at all (Clendennin, 1991; Sillar, 1994; Baxter, 2008; Bray, 2009; Holbroad, 2009).

'Bildung' and the burgeoning of childhood

Our contemporary configuration of childhood in the West would seem to be, of course, radically different from the ancient Incan and Aztec examples cited here. It will not be possible to settle finally and definitively the nature of modern childhood, fraught as it is with contradiction and complexity. The configuration of childhood is, nevertheless, a vital feature of our social landscape. Any understanding of contemporary practices, policies and institutions must take into account the strong correlation between childhood and education from the early nineteenth-century preoccupation with the process of 'Bildung' to the present day array of 'expert' discourses, institutions and practices.

In European culture, some of the most vivid extant pre-nineteenth-century images of childhood, as such, are found in Bruegel's (1525–1569) paintings: the painting known as 'Children's Games' stands out for its detailed portrayal of children at play. Composed c. 1560, it depicts a town full of about 250 peasant children playing 84 different games. Clearly, the painting signifies that children's play was itself deemed worthy of the unusual kind of artistic genre representing scenes of 'ordinary' life. The strangeness of this example is that it presents a world populated only by children at play. Nevertheless, the role of child's play in culture is evident in several other Breugel paintings, where children are seen at play in various settings among adult activities. In these examples, play is seen as a 'proper' activity of children. 'Peasant' life includes a technology of play. We may be tempted to see in Breugel's paintings, in their representations of both children and adults at play, a pre-modern world where the forces of carnival are set against the demands of work and religious observance. Breugel's world doesn't seem to be at all a world that makes the automatic correlation between children and education that our world constantly proposes.

There may appear little that is carnivalesque about another unusual, relatively early European image of childhood, Velasquez's paradigm painting 'Las Meninas' (1656). In this famous image, the figure of the child is at the centre. Yet, as Foucault has elaborated, it is not at all clear the 5-year-old infanta is the 'subject' of the drama. This child – a bright-eyed, very central image – is beset by a number of figures, including the artist, who frame her existence and suggest – particularly the dark figure on the stair at the rear of the painting – a sombre and serious setting for childhood radiance. 'Las Meninas' is a court painting and yet is also imbued with symbolic significance beyond that world. Foucault's detailed commentary on this painting asserts that it belongs to classical representation. It is remorselessly 'realistic' within a certain tradition of perspective. At the same time, with its proliferation of images of representation – the figure of the painter, the mirror, the numerous paintings within the painting, including the canvas the painter is working on and the mirror that reflects the shadowy figures of the child's parents – 'Las Meninas' appears to celebrate and problematize both the business of representation and the figure of the child.

A comparison can be made to John Singer Sargent's 'The Daughters of Edward Darley Doit' (1882). Sargent had scrutinized 'Las Meninas' intently before completing his own painting. At the centre, as with 'Las Meninas', is a 5-year-old girl sitting very casually on the floor, doll in her hands. She is separated in the image from her sisters, one of whom stands off-centre in the light, looking out at the spectator, while the two elder sisters are removed towards a dark background where the attention of one is directed outwards and the other (the eldest girl, perhaps no longer a child) is looking into a dark interior space. This painting has been interpreted as both a celebration of the delightful freedom of childhood and as a representation of the contrast between the vulnerable informality of early childhood and the troubling transition of adolescence. One key difference between Velasquez's seventeenth-century painting and Sargent's nineteenth-century painting is the separation of the children from the adult world. Sargent's painting is haunted by this idea of a world of childhood.

* * *

Current understandings of childhood may be traced from the end of the eighteenth century when the 'image of childhood' began to proliferate in various forms of representation. This rich inheritance contributes to our current sense of what is 'proper' to childhood (Coveney, 1967). The image of childhood becomes a means for various claims for a certain model of childhood – often through negative images of industrialization and urbanization, representing what childhood should not be. In these contexts the child is represented as a figure worthy of pity, concern and care, but also – in the case of the 'street child' – as a figure to be feared (Steedman, 1995: 112–29).

In the eighteenth century, Locke was among the first to articulate an explicit theory of childhood. Locke asserted that while children are born with particular faculties, tendencies and possibilities, the child has no inborn information or self or world but must acquire these in relation to the world. The attainment of reason is made possible through the light of nature, but only by being overlaid with the accoutrements of education that activate rationality. This supervention is the condition for freedom of action and morality.

> The well educating of their children is so much the duty and concern of parents, and the welfare and prosperity of the nation so much depends on it, that I would have everyone lay it seriously to heart and . . . set his helping hand to promote everywhere that way of training up youth . . . which is the easiest, shortest, and likeliest to produce virtuous, useful, and able men in their distinct callings. (Locke, 1996: lxiii)

Locke's advocacy of education is predicated on a thoroughly empiricist emphasis on the primacy of experience. It is experience that primarily shapes and defines what we are and what we may become. This relatively modern emphasis gives special importance to education.

Locke's rationalism explored the essence of the child in an incorporeal, ideal world. By contrast, Blake's later vision of the experiencing child is far from ideal. Blake's child is set upon by industrialization but also by a morally corrupt world of inequality. The vision Blake presents is uncompromising: 'babes reduced to misery'. London is a place of blood and sexual vice where the newborn 'infant's cry of fear' resounds as an accusation. Moralism haunts and limits childhood. 'Mind-forged manacles' and material deprivation prevent the being of the child from realization. The child is beset by 'Thou shalt not', 'binding with briars my joys and desires'. For Blake, the condition of children was an index of the spiritual and moral health of the nation. Industrialization had corrupted the land and infected childhood with poverty while puritan strains in Christianity had spiritually imprisoned childhood, blocking off its access to emotional health and truth. Blake contrasted these worldly views of his actual experience with an idealized image of childhood that he represented as the condition of innocence. This vision of childhood as potentially free from the depredations of the newly forming modernity became highly influential (Blake, 1971 {1794}).

If Blake is the visionary poet of a possible freedom constrained by a reductive moralism and by depredations of poverty, his contemporary, Wordsworth, seeks to account for the child in terms of an essential at-oneness with nature. For Wordsworth, the child is particularly, even bodily, attuned to the natural world. *Lyrical Ballads* includes several significant representations of children in nature. 'Lucy', for example, is the focus of a series of poems dealing with a child at one with nature. In *The Prelude*, Wordsworth articulates a powerful and sophisticated vision of the child in the natural landscape, shaped by and attuned to a nature that provides a context for existence in a fully emotional sense and as a medium for thought. Nature is a genuine way of being; the child is at home within this authenticity. While adulthood is often a condition to escape from to get back to the free natural state of childhood, at least it includes the possibility for articulating explicitly and consciously the spiritual harmony and solace one may find in the presence and contemplation of nature, as in 'Lines Composed a Few Miles Above Tintern Abbey' (Wordsworth and Coleridge, 1798; Wordsworth, 1996).

The novel provides another dimension, above and beyond the sharp portraits of children and aspects of childhood presented by some

Romantic poets. Several nineteenth-century novels put the child at the centre. At-oneness with nature is evident again in Emily Bronte's *Wuthering Heights* where passionate Cathy and Heathcliff can be themselves and, more importantly perhaps, can be themselves in the natural context of the moors. It is the social world, in a state of potential upheaval and fluidity, that intrudes between them, inhibiting their 'natural' destiny. The tragedy of separation that unfolds is based on a clear distinction between childhood and adulthood. In Bronte's world, childhood is an intensely experienced, highly charged emotional condition. *Great Expectations* begins with the child's world 'turned upside down'. This is no sentimentalized childhood, although the novel takes the child's passion seriously. The child is presented as a highly sensitive and reflective being. The social distinctions that seek to delimit identity and aspiration are represented as arbitrary and thoroughly accidental but powerful influences on the child's emerging consciousness of the world. In the *Mill on the Floss*, a similar collision occurs between the natural bonds of the child, Maggie Tulliver, and the social forces that prevent self-realization. *Adventures of Huckleberry Finn*, set in the American context, refers back to a frontier time and explores the emergent nation through the eyes of a child struggling against the 'civilizing' forces of local culture – often presented as far from civilized. Racism, unwarranted violence, war and commercial greed are the order of the day in the adult world. The child must negotiate this world both materially and spiritually, intuitively having to forge a moral code at odds with the corrupted morality of the adult world. The novel represents the consciousness of the child as subtle, reflective, emotionally complex and vulnerable. Beset by conflicting attachments, impulses and emotions, the child struggles to adapt to – and often resist – the strange and frequently disturbing concerns and practices of the adult social world. The child's perspective here is offered as a way of 'making strange' the normality of antebellum America: it offers a wisdom frequently denied to the adult world. Use of the child's perspective as a literary device may or may not have been a conscious attempt to make a statement about childhood, but it certainly has interesting and provocative ethical implications.

Innumerable nineteenth- and early twentieth-century examples of the novel of 'Bildung' concern the growing consciousness and 'education' of the child, establishing a tradition that reviews the world from the child's perspective. What is striking in many cases is the weight given both to the child's experience and developing consciousness. It is as though the presence of the child enables a questioning of the child's world, its habitual conduct and values. There is a strong parallel in popular culture: film provides some striking examples of child-focussed accounts of formative experiences: *Quatre Cents Coups*, *Stand by Me* and *Witness* all represent the world of the child and, at times, represent the world from the child's perspective.

These various attempts to represent the experience of childhood are relatively recent. They correspond with an intense 'scientific' focus on children and the idea of childhood, as well as the development of a knowledge-based apparatus of social practices bearing upon children, including education, medical services, psychological services, therapies and safeguards. At the end of the nineteenth century, Freud presented the Western world with the scandal of childhood sexuality – a revelation symptomatic of an increasing will to trace the origins of human identity and conduct, a paradoxical extension of the Enlightenment tradition. Intense interest in childhood as the source of identity accompanied an attempt to account for the relations between inherited characteristics and acquired knowledge, a complex of ideas that had haunted European thinking since before Kant. Freud's 'promethean discovery' (Lacan, 1968: 3) of the unconscious lent an enormous significance to 'primal' childhood emotional experience and presented a 'powerful mythology' of identity as rooted in deeply structured forces at play in the child's very first encounters with the world (Wittgenstein, 1970: 41–52). One of the effects of this discovery was to insist on a continuity between adult consciousness and childhood experience and fantasy, deconstructing any clear divide between the adult and the infantile.

Freud's contribution implies that what we are now is significantly defined by our fantasy life as children. Childhood is not a condition we can entirely escape: we must always remain in the thrall of such emotional complexes and projections. Our very being must also always already be predicated on that condition of childhood. While Piaget, later, claimed that the thinking of children is animistic – that is, it belongs to a more 'primitive' order of thinking – much subsequent anthropology, psychoanalytic social theory and semiotics would claim that the distinctions between the primitive and the sophisticated, between the scientific and the animistic or between the mythological and the rational are not sustainable and that every time we begin to examine these categories the borders blur. What's more, it seems, according to the psychoanalytic view at least, childhood is part of the condition of adulthood that never gets surpassed. We seem to be both fascinated by and suspicious of the idea of the continuity.

The creation of the world of the child via commercial paraphernalia signifies the idea of a realm of experience proper to and specific to the child (Aries, 1961). One of the scandals of nineteenth-century consciousness of child poverty and industrialized oppression was the realization that vast numbers of children, required to work and contribute to family and national economy, were actively being denied such a 'childhood' (Hendrick, 2005). A moral and political panic concerning the condition of the nation's human resources gave rise to various Factory Acts, the earliest decreeing in 1802 that children between 9 and 13 years old should not work more than eight hours and that they should receive instruction for the first four years of work in reading, writing and arithmetic. The 1833 Factory Act required that children between 9 and 13 years old receive two hours of instruction per day. It wasn't until 1889, however, that legislation under the auspices of the 'children's charter' authorized intervention on behalf of children, to protect them from harm, including what might be inflicted by parents. The Act also provided regulations for the employment of children and outlawed begging. Modified in 1894, this 'children's charter' empowered the state to police the private space of the home if a child was in danger. In 1885, the Criminal Law Amendment Act had established the age of consent for heterosexual sex at 16 (previously 12, then 13) partly in recognition of the fact that younger girls were working – even being sold in some scandalous cases (Eliza Armstrong, for example) – as prostitutes. In 1908, the Children's Act established special juvenile courts and introduced the registration of foster parents. The 1908 Punishment of Incest Act made sexual abuse within families a matter for state jurisdiction.

The child that therefore I am: Divisions and the myth of community

An array of attitudinal, legal, social, cultural, economic and political changes combined to establish a historically new relation to childhood. Recognition of the special, formative significance of childhood accompanied a series of legal provisions for the protection of children and brought children within the governmental ambit of a fast-developing state apparatus. Recognition of infancy as a potentiality to be positively and productively worked upon led to an awareness that the condition of the population could be not only known but also addressed by interventions that might impact upon the very forms of subjectivity a society might produce. Such acknowledgement also defined trajectories for development and a socializing apparatus capable of operating differentially for the social division of labour. Children born into this 'mitwelt' are what they are by virtue of their specific relation to this state-sponsored apparatus. Just as naming practices signify gender and family affiliation, so the potentiality of the neonate in the enframing is wrought by the symbolic order of language and the ordering of culture that signifies social identity. In the new world order of modernity, with its juridical and veridical determination of the child and childhood, education intervenes as a practice destined, as Agamben might put it, to delimit our potentiality within a determinate range of possible ways of being.

At the same time, a sense arises perhaps more strongly than before that the child is 'other' to the adult – a different form of being. An objectified entity outside of ourselves is evident in the very designation 'the child' referring to no specific real-life child but to an abstraction, an object to be understood and categorized by science, psychology, anthropology and sociology. Forms of knowledge in the modern era contribute to the production of identities within technologies of identity. The process emerging with the Factory Acts of the early nineteenth century was allied with a growing awareness of a need to monitor, manage and control children – and perhaps more importantly to shape them, to set the parameters for their identity and to organize the possibilities of identity within a range of normative determinations. Bureaucracy, technology and a particularly powerful, embedded and enduring series of ideas have joined forces to render the child as a product of programmed socialization. These processes now begin in contemporary nursery school practices, with their norm-related curricula.

There are reasons to question this objectification of childhood, partly because as 'the child' hovers between abstraction and reality, childhood is not a given and separate condition. We ourselves partake of the identity of the child. As Derrida implies strongly in 'The Animal that Therefore

I Am', the consequences of such 'othering' can be damaging and negative. One contemporary consequence is the elaborate social technology that is both the expression of responsible concern and a restraint on identity. The determination of the child as 'other' asks a question concerning the ethics of identity. To what extent must the process of Bildung enable the otherness of the other and to what extent, on the other hand, do we have the right and the duty to shape the other according to the norms and values of the practices that we adhere to? To what extent can we be aware of and negotiate the practices, values and norms that are embedded in our own systems and culture so that they may be open to the other? Absolute hospitality to the other – in this case the child – is not possible and probably not desirable either. But to be hospitable one must acknowledge the power to be hospitable, that is, the fact of power over an 'other'.

In his review of Heideggerian ontology and reconsideration of Dasein, Agamben makes much of the condition of infancy as a kind of openness that is 'other'. The otherness of the child is always problematic in so far as the identity of the neonate infant is inchoate. The principle of 'Mitsein' – that what we are is always already predicated on being with others – is a brute incontrovertible fact of existence. The neonate enters a world of others, shaped by others. Naming and all the other rites of passage confer identity on the child signifying gender and family allegiance, for example, before the child has any say in the matter. In the process of acquiring lexis and syntax, the child effectively lives within the symbolic framework of the particular language(s) learned. Language constitutes a symbolic limit to the world, as Wittgenstein indicated. From the outset, the child's autonomy is overwritten. The condition of infancy is dependency as well as potentiality. The acquisition of a language, a culture, a world and the predicates of being delimit freedom and shape the substantive nature of the individual. This radical contingency characterizes Heidegger's account of Dasein as 'thrown', but the infant is thrown somewhere with highly specific historical, cultural conditions. And yet infancy is always in process, not yet accomplished. A powerful modern view of the condition of childhood is essentially teleological, leading towards some state of completion, but always in need of development, a substance to be worked upon, protean and inchoate.

At the same time, the mythology of psychoanalysis has told us that to know ourselves it is essential to revisit our childhood. To liberate ourselves from the kernel of childhood trauma, the mythological constructions of the unconscious must be brought to consciousness where the rational ego can supervene, at least temporarily, during waking hours, over the irrational id. Whatever psychoanalysis may offer in terms of a therapy for trauma, it relies on recognition that as adults we continue to have recourse to childhood emotions. As products of our childhood, we frequently reach for a sense of who we essentially are, cultivating this image through anecdotes, memories, photographs and intimate discourses. The child is also always subject to this temporalizing discourse: much of the practice of modern schooling is dedicated to cultivating a sense of the self as a temporal self, as a work-in-progress and as a substance to work on – often as a work of improvement.

As we embrace the child within and see ourselves in continuity with that child, at the same time the child's very existence suggests a fracturing of existence. Our 'present' selves are disturbed by this non-present trace of the child, to borrow Derrida's terms. The child as object, though, is not just a fragmentary, spectral element of our existence (although it is always at least that). The child is an object for knowledge, a specific mode of being to be understood by anthropology, sociology, ethnography, psychology and a range of scientific knowledge that will inform us about the nature of this object. We can detect here a collective will to 'manage' and work upon it the nature of the child – in order better to maintain it within the borders of the proper. The sense of outrage that occurs when 'the child' exceeds this proper limit is dramatically realized in high-profile media representations of deviant child behaviour, as with rare cases of child murderers or child soldiers. In contemporary Western culture, this fear of deviance is powerful and correlates to the powerful will to ensure the proper management of childhood.

In 'The Animal that Therefore I Am', Derrida (2002) considers the otherness of the animal, beginning by asking what happens when we look at an animal? We can transpose some of this question of identity, especially in relation to the condition of infancy, itself a particular and evocative form of otherness. What happens when we look at a child? What happens when we are conscious of the child looking back? What happens when we consider the limit between ourselves and the child?

A common sensation in relation to neonates is an instant 'emotion' of responsibility. The infant calls forth something, in a Levinasian sense, as we face the radically other version of ourselves. Our sense of the otherness of the child is compromised or at least qualified by our projection of an identity onto that child that occurs even at the moment when we acknowledge our responsibility for it. The child may be seen from the outset as an expression, even an extension, of our individual and collective selves.

The contemporary child – depending on accident of birth – inhabits a world of childhood: a world partly separated from the world of adulthood. The school in our culture configures this world in a particular way. While progressive schools may emphasize the role of relative freedom and play and the school playground enables children to cultivate their own cultural practices that have a life and continuity of their own, the world of the school exists as a preparation for the 'real' world of adulthood. In this carefully crafted milieu, a temporal projection of being is intensely focussed on childhood. The teleological process is organized into specific phases laden with specific accomplishments. Specifications for levels of attainment in national curricula define a temporal hierarchy of norms in an age-stratified context. Childhood is thus beset by the developmental imperative. Norms of attainment are deemed elements in a chain of development. This progressive, developmental order belongs to a particular conception of being that the specific being of the child is now predicated on. The progressive accumulation of accomplishments and, equally important, the development of a managed disposition are essential to the contemporary projection of childhood.

The postmodern condition proposes that the mobility of people, ideas and entities characterize the contemporary world. In Bauman's terms, the nature of the world is 'liquid', uncertain and unstable (Lyotard, 1985; Bauman, 2000). The postmodern condition and 'liquid modernity' speak of the destabilization of identities. Things get mixed up: hybridity is the fundamental condition of being in the 'global village' where communications technologies and transport systems have foreshortened distance and imploded time. A symptom of this condition is the detachment of belonging from community and the emergence and priority of networks, self-producing forms of solidarity that exist in virtual rather than 'real' space. In spite of persisting visions of 'a deep, horizontal comradeship' (Anderson, 1983: 16), alternative accounts of community have problematized the very possibility of community as an expression of coherent collective identity that is not totalitarian and exclusive. What's more, many claim, community does not correspond with collective entities in modernity or postmodernity and is always a forced, violently sustained entity. Both Nancy's political projection of 'community without unity' and Agamben's messianic 'coming community' point towards the difficult social and political question concerning how to proceed with the development of a collective future (Nancy, 1991; Agamben, 1993). Nancy emphasizes the implicit violence in contemporary efforts to design society according to pre-planned definitions. Nancy argues that

> the community that becomes a single thing (body, mind, fatherland, Leader . . . necessarily loses the in of being-in-common. Or, it loses the with or the together that defines it. It yields its being-together to a being of togetherness. The truth of community, on the contrary, resides in the retreat of such a being. (Nancy, 1991: xxxix)

Agamben similarly advocates 'the coming community' – 'without destiny and without essence' – as a fragmentary community of singularities whose being-together 'is mediated not by any condition of belonging . . . nor by the simple absence of conditions . . . but by belonging itself' (Agamben, 1993: 85). For both Nancy and Agamben there can be no terms, concepts or representational axioms to represent this community. This anti-foundational mode of thinking about being-together, or Mitsein, poses serious – and seriously ethical – problems for contemporary technological, norm-saturated modes of enframing the child and childhood.

Collective responsibility and new technologies of childhood

For Plato, children are the property of the state; for Aristotle, children were essentially the property of the father. Locke suggested that parents hold their children in custody from God. We contemporaries often define children as subjects of discursive, legal and institutional frameworks. From the late nineteenth century onwards, children have been held within a series of governmental practices or social technologies. Technology in this sense is to be understood, as Heidegger – drawing on Aristotle redefines it – as a bringing forth, a way of making things happen as well as a way of making things. It is easy to see how an institution such as a school, with its shaping and determining of identities, can be conceived of as a social technology, as a mechanism or – to use Foucault's powerful concept – an apparatus. Such a technology stands in a specific relation to its social environment. As Sherlock Holmes noted, the grand buildings of elementary schools rising above the grey slate roofs of the urban landscape signify a new technology belonging to a new world order.

Heidegger saw modern, machine technology, based in science as a will-to-knowledge and a will-to-power, as a 'technological enframing', producing a condition of acquisitive nihilism. Its tendency was to bring everything within its ambit, to draw everything into its power – for use or potential use. Urban populations were rendered useful and productive through schooling. The school and the process of schooling constituted a particular 'enframing' in childhood. Accumulated legislation, institutions, a powerful bureaucracy and an array of practices formed a rational enclosure enacting a radical change in the nature of the state–population relation.

The later expansion from elementary schools via the tripartite system towards comprehensive schools (1944) charts the progress of an all-embracing social technology. Following the model of the 'village college', the community comprehensive school was designed to be the centre of local life. Accompanied by Further Education (FE) to oversee routes from education to labour and the enormous expansions of the accessible university system, education came to embody an ideal of rational, progressive development. Setting in motion a new temporal organization of life with a new emphasis on rendering time productive, education worked on the plasticity of identity rendering individuals and communities useful according to changing economic agendas. The overriding ethic of self-refashioning gets put to work within the changing demands of the labour market giving rise to a new ecology of identity.

Governmentality, as Foucault has designated the above condition connotes a form of government dispersed to intervene into intimate dimensions of life via bio-power to effect a regulation of everyday life, extending the principle of the panopticon. Two recent UK examples of attempts to address the condition of 'disadvantaged' children through state-funded projects are indicative of relations between the contemporary Western state and childhood. In both instances, childhood is treated as both a proper and urgent concern of the state. Significant resources are dedicated towards management of particular groups of children at the edges of the economic, social and cultural mainstream.

Sure Start constitutes a major UK education-focused initiative designed to address the 'health and well-being of families and children from before birth to four . . . concentrated in neighbourhoods where a high proportion of children are living in poverty'. Sure Start schemes are set up 'so children are ready to flourish when they go to school'.

> Sure Start is the cornerstone of the Government's drive to tackle child poverty and social exclusion working with parents-to-be, parents/carers and children to promote the physical, intellectual and social development of babies and young children so that they can flourish at home and when they get to school. (Sure Start, 2008)

Sure Start targets a specific age group and socio-economic sector and intervenes to offset the effects of 'living in disadvantaged areas' in a state of 'deprivation'.

> Sure Start local programmes work with parents and parents-to-be to improve children's life chances through better access to:
> Family support
> Advice on nurturing
> Health services
> Early learning. (Sure Start, 2008)

The first wave of Sure Start programmes began in 1999. Districts were selected according to 'the levels of deprivation within their areas' (Sure Start, 2008).

Targeting specific geographic, socio-economic contexts, Sure Start has offered families with preschool children supportive interventions to ensure their children get 'the best possible start'. The interventions include access to specialist playgroups, parental advice, toy libraries, speech and language therapy, specialist educational provision, physio-therapy and many others. While directed explicitly at socio-economic deprivation, the whole scheme is intensely focussed on human resources, on the children and families themselves and their potential for development, rather than on the material conditions of their existence.

Sure Start has been brought within the dominant governmental technology of target setting and performance auditing. The emphasis is on self-assessment, and this is indicative of the ethic of self-improvement that guides the scheme. Sure Start monitors itself and produces its own self-advertising literature, claiming success for itself and pulling together statistical data to verify its claims. It is predicated on a logic of improvement that determines success in terms of the triumphs of its own initiatives but not on any indicative measures of overall improvement of the socio-economic conditions of the deprived areas it addresses. The contemporary drive to eradicate child poverty in the United Kingdom, for instance, is based on a host of initiative designed to provide interventions of care and development. This same logic can be seen in a range of historical initiatives and also in initiatives in other contexts, most notably in the long-running US Head Start initiative. Head Start, like Sure Start, generates its own world of conferences, programs, services, research, statistics and publications – all designed to sustain the socio-moral purpose of the initiative in its stated aim to serve 'the child development needs of preschool children (birth through age 5) and their low-income families' (Sure Start, 2008).

Given their national scope and scale of funding, Head Start and Sure Start appear to constitute a huge investment of resources and energies. Yet, while they recognize through their targeting that needy children are produced in deprived socio-economic areas, they are not empowered to address such socio-economic conditions. They are both predicated on a self-assurance that education remediates poverty and its attendant social problems.

Sure Start is organized in relation to the key notions of partnership, prevention and participation that have come to define the policy drives in such initiatives designed to address social exclusion. The prevention dimension signifies a governmental determination to address social exclusion via mechanisms of norm-related containment. Participation ensures that a strong element of engagement and responsibility is cultivated in the participants or 'service-users' themselves. Participation is a social technology designed to tie in such subjects and their aspirations with the aims of the scheme and with inclusive, positive social trajectories.

These schemes present education as the key mechanism for cultivating the self-governing and self-directing citizen. Areas of 'social exclusion' where children and young people may reject the mainstream norms of development that are conditionally on offer to them face the danger of potentially costly delinquency. Keeping such children, via their families, 'on track' (Sure Start, 2008) is a major feature of the proposed enhancement of governance represented by extending interventions to include preschool children and by the specific targeting of markedly deprived areas.

As indicated, the dominant ethic of such initiatives is one of social amelioration. Improvement is predicated on the state and its agencies supplementing and managing family socialization. The positive provision of developmental practices within communities through a range of formal and informal institutions carries out this function. Advice on nurturing, general support for the family and models of early learning are provided. A professional ethic binds practitioners to the individual cases they encounter, with a more optional faith its larger social purposes.

Sure Start sustains its 'world' through the determination of objects, identities and practices that constitute it (Dreyfus, 1991). This world is sealed off from any knowledge threatening its purposes and reasons for being. Education figures as the key to social amelioration. In its remedial drive, Sure Start claims a correlation between effective learning and 'appropriately developed speech and language skills' (Sure Start, 2008). This world of practice is suffused with knowledge taken to be self-evident, in effect creating a powerful 'force-field' defining what is and is not significant. In the case of Sure Start, the focus on language provides material that can be forged into empirical data, giving a 'scientific' validity to the intervention process, even though such data is essentially derived from metaphysical formulation. Faith that such interventions can 'improve' language and thereby produce more beneficial educational trajectories for socio-economically disadvantaged children is precisely that: faith.

Sure Start interventions address language acquisition in an educational mode. Childhood is the necessary focus of this remedial work.

'O' Imposition Inner Signature

The child here is a representative figure for the whole. Remedial work addressing the child's language expresses an anxiety about the linguistic, cultural well-being – or hygiene – of the communities in question, actually the economically and socially most deprived areas of the country, reactivating an anxiety that reaches back to the Newbolt Report of 1921. Intervention in language acquisition is linked with socio-economic remediation. This link is an ontologically indispensable element of the world of Sure Start.

The justification for the engagement with language acquisition is, however, unfounded. No evidence within the extensive research literature supports the contention that language acquisition is effected, accelerated or enhanced as a result of the language teaching practices of adults, however broadly those practices might be defined. Children's language acquisition is not dependent upon following 'practitioners'' guidance and planning as described in an array of documents provided by the former Qualifications and Curriculum Authority (QCA)[1] and other educational and government bodies. Language acquisition studies of individual children, such as Dromi (1987) and Clark (1993), as well as studies based on the language profiles of 1,800 normally developing children (Dale, 1991; Fenson et al., 1993, 1994; Bates et al., 1994, 1995), have shown that all children, regardless of their backgrounds and the culture of the language input of those backgrounds, pass through the same phases of language development and that these phases occur for all children at the same time, or at least no more than a few months apart. This finding is consistent and has been replicated in the literature from studies as early as 1928 (Stern and Stern, 1928) to 1990 (Radford, 1990) and beyond.

Why then does Sure Start persist in manufacturing a language policy and practice that is effectively vacuous? And why is this regarded as educationally verified and viable? From within the onto-institutional domain, or 'world', of Sure Start it is language interventions that justify the existence, the practices and the products of this world. In onto-institutional terms with regard to language acquisition, questioning such tacit assumptions threatens the nature of the project and its existence.

---

1 Between 2009–2010 in England QCA was split into the Qualification and Curriculum Development Agency, QCDA, and Ofqual, the Office for Qualifications and Examination Regulations.

The attempt to intervene towards a culturally determined and institutionally controlled goal, particularly with regard to language, has long been a condition integral to education, especially state education. A number of assumptions are attendant upon this goal. These include the notion that such interventions are effective, and that they are related to – even grow out of – knowledge of empirical data that confirms a given course of action. As already outlined, however, no evidence exists that confirms the effectiveness of pedagogic or pedagogically supportive interventions influencing the rate, nature or even possibility of children's language acquisition – quite the reverse, in fact. Language acquisition occurs by quite different means. Again, as already outlined, the evidence that supports this conclusion is abundant and has been abundant and consistent for a long time. Children who are not exposed to the management of 'natural interactions' acquire language in exactly the same way, within exactly the same time frame, as children who are subjected to this bureaucratically organized and registered experience.

The Children's Fund presents a parallel instance of systematic intervention into the worlds of children deemed to be in need of institutional support to retain their identities within the educational order and the attendant order of governance. The Children's Fund is a large-scale and diverse UK programme set up in 2000, its explicit aim to engineer what have been referred to as 'joined up responses' among practitioners in the provision of services for 'children and families' deemed to be 'at risk'. While Sure Start aims to begin early in the lives of children, the Children's Fund aims to escort children with specific social problems through a 'proper' educational trajectory in site of their specific difficulties.

Practitioner participants are identified through social work, child protection, police services, education, housing and health, as well as a range of non-statutory forms of service provision. The strategy of realignment involves collectively defining the 'objects' of their now-integrated practice. The impetus for the Children's Fund came from *Victoria Climbie Inquiry*, published following the murder in London of 9-year-old Victoria Climbie. The significance of this case was thought to hinge on the fact that despite being known to and registered as a 'case' by several different services, including specialist child protection teams, Victoria was unprotected, as a multiply excluded child. The Children's

Fund was designed and implemented as a key strategy to tackle 'social exclusion' so that its remit extended beyond the prevention of extreme cases such as that of Victoria Climbie. In both extreme and more generalized focusses, however, emphasis fell on shifting the attention of services towards prevention. And while much of the emphasis in both official and less official statements about the remit of specific Children's Fund schemes has been on 'children and their families', there is clearly a further dimension of 'community' to be addressed. Children's Fund schemes have frequently been located within communities that are deemed to be problematic in terms of social profile and in relation to the governmental demand for social inclusion.

The remit of the Children's Fund extends beyond mere protection towards providing conditions for the realization of general aspirations on behalf of children, including enjoyment, achievement, 'positive contribution', 'economic well-being' and the norms of welfare and productivity. What's more, to ensure the inclusion of the potentially disincluded, there is a drive towards the participation of children and young people in relation to the services provided as well as decisions that may impact their well-being:

> This means that the organizations involved with providing services to children – from hospitals and schools, to police and voluntary groups – will be teaming up in new ways, sharing information and working together, to protect children and young people from harm and help them achieve what they want in life. Children and young people will have far more say about issues that affect them as individuals and collectively. (ECM, 2006)

Children are expected to take part in their own governance in light of the norms implied above. Local authorities and service providers will be subject to a regime of inspection to ensure that such active participation is being developed:

> Over the next few years, every local authority will be working with its partners, through children's trusts, to find out what works best for children and young people in its area and act on it. They will need to involve children and young people in this process, and when inspectors assess how local areas are doing, they will listen especially to the views of children and young people themselves. (ECM, 2006)

We can see that a significant strand in this post-2000 reformulation of children's services is the new emphasis given to 'the child' as a unit not simply of governance and care but also of self-governance.

The three key terms of the children's fund have their roots in much more deeply embedded ideals of governance that can be traced to changes in the nature of government – roughly from sovereign power to capillary bio-power – in the modern period (Foucault, 1977). They open questions concerning the role of the school and educational services in relation to the changing topography of governance implied by new governmental formations under the concept of 'partnership'.

We may interpret the Children's Fund as part of a relatively new way of engaging with the governance and the politics of childhood. Increasingly, in governmental documentation, concern for 'children' addresses 'the child', a significant shift. The child is being represented as a self, capable of being addressed in terms of self-governance. In recognizing the agency of the child and in seeking to promote 'the voice of the child', broad, powerful tendencies in the juridical and veridical dimensions of governance amplify the established and now firmly ingrained human technology of the school. Since the inception of the modern school in the second half of the nineteenth century, the 'deep grammar' of schooling has been concerned with the formation and refashioning the 'self'. The Children's Fund has been able to propose new working arrangements – effectively modelling these new arrangements rather than fully instituting them – that are entirely consistent with that traditional telos, but that indicate how the subtle deployment of a range of services offers new possible flexibilities towards ensuring that exclusions and the casualties of social order can be better avoided. In this we can also see the invasion of governmental practices further into the 'interiority' of the child – a psychological space that has, according to many significant commentators, been developed in large epistemic shifts of the past 200 years in the West (Foucault, 1988a; Taylor, 1989; Steedman, 1995).

The discourse of self-improvement in social services working under the rubric of 'prevention' correlates strongly with what Rose has referred to as 'governing the soul'. The Children's Fund extends to 'governing the soul' of the community (Rose, 1990; 1999). For Rose, emphasis on 'government through community' is predicated on the move towards governmental address of 'problem' communities (as locations of social exclusion). In this discourse – and the array of attendant practices – 'a sector is brought into existence' (Rose, 1999).

In the context of what Giddens has defined as 'reflexive modernity', we can see the extension of the government into the community through various satellite institutions and practices designed to address more recalcitrant individuals, families and communities. State administration – 'police' in Foucault's sense – of individuals, families and neighbourhoods occurs through normalizing agencies of social welfare in arrangements that are both more flexible and more oriented towards self-corrective techniques of person and community management.

On the one hand, these general tendencies – realized in detail through Children's Fund projects – modes of thinking and practices seem to enhance the agency of the 'self' that is required to effect its own transformation and reorientation out of unproductive or negatively productive exclusion. On the other hand, as the gaps in provision are healed, we can also see clearly reinvigorated disciplinary mechanisms that seek to keep the project of the self (and/or community) 'on track' and properly oriented towards norms of positive development. Multi-agency working – 'partnership' – offers multimodal 'worlds of care' as a new dimension in the changing topography of relations between services. For innumerable children, institutional cultures come into new relations that enable a programme of care to be more flexible, more effectively governmental. No longer contesting the determination of the 'object', such disparate entities as the school and a youth work scheme become partners in a juridically and veridically agreed pursuit of a common end.

At the same time, the foregrounding of prevention intensifies the normative telos of such flexible systems of care – or 'services' as they are officially designated. The increasing emphasis on the metaphor of 'voice' – the guarantor of participation – as the expression of self is misleading in so far as 'the voice' of participation must be trained to express itself in the language of self-enhancement, and must inflect with the accent of self-management and, ultimately, normative self-renewal.

In so far as services dedicated to prevention address 'communities' or 'the community', they address communities or the community under stress – 'communities' defined by their likelihood of producing exclusion or excluded individuals. Such communities – and the individual children and families they generate – are entities remote from the Hegelian ideal where the community and the state coalesce in mutual expression of one another: such communities are in fact defined as communities by their proximity to the zone of exclusion. Community, as suggested above in the sense of determinate identity relating to 'ethnos', has become entirely problematized in a host of recent rethinkings: in Nancy's idea of the *communauté désoeuvrée*, in Sennet's problematization of the imperative of community and in Rose's definition of community as inhabiting the newly emerging neoliberal governmental discourses of contemporary population management. It may be that – for socially excluded children, at least – community now signifies a context to escape from via a scaffolded attachment to normative aspirations. For those same children, it may also be that education makes an offer they cannot accept.

A programme for the future

In *Liquid Modernity*, Zygmunt Bauman presents a vision of the contemporary world in an alarming state of uncertainty: a world where familiar structures, identities and practices are constantly under reflexive review, where constant problematization of purposes and boundaries of the 'proper' creates an anxiety inducing an atmosphere of uncertainty and fluidity (Bauman, 2000). Nevertheless, in this liquid condition, the logic of governmentality prevails and becomes more 'liquid', flexible and far-reaching – hence the emphasis on participation that seeks to bind the governed to the processes of governance *Liquid Modernity* announces the apotheosis of the self-fashioning individual: hence 'guidance-hunger' and proliferation of the Jane Fonda factor (Bauman, 2000: 67–8).

There is a strong flavour of this ethic of self-formation promoted through contemporary governmental practices relating to children. This is especially the case for children who are deemed to be in danger of crossing over into the perilous zone beyond normativity that has come to be referred to as 'social exclusion'. Such children, if they can't or won't be offered redemption from actual poverty, can overcome its effects by the cultivation of 'resilience' and by being retied to the project of improvement that promises redemption.

The rise of intense governmental concern for the child, entailing an extensive and omnipresent apparatus to manage identities and sustain norms of being and norms of development, has been a key feature of modernity's attempt to secure a predictable and knowable order. A bureaucracy worthy of the name of Weber's 'iron cage' has been established to render, as far as possible, the future development of the child stable, knowable and containable. Technologies of childhood have conspired to contain children, inchoate and potentially unpredictable, within the defined order of legitimate trajectories within the social division of labour. This confinement corresponds to Heidegger's idea of the 'enframing' as a determinate way of being delimiting possibilities and within its order.

Recent educational initiatives, forged in the name of pastoral concern and educational access, have worked to ensure that children as subjects of education are kept within prescribed limits. Social exclusion has come to signify a danger zone of non-existence, beyond the pale of remediation, beyond the reach of normativity that defines all officially sanctioned forms of identity. As education seeks to enfold more and more of life and to become an ontological principle defining what the human being essentially is, such exclusion is represented as a mortal danger to both the self and its world. Protection is essential for children, but is not a simple issue. (Consider the difficult, intensely poignant thesis of *The Private Worlds of Dying Children* [Bluebond-Langner, 1980]. Adults, seeking to protect dying children, withhold information that the children already know about their real conditions of existence, but do not reveal that they know to protect the adults that care for them). Ethical questions about the rights of education and the right to determine 'proper' development arise from the enframing of childhood. Onto-logical-ethical (onto-ethical) concerns also arise from the attempt to guarantee a programmed future that closes down other potential ways of being, that promotes – as Derrida might put it – a knowable '*futur*' rather than a more open and hospitable '*avenir*'.

Essentially, what remains after our deconstruction of education in its technological relation to childhood is the question of the relation of children to technologies. To what extent must this be fixed? To what extent must the established technologies of care and protection for children continue to exert their power over children in the enframing? Is it possible to envisage an alternative that is more hospitable to differences, that is less closely tied to a technology of social distinction, that is less concerned with closing off forms of knowledge and that is less rabidly normative? These questions really depend on the concept of responsibility and on a fundamental question of rights. Who has the right to determine what sort of future is to be programmed for children and for childhood? And what kind of collectivity could exert such responsibility?

In the influential *Centuries of Childhood*, Aries (1962) associated the rise of childhood with industrialization. A significant question in the West now concerns the future of the post-industrial child.

Educational Research: Improvement and Metaphysics

4

Chapter Outline

The metaphysics of mainstream educational research

In the developed world, the state sponsors educational research. This is generally seen as a normal state of affairs. For example, departments of education in the United States, United Kingdom, Australia and South Africa fund, manage and disseminate a range of educational research programmes, mostly dedicated to general improvement. One of the questions we want to ask about the current educational hegemony addresses the relation between educational research and its own framework of understanding. Our ontological approach leads us to question the idea that the kind of research currently advocated, funded and used in educational settings is necessarily fruitful and thus necessarily deserves its existing status and power.

Not all educational research has this hegemonic character. National and continental educational research associations frequently express a more heterogeneous understanding of what educational research is, should and might be. Their structure tends to be more or less decentred, although less practice-oriented modes of research still occupy a marginal position. In philosophy of education, itself now a significant research area, a hegemonic structure still tends to privilege research oriented towards improvement, promoting educational reform rather than posing the more problematic ontological questions.

The power of state-sponsored, hegemonic educational research is ontological, declaring what has the right to exist and thrive. This power projects its understanding of how things are onto the world, excluding elements that disturb its world view. This ontological force sustains research modalities that agree with mainstream ideas and values, and that ultimately project a ruling vision of the world of education.

A brief examination of the UK's National Foundation for Education Research (NFER) offers insight into contemporary educational research ontology. NFER is a not-for-profit charitable organization founded in the 1940s. Today it claims responsibility for much educational reform. As the leading institution in the United Kingdom supporting evidence-based research development of educational practice, NFER undertakes over 200 research projects every year, spanning all sectors, each dedicated to the improvement of 'children's lives'. In this claim we can see the direct correlation between education and life. In relation to children, according to the NFER, the two are synonymous (Griffiths, 2003).

NFER represents educational professionals as necessarily in need of improvement and dedicates itself to 'ensuring our work improves the practice and understanding of those who work with and for learners' (NFER, 2010). Clearly aligning itself with the improvement agenda, in the use of the word *our*, NFER conceives of 'work with and for learners' as a collective and unified enterprise, a common cause addressing those whose work stands in need of improvement. NFER is sure of the value it produces: 'Our work enables policy makers and practitioners to make better, more informed decisions, drawing on sound evidence and accurate information' (NFER, 2010). The confident use of the word 'learners', an abstraction evident in all the NFER documentation, forecloses any kind of sociological analysis of educational failure and

'underachievement'. Of course, sociological analysis cannot be counte-
nanced by the unwavering positivism that NFER professes and demands.
Its ontological horizon would be fatally breached by such recognition.

NFER insists that its dedication to improvement is ethical, although
it never articulates its ethics. NFER has never asked the ontological
question concerning research ethics: what is a proper research ethic?
This absence must be attributed to foreclosure. It has never occurred
to NFER to question the foundational idea that it works most closely
with. Improvement implies the ethical, as NFER confidently promotes
research informing 'development activities that we believe will have a
positive impact on society' (NFER, 2010). The elliptical logic of the alignment of educational research with improvement could not be clearer.

NFER expresses its commitment to assessment and testing without
shame:

> NFER undertakes assessment-related projects of importance to national
> and international educational policy and its implementation, involving
> pure research, the development of assessment instruments and the evalu-
> ation of assessment initiatives. (NFER, 2010)

Its research interests cover what it refers to as 'the whole range of tests
and other assessments, including high stakes tests, assessment banks,
e-assessment and assessment for learning', entirely adopting the questionable, yet hegemonic, idea that learning is fundamentally dependent on assessment (NFER, 2010). So NFER declares itself at one with
'the technological enframing' that has occupied mainstream education
and decisively organized its institutions and practices. Subscribing to
the notion of 'assessment development', NFER engages in test developing 'for many different purposes, including national curriculum test
developments, tests for publishers, e-assessments and assessment tasks'.
This obsession with testing is indicative of an ontotheological commitment, a faith in a rational ordering of the world and in the positive
value of rationally construed interventions. Under this faith, the business of assessment is understood as essential to educational progress. If
you don't have assessment, you don't have the data that assessment provides – you can't measure progress. And if you can't measure progress
and decisively verify its existence, its existence must be in doubt. This is
the essential logic of NFER's fundamental belief system.

NFER's assessment commitment extends to piloting test materials and subjecting informal trial and 'pre-tests' to statistical analysis, claiming that it does all this 'to select items that work well'. The commitment to assessment is unwavering, but entirely pragmatic, never philosophical. The organization never questions the value of assessment development as the basis for improvement and progress. We may be tempted to ask why assessment is so much and so constantly in need of development, as though existing assessment is not yet perfected. Nevertheless, it seems, this less-than-perfect phenomenon, assessment, and its necessary supplement, testing, seem to remain worthy of unquestioned commitment. Isn't this commitment to assessment and to researching in order to improve assessment, then, in need of review?

Just as NFER's commitment to advancing the work of practitioners, in order to improve the 'lives of children', implies an existing gap between what's possible and what occurs, NFER similarly implies that assessment is always in need of improvement. NFER's mission eschews 'pure research', having already decided what educational research essentially is. Assessment is the key to all educational improvement mysteries. NFER's research mythology relies on piloting as its key research instrument, since piloting provides reliable evidence to inform developments of assessment. A certain circular logic is at work here. In a world enclosed by the dominant idea of assessment, the piloting and testing of assessment takes centre stage and becomes itself a raison d'etre. NFER claims its right to be the arbiter of assessment – its own founding principle – undertaking what it considers to be exemplary evaluations – assessments of assessment – to express its ontotheological commitment to assessment as the principle of education.

Heidegger: Ontological difference, anxiety and world

Is the faith in research as an instrument of improvement justified? In the general field of education, especially education in Higher Education (HE) departments, this question seems unaskable. Within its own horizon, educational research is inevitable and essential. It is inevitable and essential to improvement, while improvement is the necessary goal of educational endeavour. An important question, however, concerns how research, within the general ethic of improvement, is configured in a very particular, limited way that defines what research itself is.

Is it the case that every aspect of educational practice is in need of a research basis in order to authenticate its being, provide it with foundations and enable it to flourish? A leading theorist/administrator in the United Kingdom believes that teaching, for instance, does stand in need of such a basis:

> Teaching is not at present a research-based profession. I have no doubt that if it were, teaching would be more effective and more satisfying. The goal of enhancing effectiveness and satisfaction can be achieved only by a combination of various means of which an adequate research base is just one. It is in my view an extremely important one. (Hargreaves, 2000: 200)

This claim is worth exploring from an ontological view. Its unquestioned assumption is that the current state of teaching is lacking. All other ontological conditions – the constrictions of the curriculum, the limitations of the institutions, the insistence on age stratification, the determination to render school learning norm-defined, the obsession with assessment – can be put aside as the effectiveness of teaching abstracted. Not only that: it is research that can best provide the necessary impetus for the desired improvement. We might call this condition ontological foreclosure. The statement expresses a faith that empirical research can show the 'way forward' towards improvement and beyond towards a more 'satisfying' world of practice. There is no recognition that the focus on the empirical gives no purchase on the ontological conditions that make the empirical seem like a given reality. Without questioning the very form of reality that constitutes the world of practice that research addresses, there can be no thinking other than within that enclosure.

Our analysis of the ontological conditions of the role of the empirical in educational research draws on Heidegger's general ontology, starting with the attempt to define the nature of fundamentally different types of knowledge. 'What is Metaphysics?', Heidegger's 1929 exploration of science, gives special attention to the 'nothing' that lies beyond the attention of science. This analysis has implications for the understanding of the foundations of knowledge – its ontological conditions. In staking a claim for metaphysics, Heidegger's argument moves against the idea that science alone can be the paradigm for knowledge. Only metaphysics can provide the thinking necessary to renew the pursuit of truth that connects knowledge with being, above and beyond amassing and classifying bits of knowledge and fragmenting them into specialization. Charged with this essential role, metaphysics comes up with some uncomfortable realizations. If specific sciences deal with particular realms of things, then beyond that they are necessarily concerned with 'nothing'. Strangely, Heidegger wants to interrogate this nothing, asserting that metaphysics must concern itself with the nothing that science must not concern itself with. This nothing, as it turns out, is both troubling and persistent. Although it may in effect be largely ignored, it has an unavoidable tendency to make itself felt as a troubling absence. It turns out that the nothing is much closer to home than initial consideration suggests.

Heidegger claims that intellectual understanding is actually and necessarily predicated on forms of understanding that are not intellectual, but belong to what we can provisionally call moods or attunement ('mood' is Heidegger's translation of Aristotle's term *pathos*). Heidegger's ontology demands that consideration of the fundamental condition of Dasein as 'the entity which we ourselves are' is crucial (Derrida, 1987: 17). Problematizing the conventional notion of the human subject as a transcendental entity, Heidegger refers to the human being as 'Dasein', a move that is essential to the project of the question of being, since it is only via the specific being of Dasein that the question of being gets posed at all (Heidegger, 1962: 71–7 {44–52}). In *Being and Time*, Dasein is structured by mood. For Heidegger, 'mood' is not to be understood as a transient emotion. Mood is fundamental to Dasein's experience of being-in-the-world (1962: 172–8{134–9}).

Heidegger asks if is there a mood that corresponds to an understanding of the nothing beyond the limit of given knowledge: 'Does such an attunement in which man [sic] is brought before the nothing itself occur in human existence?' The answer is 'anxiety' – not anxiety about something in particular, which Heidegger categorizes as 'fear', but the 'fundamental mood of anxiety' (Heidegger, 1993c: 100). This generalized anxiety may only trouble us at certain times of solitude or alienation. It

relates to the nothing of all things, all enterprises and worlds. Contingent on non-existence or death, this existential anxiety is at the same time productive, giving rise to the world-making activities of Dasein.

The 'fundamental mood of anxiety' as the state 'in which the nothing is revealed' (Heidegger, 1993c: 101) belongs to Dasein's nature as 'being-towards-death' (Heidegger, 1962: 299–311{255–67}). Death is defined as: 'an end beyond all completion, a limit beyond all limits and as 'this uncanny thing' (Heidegger, 2000: 168). There's 'no way out in the face of death' (Heidegger, 2000: 169). The confrontation with this inescapable nothing occurs 'not only when it is time to die but constantly and essentially' – hence the term *being-towards-death* as a way of defining Dasein ontologically. Death is experienced as foreknowledge of one's own end, but also as a metaphorical expression of the nothing. As the 'nothing' that Heidegger identifies is an indispensable condition of Dasein's knowledge, so being-towards-death is identified as a fundamental condition of Dasein's being. What's more, anxiety-towards-death is experienced metonymically, in all the possible and actual anxieties about endings, non-belongings and dissolutions. While none of this anxiety is necessarily conscious it continually operates.

For Heidegger, metaphysics must include attention to the conditions of Dasein's being – or world as a phenomenological category rather than as a given totality. Being-in-the-world for Dasein is always a matter of being situated. We are always ourselves somewhere: spatially, temporally and culturally within our specific world. Against the subjectivist tradition of picturing an individual as an ego or self, and against the Cartesian subject as a transcendental unity of apperception, a mind or a consciousness, Dasein exists entirely in its world within the medium of spatial and temporal finitude and belonging.

The world is not a totality within the scope of our transcendental apprehension. Nor does the world entirely precede our being in it: our being is constitutive of our world. Dasein is always already constituted by and embedded in, to use Husserl's (1970) phrase, its lifeworld. Dasein's 'thrownness' emphasizes the contingent, historically specific nature of understanding, knowing and acting. For Heidegger, the subject is always of the world; so too the world is of the subject. Just as there can be no 'worldless subject', there can be no 'subjectless world' either (Zahavi, 2001; Alweiss, 2003). Except that for Heidegger it does not make sense to refer to this independent entity, the subject. The use of the term *Dasein* is, among other things, an attempt to avoid the category of the subject with its metaphysical potential for worldless abstraction. Dasein inhabits a 'Mitwelt' – always already engaged with others and with the things of its world which constitute the horizon of its being.

Another way of defining this complex sense of world is found in 'The Origin of the Work of Art', where it is asserted that a stone is world-less (Heidegger, 1993a: 170). Derrida's reading of Heidegger in *Of Spirit* presents the following expansion:

> 1. The stone is without world (*Weltlos*). 2. The animal is poor in world (*Weltarm*). 3. Man is world-forming, if one can thus translate *Weltbildend*. (Derrida, 1989b: 48)

In this formulation, we see the implication of Heidegger's claim that Dasein is world-forming. In contrast we can say that for Husserl's phenomenology, objectivity stands in a transcendental relation to subjectivity. Subjectivity is able to bracket the attendant world of experience and desire that constitutes the subject's immediate being. For Heidegger, no such bracketing is possible; it makes no sense to speak of a subject detached from the life–world. The everyday life–world is the very condition of knowledge. For Dasein, being-in-the-world is always already structured by knowledge of things, or 'foreknowledge' (Heidegger, 1962: 190–3{149–52}). Dasein does not experience a sudden encounter with the entities of its world, as in the classic representation of subject encountering object. On the contrary, Dasein is always already oriented with its world, and this is an inherited disposition. The 'facticity' of this world inheres in its 'things' as they give shape, form and colour to the world of Dasein, but such things are themselves already shaped by the world-forming activity of Dasein.

'World' has far-reaching ontological implications for Heidegger. Through the world-creating condition of Dasein, the things of the world are not simply there in some inert and pre-given way. The things of the world are the products of the contingency, anxiety, labour and attendant care of Dasein. It is this care (*Sorge*) that invests things with significance, imbues them with specific meanings and animates them within an inherited but actively inhabited world. While anxiety, apprehension of the nothing and being-towards-death generate the 'uncanniness' that may disturb the everyday consciousness of things, they are the pre-conditions for care and the production of the world.

The related concepts of anxiety, care and world imply a phenom-enology that enables us to rethink the ontological status of research projects in education above and beyond their own characteristic self-descriptions. Any educational research project creates its own world, determining its objects and the specific nature of its care. It partakes of the larger world of educational initiatives oriented towards fields of practice and that organize knowledge, research, professional expertise and identity. Educational research is structured by this drive to ground itself and define its purposes in relation to the field of practice. This desire to address and transform the social can be seen in the current, global growth of the professional doctorate. Specifically designed to accommodate practitioners and to engage with the field of practice, pro-fessional doctorates insist that while students may engage with theoreti-cal knowledge addressing critical issues, essentially they will adopt the social missionary purpose of producing 'a range of solutions relevant to their professional practice'. Such knowledge is solution oriented, for example:

> Research undertaken as part of the professional doctorate is geared to directing and informing change, and to making a difference in the work-place and/or professional context. (UniSA, 2011)

Here research stands in a perfect symbiotic relationship with practice, and we can have no doubt of the ameliorative force of the familiar phrase 'making a difference'. A US e-learning doctorate declares an unembar-rassed existential purpose: 'to better assist your own students in the self-actualization process. Emphasis is on services (Walden University, 2011). But this is a typical statement: social amelioration, so the story goes, can be realized through strategies of intervention and their attendant tactical, technical practices informed by practice-oriented, evidence-based research and knowledge production. This circular logic demands a firm faith in the beneficent effects of the application of research-based knowledge, faith that knowledge can redeem practice even when research-based knowledge may fatally puncture the positiv-ism of that faith. The focus on practice and improvement banishes that dangerous kind of knowledge.

Consideration of the ontological conditions of knowledge in improvement-oriented educational research suggests a self-enclosed world imbued with ready-to-hand understandings. 'World' in this sense constitutes a limit for what can be known, thought and produced. If certain kinds of empirical data trouble the positivist assumptions of the world of ameliorative education, recognition of the difference between forms of knowledge opens awareness of otherness in the form of alternative horizons (Gadamer, 2004).

Troubled times: Metaphysics and educational research

Nothing is more instructive . . . than the way Spinoza conceives of the common. All bodies, he says, have it in common to express the divine attribute[s] of extension . . . And yet what is common cannot in any case constitute the essence of the single case. Decisive here is the idea of an *inessential* commonality, a solidarity that in no way concerns an essence. Taking-place, the communication of singularities in the attribute of extension, does not unite them in essence, but scatters them in existence. (Agamben, 1993: 18–19)

'The simple', Bachelard used to say, 'is never anything more than the simplified'. And he demonstrated that science has never progressed except by questioning simple ideas. (Bourdieu, 1990: 139)

Contemporary educational research philosophy is troubled. An essentially instrumental view of educational research perceives delinquent theoretical research as turning its back on practice. Within educational studies, the prevailing common sense perception is that without a dedication to practice and a focus on improvement, there lurks crisis of purpose and absence of criteria for quality. A certain ontological fragility has accompanied what has often been a hostile polemics questioning the value of any educational research unmoored from its proper focus on improving practice. In recent times a discourse of crisis has arisen among mainstream commentators deploring the fragmentation of the field. The apparent loss of a centralized and consistent programme for educational research has been lamented as a dangerous sign of potential anarchy. Divisions between research orientations are seen as divisive, even pernicious and potentially fatal (Pring, 2000; Carr, 2007; Hammersley, 2007).

Critical differences between qualitative and quantitative approaches to educational research persist. The panacea of 'mixed methods' orientations has not eradicated the 'q' division that is seen as but one among many divisions: between empirical and theoretical, positivist and constructivist, realist and post-structuralist, for example. These labels define approaches often represented as being in conflict, having different orientations to knowledge. They are also deployed as handy frameworks in research guides. Much mainstream educational research remains locked in an overburdened empiricism, relying on data sets to verify its truth, with nodding reference to ideas as ways of seeing. From certain points of view, the traditional, empirical grant-attracting models are simply useless in terms of answering historical, sociological and political nuances. They are politically myopic, philosophically naïve and methodologically too narrow and reductive.

Theoretical, interrogative research is frequently seen as threatening the integrity of the whole enterprise, toying with big but empty ideas and rife with neologism. Essentially irrelevant in terms of practice, according to some, they deserve nothing less than banishment from the 'community'. In addition, there is an increasing solidification of approach in the ready-to-hand guides that evade all fundamental ontological issues. Educational research handbooks provide a process menu for the would-be researcher: choose your orientation, produce your design, gather your data, set your mode of interpretation, produce findings, display and disseminate. In this neat account, research theory choices get presented as methodological binaries: quantitative or qualitative, positivist or constructivist, Enlightenment or postmodern. These are represented as exclusive 'orientations to meaning', as codes offering different accounts of the world, in Bernstein's terms (Bernstein, 2000: 185). Postgraduate research courses rehearse and confirm these positions.

Latterly, in the wake of a potentially distracting array of 'paradigms', the role of theory has been particularly questioned in favor of a more pragmatic and 'creative' form of research for education. Some have advocated a return to a more restrained, more modest, more 'proper' practice-based – really, Aristotelian – model of educational research (Thomas, 2007).

Others proclaim darkly, in the face of what is represented as a distortion of the proper by intrusive burgeoning of theory, that the real distinction is between high-quality, well-designed, relevant and purposeful – essentially empirical – educational research and poor quality, directionless and pointless 'non-research'. These self-appointed in-house arbiters of excellence declare that, in fact, most educational research is both poor and pointless. Pointlessness can only be averted, it seems, by keeping the worlds of practice and policy in view pointless (Gorard and Smith, 2006).

The crisis in educational research about what it is, what it is for and how its 'proper' value might be arbitrated remains far from resolution. Inevitably, the turmoil in educational research has an ontological dimension. Questions about what educational research is are usually concerned with what it should be, producing differences and hostilities about the proper. Most frequently, questions and differences get resolved by affirming that what is proper to educational research is its connection with educational practice. Heavy moral overtones, frequently drawing on the rhetorics of 'social justice', reverberate through such assertions.

The ethic of improvement has been influential in affirming this priority of the pragmatic. Education is seen as an essentially practical business. The system exists, the ideas are founded, so the main consideration is to improve efficiency and to be more inclusive, in the name of social justice. The anti-inclusive element tends to be foreclosed; it never appears as an issue. But who would want to question improvement? And who would want to argue against the rhetoric of social justice?

As ontological questions, about the nature of the contemporary educational enterprise and the fundamental nature of its institutions, are fundamentally theoretical questions concerned with the interpretation of identity, they cannot be comfortably entertained by a will-to-improvement. Much intellectual energy and resources, then, go into refining research methods in order to produce reliable data and data sets that can be deployed in the good work of improvement. This tends to mean that certain ways of thinking – especially the ontological – that problematize the grounding of the improvement enterprise get excluded. And yet, concern with ways of thinking necessarily bears on all aspects of research. Dependant on convictions about the nature of the enterprise, research is always ontological. Any empirical methodology is also the articulation of a position, a statement concerning the production and generation of knowledge predicated on an understanding of the 'world' of education, predicated on an understanding of the 'proper' relations between educational research and educational practice. The ontological dimension cannot be elided by some pragmatic sleight of hand. Questions of method are not simply questions of 'craft' but are always also questions engaging metaphysics, questions concerning how things are.

Educational research manuals, procedures or advocates may try to suppress or banish the metaphysical question to facilitate pragmatic activity, but metaphysics must always haunt research endeavours. No educational research exists without some reliance – explicit or implicit – on ideas about the specific world of practice it addresses. Such ideas in turn depend on ideas about the nature of the world in the larger sense. The early philosophy of Derrida frequently insists that metaphysics is not the exclusive property of philosophy: our everyday language is already laden with metaphysical concepts. Metaphysics gets played out in the most humble everyday exchanges as much as in the most rarified academic discourses (Derrida, 1978). Matters of research craft are already metaphysical, just as metaphysical questions have strong implications for craft. In the context of any form of research this interplay is likely to be intense, even when – as with much mainstream, influential educational research – the relation is suppressed and unaddressed.

Danger may attend the ontological dimension, of course: questions of foundations can be tricky, casting doubt upon the very enterprise they address. Mainstream educational research, it seems, cannot bear too much of this kind of interrogation. Given the claims it frequently makes for social and ethical significance, it needs to resort to certainties of purpose and identity. One tactic deployed to keep perspectives dangerous to the mainstream enterprise at bay is to dismiss them as known irrelevances – post-structuralism or postmodernism, for instance. In this guise their contents can be reductively simplified, dismissed as frivolous and subjected to a shallow discourse of derision.

In fact, much of the energy of ontological thinking comes from what is often called 'continental philosophy', offering numerous approaches from specific generative paths to research philosophy, especially in terms of opportunities for 'thinking otherwise', to paraphrase Levinas (Levinas, 1981). Continental philosophy is – rightly – a disputed designation (Critchley, 1997), but this de facto category refers to a tradition that has generated exceptionally productive lines of thinking. Marx's, Nietzsche's and Heidegger's philosophies – different as they are – provide strong lines taken up and developed in post-structuralism and postmodernism. These broad and contested lines of thinking arise from rich veins in the recent productivity of Western philosophy: Derrida, Foucault, Lacan, Levinas, Lyotard, Deleuze, Agamben, Baudrillard, Badiou and Butler, for instance. The lines of thinking these names represent have impacted various disciplines traversing the study of education. One of their virtues lies in their potential to provide ways of interrogating anew both the protocols of research design and method and revisiting ontological foundations of research. Such thinking activates a 'hermeneutics of suspicion' to address fundamental questions (Gadamer, 1984).

Above all, such lines of thinking have insisted that the dimension of meaning cannot be elided, avoided or negated. Derrida has demonstrated that ontological decisions are functions of our own responsibility in the face of unknowable premises and consequences. In the context of research, decisions about what we are interested in, our 'topic', our stance, and how we may and do proceed must always (in order to be decisions) be made decisively in relation to some ontological commitment. In other words, decisions cannot be responsible if we are automatically prompted to make them according to what appears to be an irresistible logic (Derrida, 1995a). This includes all decisions made pragmatically in the most constrained circumstances.

The discourse of crisis in educational research

In educational research contexts, many have recently identified theory as a malaise on the grounds that knowledge grounded in *phronesis* is most proper. Practice set a stabilizing limit for procedure and reflection (Carr, 2007). Advocates of theory, on the other hand, claim that practical knowledge is necessarily unaware of its own theory-bound condition, since *theoria* is the ultimate virtue that promises to liberate practice from its own embedded limitations (Anyon, 2008). Pragmatic resolutions of the divide between theory and practice have sought to renegotiate the relation in terms of the specific purposes of educational projects, where aim and function have the status of transcendental organizing principles (Pring, 2000). Equally, a supposedly ethical principle – 'social justice' as educational research commonly affirms – provides the organizing centre for method and criteria of value (Griffiths, 1998).

This resolution of the practice/theory divide is achieved by the elevation of purpose and function as the overriding principles. The argument declares or implies that the business of improving education, often in the name of social justice, is the ultimate aim. All else is to be pragmatically subsumed under that noble mission. Improvement here cannot stand as a simple, neutral term. It automatically entails a shift in the relations between education and the socially and economically disadvantaged, even when there is no basis at all for this assumption. Such a problem-solving view of improvement for social justice is ontotheological: it has already decided both how things really are and how they should be. It regards the difference between how things are and how they should be as an unfortunate glitch in the 'proper' working of things. Regarding its own vision of how things should be as the proper end point of all development, it carries an ethical, ontological and teleological force.

If educational research 'should be' practice oriented and driven, the pragmatic position outlined above can determine what is good, useful, productive and relevant and what is not. What is not can then be dismissed as irrelevant, trivial and or useless. It can be castigated as a form of deviance from the real path to fulfilment. At its worst, this position operates as an intellectual McCarthyism seeking to clear out the improper intruder.

In recent times, Engestromian Activity Theory has offered an influential resolution of the practice and theory divide in educational research with its portable research model and its commitment to built-in expansiveness (Engeström, 2003). Activity Theory offers a ready-to-hand, universally applicable research template for improvement. The problem with Activity Theory, though, is that in its radical pragmatism it strictly limits its own resources for the thinking that will frame and inform its research practices (Peim, 2009). It is, in other words, ontologically constrained.

The automatic assumption of improvement as a condition of systems of activity that is evident in Engeström's Activity Theory is symptomatic. It is founded in an act of faith rather than in any special grip on reality. It is 'ontotheological', to borrow Heidegger's term. It projects its belief of how things are onto everything, shutting out alternatives. For while the ethic of improvement – impelled by its self-proclaimed social purpose (Fullan, 2001; 2003a) – dominates much contemporary educational research, there is little evidence indicating progress towards the desired state. The improvement drive carries an ethical flavour reinforcing the value and significance of research elevated to an ameliorative social project. As an expression of social conscience it transcends the merely academic. Devotees of the improvement ethic, however, fail to see beyond the necessarily limited horizon of their own world.

In education, the dark ruminations of Foucault on bio-power and governmentality, for example, disturb the more confident assertions of the improvement set. The classical sociological analysis of Bourdieu about schooling, social reproduction and cultural capital – still relevant and powerful in contemporary accounts of the social discrimination of education – or of Bernstein concerning code modalities and the exclusionary force of knowledge structures and their institutions has not been superseded, in spite of all the school improvement research effort of the interim. But those who eschew the ethic of improvement and confess their own ambiguity concerning the now key factor of research 'impact' are often cast as irrelevant or frivolously self-indulgent. What's the point of rehearsing gloomy and difficult social theories if they can make no difference, especially if they actually interfere with the ongoing work of progress?

Notwithstanding the dominance of the ethic of improvement in mainstream educational research, especially in research projects funded by major national bodies, a discourse of crisis in educational research has arisen in relation to the role of philosophy and theory. This crisis is partly generated from a sense that general agreements on the central role of improvement and on the existence of a common cause are both in trouble. Influential commentators in the field of educational research have expressed concerns about a loss of coherence and common purpose. The crisis refers to fear of a loss of a sovereign, dominant perspective and proper purpose in educational research. Uncertainty, division, contradiction and proliferation of differences within the field are identified negatively rather than as signalling a potentially productive 'cosmopolitan' condition. The key area of contention is the relation to thinking, theory or philosophy – that dimension of research we might entitle metaphysics. The often assumed separation between method – as technique or craft – and metaphysics – as engagement with ideas – reaches back deep into Western thinking. It is there in the split between rationalism (e.g. Spinoza) and empiricism (e.g. Hume). Through the Enlightenment attempted resolution of Kant to the present day, this division has been worried, worked on and continues to be rethought. It is experienced as crisis when there is a perceived need for coherence, singularity of purpose and cohesion.

Fear of impasse (aporiaphobia) and community as salvation

A fear haunts contemporary educational research thinking. Problem of foundations, purposes and intellectual coherence have generated a strong desire for a return to the 'proper' – a recovery of the proper grounding, mission and criteria for quality. A frequent realization in the expression of this tension is that a proliferation of modalities and perspectives has in effect decentred educational research so that universal criteria cannot be invoked or applied. This recognition has been mostly lamented as a negative condition that threatens integrity and common purpose. In all cases, solutions to the present crisis are proposed based on the assumption of a need for reform and recovery.

A symptomatic account begins by asserting a crisis in 'qualitative research' concerning its relevance and quality. Expressed in terms of the familiar but questionable distinction between modes of educational research, this account asserts that qualitative researchers need to give more attention to matters of validity of knowledge claims. A proliferation of perspectives has given rise to incommensurable paradigms, a condition generating 'fundamental differences that it may be impossible to bridge' (Hammersley, 2007: 299). In sorrow, an appeal made to an external value such as 'the political' only masks the 'real' problem (Hammersley, 2007: 299). At the same time, it is felt that guidelines for judging value and quality of qualitative research are desirable. The melancholy recognition that 'the barriers to our being able to produce any set of common guidelines, even among qualitative researchers, are formidable' leads to the unqualified affirmation that 'we should not simply accept methodological pluralism at face value, reinforcing it by treating each approach as having its own unique set of quality criteria' (Hammersley, 2007: 299). Acknowledging the difficulty of reaching universal agreement among educational researchers for protocols of authenticity, we meet a desire for the research community to continue to work towards this impossible desideratum. This drive is, oddly, a necessity unable to articulate its own grounds but is the pure expression of an ontotheological preconception about the value and purpose of educational research. With no ready-to-hand cure, all that's left is to appeal to the research community to carry on the hopeless quest for the absent protocols that might salve the wound. What else can be done? The half-solution offered relies entirely on the not-necessarily-correct assumption that there is an educational 'research community' that wants to work recovering its collective mission.

This thoroughly familiar position clearly arises from a belief system rather than any philosophically necessary argument or irrefutable research data. One alternative solution to the same perceived crisis has been to return attention to the 'proper' domain of educational research: the realm of practice. Impatient with the irrelevance of theory, those who hold this position affirm that educational research is to be both judged and saved in terms of its authenticity as practical science. The crisis would be resolved by handing the practice of research from the theorists back to practitioners whose situated practice could be reflexively reviewed and evaluated 'on the basis of a coherent and clearly articulated point of view' (Carr, 2007). The problem is that this new educational research order is to be informed, from the outset, by 'an understanding of what education is' with no apparent recognition that the 'is' carries a tremendous burden (Carr, 2007).

This need to return to a proper condition for educational research is expressed in urgent, if wistful, terms:

> Although educational researchers often behave as though they belong to a single intellectual community, the sad truth is that educational research now embraces so many traditions, paradigms, theoretical perspectives,

> methodological frameworks and academic disciplines that it cannot claim
> to meet even the most minimal criteria of homogeneity that any notion of
> a 'research community' presupposes and requires. (Carr, 2007: 273–4)

Exasperation ('even the most') and lament (the truth is 'sad') characterize the mood here. The word *now* suggests a nostalgically idyllic past
when this sad state of affairs was not the case; it also implies a future
when homogeneity can be restored. By the end of the article, 'the vision
of educational research as a practical science' is reaffirmed, with the
claim that this model of educational research does not reign supreme,
largely due to a failure of reflexivity (Carr, 2007: 272).

Unphased by the scale or nature of the ontological problem, untouched
by the consideration that what practitioners determine education to be
and how they configure the proper purposes and orientations of educational research may not be the end of the matter, the 'practical' solution turns out to rest on the faith that practice is the privileged position
from which all educational research and knowledge should be judged. To
achieve the desired, reflective, practice-oriented condition – free from all
the other improper business it identifies as 'traditions, paradigms, theoretical perspectives, methodological frameworks' – it must delimit the
very being of educational research. The desired 'practical philosophy' is:

> simply the name of that tradition of inquiry which, by promoting histori-
> cal self-consciousness, enables each generation of practitioners to make
> progress in achieving excellence in their practice and, by so doing, ensure
> that tradition through which it is sustained progressively evolves. (Carr,
> 2007: 281)

The desire to centre what has become decentred thus appears as a
vague affirmation of 'historical self-consciousness' or knowing where
you come from, directed towards an unproblematic 'excellence'. Thus
a familiar, influential idea about what educational research should be
is expressed, assertively rather than interrogatively, as practical 'reflection' based on a commitment to 'excellence' and fidelity to a tradition.
These values are all predicated on the familiar assumption of a presently
scattered but properly gathered community. According to this line of
thinking, that community needs to harness its differences to the common project in order to recover its given mission. As one educational

philosopher puts it, such a project demands the existence of 'the forums in which researchers, politicians, teachers and the community can come together for deliberating practice and policy in the light of the best evidence available' – as though practice and policy were the essential focus and as though such spaces of deliberation could reconcile all present differences to advance the improvement agenda (Pring, 2000b: 501). This kind of thinking is only possible by foreclosing the ontological questions that beset the enframing of education.

The desire to express universal values for educational research constitutes an attempt to provide a lost world with a centre (Derrida, 1978). Other ways of thinking about the relations between educational research and the privileged idea of community may be gleaned from some philosophical arguments from continental philosophy that have strong implications for the consideration of community in any context.

The influence of ideas of community in Western political thinking is questioned in Nancy's identification of a persistent myth of 'original community' (Nancy, 1983). This imaginary, lost way of life is perceived to have been an immediate 'being-together': intimate, harmonious and in direct emotional opposition to the depredations of contemporary difference. Although the idyll is lost, it returns in idealized form in accounts and images of the natural family, the village, the polis, the people or the republic. A parallel, contrary approach to questions of community occurs in the writings of Agamben, who proposes the idea of a 'new' community based on the notion of belonging 'without identity'. This is a community of singularities and fragments: it is a 'community . . . mediated not by any condition of belonging . . . nor by the simple absence of conditions . . . but by belonging itself' (Agamben, 1993: 85).

The view Hegel promoted envisioned the ideal state in terms of the ideal community. Contemporary communitarians, like MacIntyre, similarly advance community as a means for restoring identity and recovering political purpose in various domains of existence (MacIntyre, 1984: 190–1). Nancy's analysis reminds us, however, that community does not always entail a warm embrace: it can also be characterized by a violent affirmation of identity and a potentially stifling insistence on universal norms. Community is frequently founded on the myth that a lost idyllic or heroic past can, in some messianic future, be recovered. The longing for universals, for common criteria of value and for a shared sense of purpose heard in troubled accounts of the present state of educational research is linked, as shown above, with the desire to restore a proper, cohesive community. But a totalizing community based on shared identity must always police its borders and eradicate the dangerous and different other.

The longing for a proper 'academic' identity can lead to symbolically violent exclusions and negations: dangerously unanchored relativists or exorbitant neologists can be degraded, McCarthy-like, as non-researchers. Not to speak the same language, not to share the same culture, not to engage in the self-regarding, essentially enclosed pursuit of 'excellence' in 'our' terms threatens the regional identity and the social solidarity of the educational research 'community'. But the perceived lack of centre or centring principle for educational research (Carr, 2007; Hammersley, 2007) can be looked at in quite different terms. Rejecting a kind of hardware (body)/software (mind) dualism, Lyotard sees human thinking as actually impelled by desire arising from the fundamental lack of centre or cohering principle in being itself (Lyotard, 1991: 23). For Lyotard, this fundamental lack is the very condition of creativity: thinking is not simply digital, data sorting, logical or problem solving; thinking is the uncomfortable, troubling drive to engage with the lack, and to construct and create anew what has not been thought before. This questing is analogical, lateral, intuitive and inventive. For Lyotard, the world of 'inscriptions' (what's already there) and ready-to-hand traditions is never sufficient: 'there's still something missing in this plenitude' (Lyotard, 1991: 20). Knowledge and indeed culture itself are always already – and empirically – incomplete. What would an account of the condition of contemporary educational research make of this perspective: would it, as so many mainstream commentators do, lament the proliferation of 'many traditions, paradigms, theoretical perspectives, methodological frameworks and academic disciplines' as a kind of hopeless disorder?

Educational research and technological enframing

In Heidegger's (1954) lecture 'The question concerning technology', he scrutinizes the role of 'machine technology' in modernity. Redefining the relations between human beings and technology, Heidegger pays attention to modern forms of the technological with their characteristic ways of accounting for and organizing identities, purposes and practices. Such practices, as Weber also noted, have invaded modern forms of life, especially visible in bureaucracies that seem to have a system, power and will of their own, independent of any controlling will. Modern technology, with its determination to know and order everything and put it to use or hold it in reserve for future use, is seen as an extreme form of disembodied will-to-power. Heidegger refers to this condition as 'technological enframing', as we've already suggested, a provocative metaphor for strong tendencies in the contemporary condition of education at large. But it is easy to see how much formulaic research – and much research done in the name of greater 'performativity', including NFER and national research council-funded research – falls within that 'technological enframing' designation (Heidegger, 1993b).

In Heidegger's account, though, what technology is remains an open issue. In one sense, it is the product of human activity, but in another sense technology defines a boundary for what it is possible for humans to do and to be. Heidegger famously asserts that 'the essence of technology is by no means anything technological' (Heidegger, 1977b: 4). It is possible that Heidegger means to emphasize the fundamental relation that technology has with the meanings human beings make in their world or worlds, both with what they inherit as 'given' (as with Lyotard's account of culture summarized above) and with what they may create collectively with that heritage. It is not too great a leap to indicate that educational research can be defined as a kind of technology of knowledge. Questions about research are always questions about significance and value: about our essential relation to being-in-the-world. Such questions cannot help but therefore touch upon metaphysics. As soon as we begin to describe how things are, ontological questions arise. As soon as we declare anything about how we know things are as they are, epistemological questions are in play. As soon as we begin to enquire about how we stand in relation to what is and to what we know, phenomenological questions come up. To leave these aside, as taken for granted and assumed, may frequently be necessary, but at some point any research enterprise must confront them. Even the preferred term *reflection* cannot avoid reflecting on the very terms and conditions of the research object, the research enterprise and the researcher.

In another sense technology is an apt analogy or synonym for research. In the tendency for research to be represented as a technical process, a series of 'craft' procedures to be applied to reveal meanings that are essentially separate from such techniques (Booth et al., 1995; Scott and Usher, 1996), a distinction exists between techniques of method and the symbolic domain of interpretation. This distinction has its roots deep in the history of Western thinking, in the classic and persistent divide between 'the sensible' and 'the intelligible' (Derrida, 1978). This divide is not reduced by the contemporary proliferation of handbooks on research. There is a deep-seated tendency for research training and thesis production to divide into the familiar segments: literature review, research design, methodology, method, data and findings. This seems designed to promote a separation from thinking that often gets relegated to epistemological framing, clear argument or necessary logic. But there can then be no method that can neutralize its own relation to its onto-logical foundations, and this means, for example, taking into account the problematic nature of the object of research in its relations with the subjects of research and their world(s). In an earlier version of contem-porary understandings of what counts for us as perception, knowing and understanding, Kant concluded that there must be distinction between what we know and what exists. In Kant's view, we can only know things within a framework of knowledge that we ourselves create: things-in-themselves remain forever beyond our grasp. Hegel challenged this view. From his essentially historical outlook, Hegel saw knowledge as culturally and temporally relative but also argued that the ultimate – and most proper – object of our knowledge is consciousness itself. Absolute knowledge is both possible and desirable but can only ever be knowledge of our own consciousness. These two positions, Kant's and Hegel's, have furnished the grounds for philosophical engagement with fundamental questions about knowledge, discovery, language and the history of ideas that is far from exhausted. The point here is that after Kant and Hegel it is no longer possible to espouse an empiricism that erases the distinc-tion between what we know and what exists. Furthermore, the tradition of continental philosophy offers ways of engaging with such issues that go beyond the impasse and exasperation of those who would restore a common purpose and tie educational research to the grand mission of school and general educational improvement (Hegel, 1977; Kant, 2003). Continuing to engage with philosophical issues opened up in modern thinking by Kant and Hegel, drawing on contemporary resources for such thinking, in fact challenges the constricting 'enframing'.

Philosophy explicitly entered the formal space of academic educational discourse in offering a space for the review and rationalization of practices (Hirst and Peters, 1970). Its 'proliferation' can be seen as both expanding and complicating that necessarily indeterminate space. For some, this 'crisis' calls for a return to commonly shared values and cries out to reaffirm the proper orientation and focus of educational research. From another perspective, the crisis is both inevitable and productive: it signals the potential demise of centralized control – the 'technological enframing' of practice and discourse – and heralds an end to an exclusive intellectual McCarthyism that enables some to define the work of others as empty and meaningless.

One significant question for educational research now may be whether the indeterminate space of educational research forecloses certain kinds of thinking and engaging with ideas with tighter border controls, or whether that space remains open to what may seem foreign, intrusive and improper, in a cosmopolitan spirit of hospitality (Derrida, 2000; 2001).

Ethics in educational research: Ontology and the question

Various philosophical takes on ethics have important implications for educational research beyond current concerns with procedural conduct. Codes providing a checklist of research behaviours may displace ethical thinking with a ready-to-hand ethical procedure (ESRC, 2011). This delimitation of the ethical dimension is a strong tendency in educational research that arises from the foreclosure of ontological thinking.

A major problem in ethics that is reflected in much educational research derives from the legacy of platonic thinking whereby the real world is seen as the manifestation of a more real world that lies behind it – a really real world of essences or forms. According to this view, articulated most substantially by Plato, the world or 'nature' is 'but a spume that plays upon a ghostly paradigm of things' (Yeats, 2000). In other words, behind the messy reality of any given object, situation or process is an ideal version of that thing. The task of philosophy is to understand this difference and to seek the ideal form so that thinking can measure reality against it. This thinking implies that the answers to research questions and the solutions to research problems already exist out there somewhere, as yet unrevealed. The task of research is to uncover their existence, to reveal the truth that they embody. Plato stands as an early exemplum of philosophical enquiry, whereby the good pre-exists the search for its essence. Curiously, much contemporary social science research follows this model. Appearances are to be probed to reveal the truth of their form.

But at the heart of Plato's thought is a paradox, expressed in the dialogues' constant to and fro of question and answer. Plato's dialogues are skewed by Socrates' dominance, controlling the dialogic process, driving it towards a specific end point. Socrates insists on the process of questioning, implying that our grasp of essences is partial and our representations produce partial resemblances. At the same time, the good life, for Plato's Socrates, is incompatible with the unexamined life, in the well-worn dictum. What this means exactly is uncertain, however. For Plato's Socrates, all good comes from questioning one's presuppositions, from interrogating everything that is conventionally speaking held to be the case. In this respect, and in spite of the theory of forms, Plato's metaphysics is ontologically interrogative. It is at odds with much of what formally and officially goes by way of mainstream educational research with its constant reaching for conclusive data. There is a powerful ethical dimension to this: for Socrates, for Plato, to put things in question itself is the ethical, the conscientious, if endless, pursuit of the truth about the good. This is uncomfortably problematic for the certitudes that the ethic of improvement is founded on – especially in education.

For Kant, the source of the ethical is not outside and unreachable, but within. There it is, a mysterious, inexplicable but undeniable presence, one that is worthy of wonder, just as is the starry firmament. To be ethical is a given faculty. The way that it is possible or desirable to be ethical depends on being attuned to one's environment, to the specific conditions of one's time, place and culture. Kant's position presents the problem of ethical responsibility in a form that still resonates in contemporary thinking, with its emphasis on aporia and undecidablity, with the ethical as the problematic but essential ground of both action and thought. Kant does not doubt the inbuilt ethical imperative but at the same time offers no guarantee as to what form the ethical will take, what particular decisions it will lead to. In this difference between the imperative and the contingent there is a world of trouble. Nevertheless we might say that a properly Kantian approach to educational research ethics would adjure us to attend to the ethical call while also interrogating the very conditions we find ourselves in that frame our ready-to-hand ethical decisions (Kant, 2003).

Heidegger's emphasis on ontology as the starting point informs much contemporary ethical thinking. For Heidegger, thought begins with and sustains itself with the question, the 'the piety of thought'. In *Being and Time*, Heidegger (1962) had attempted to outline Dasein's radical contingency: any ethics arising from this interrogation cannot come from some unbidden force within nor can it reside in the external universe. For Heidegger, ethics arises from and is a product of the same particular mode of being that is opened by Dasein as the question. In questioning, Dasein takes on a hitherto unknown way of being that is the product of its own openness to the nature of things, to being. This way of being is not guaranteed but is, rather, the ultimate responsibility. In terms of research ethics, this means that research is ethical from the very beginning, not just in terms of following procedural codes, but from the act of questioning. This ethical questioning carries the possibility that the question, in being posed always from a contingent position, can rise above its own contingency in so far as it doesn't rest contented that the order of things as given is necessary. The piety of the question demands, then, a condition of ontological awareness, and this of course involves thinking and rethinking the grounds of our knowledge and understanding and the openness to being that they imply or enact (Heidegger, 1993c).

Wittgenstein, the great pragmatic philosopher of modernity who would probably seek to cure Heidegger of his philosophical anxieties, might refer instead to the untroubled and plentiful nature of much ethical conduct carried through without reference either to formal codes or to internal, troubling questions. The later philosophy of Wittgenstein, concerned with language games and their rootedness in forms of life, is also concerned with articulating the embedded nature of practice. Much ethical conduct simply arises from being at home in a way of life and knowing what to do next; in other words, it is the outcome of situated contingency and mostly requires no explanation or justification. When we do articulate our ethical conduct we resort to the ready-to-hand ethical discourses furnished by our specific 'form of life'. Wittgenstein was always interested in the unspeakable dimension of certain aspects of life, concerning what we can know or do without necessarily being able to produce criteria or an account in language. On this model, ethical knowledge and its application is managed much like making moves in a game in which the rules are understood implicitly and knowledge of what to do and say are matters of practice (Wittgenstein, 1953; 1994).

In modernity, however, any reliance on the domain of practice as an arbiter of ethical action is problematized by various analyses of a modern 'form of life' that depends on a procedural logic to pursue 'efficient' practicalities that may be informed by ethical intentions. The early twentieth-century work of Max Weber carries a dark warning concerning such pursuit of rationality as an end in itself. Rationality, for Weber, is closely associated with the idea of a will to 'mastery', where knowledge serves this will. Within a means–end logic, knowledge is subsumed to the cause of a disenchanting efficiency that sweeps aside all other considerations in its relentless, calculated drive. Far from expressing human freedom, this condition – intensified by modern forms of knowledge, including science and technology – constitutes an 'iron cage' where all ethical questions – including all fundamental ontological questioning – are subordinated or eradicated in the name of rational efficiency. The impersonal nature of modern bureaucratic systems – the condition of their 'virtue' – means that the intervention of conscience is foreclosed and the ethical dimension subjugated to procedural logic. In Zygmunt Bauman's more recent, Weber-inspired retrospective on modernity, this bureaucratization can have fatal consequences on an alarming scale. For Bauman, modern bureaucratic systems, by their removal of the face-to-face encounter and in their very impersonal rigour, tend towards a dangerous implacability, one that is insensitive to differences and nuances and can only recognize authentic identities in its own image (Bauman, 1991).

New impetus has been given to ethics in recent continental philosophy. Following – but rethinking – Heidegger, Levinas proposes a rethinking of ontology, positing the ethical relation to an Other as what occurs logically before anything else. Ethics in Levinas is primary: it arises from the recognition of an Other that ties us to existence and demands a response. Derrida writes:

> Levinas does not seek to propose . . . moral rules, does not seek to determine a morality, but rather the essence of the ethical relation in general . . . in question, then, is an Ethics of Ethics [which] . . . can occasion neither a determined ethics nor determined laws. (1978: 111)

The ethical cannot be derived from or subordinated to the conditions that give rise to any social context. It is always already there. This line of thinking, that has some possible correspondences with Kantian ethics and with some of Wittgenstein's less pragmatic statements, has been productive for a range of themes, especially Derrida's questions of law and justice. Derrida proposes that the privileging of the question as the source of philosophy in Heidegger misses what comes before the question. To ask a question presupposes a relation and a promise. The question actually presupposes an ethical relation to the Other, a recognition that there is something that makes a serious call on one's resources, on one's being in the world and on one's capacity to respond. For Derrida, responses are echoes of a special kind of responsibility towards what cannot be either evaded or – to use one of Derrida's own inventions – deconstructed. This responsibility, ultimately, is towards justice, an ultimate, non-negotiable, non-questionable principle, the only thing that stands beyond deconstruction. Justice cannot be reduced to anything that is given in advance: it is not to be equated with the law. On the contrary, justice stands in a problematic, always questioning relationship to the law. This means that there is always a difference – and often a decision – between the law and justice. As a result, ethics implies thinking otherwise, thinking beyond procedures and standard positions towards the question, the ontological and the relations that the question presupposes. One of the disturbing consequences of this line of thinking for educational research is that the easy equation between the improvement agenda and social justice is necessarily problematized. It cannot remain beyond the question, beyond interrogation.

Educational research, the ethic of improvement and the role of ethics beyond the question

For educational research, there exists at present, within the contemporary world order of education as institution, a dominant 'ethic' or way of thinking and conceiving of the 'good' that is predicated on a will-to-improvement. This ethic is evident in many places and in many ways. It is there in the continued existence of league tables for school performance. It is there in quality assurance systems that have penetrated to the heart of university teaching. It is there in comparative accounts of educational performance that drive an ethic of national and international competition. It is there in the injunctions to young people in educational institutions to improve themselves constantly, to develop their capacities, to be more responsive to the demands of the national curricula and the performance targets for their age group. It is there in the drive to render the whole of life – through lifelong learning – subject to the law of improvement through which the human subject stands always to be judged before the court of education in terms of competences, accomplishments and formal credentials. It is there also in the attention given to CVs in work environments where the CV offers not only a resumé of achievement but must also include a forward trajectory emphasizing new directions, new motivational paths. It is there in national research council funding specifications that want to tie educational research securely to current practice, frequently assuming that current practice is simply a given rather than a questionable condition. Within mainstream educational research the commitment to an ethic of improvement that displaces and overwrites any questioning of the rights of education and the necessity for the logic of improvement and all its modernist, highly questionable, bureaucratic machinery is not open to question at all.

According even to this brief account of ethics and philosophy, one may ask a seriously ethical question about the unthinking commitment frequently being demanded by and given to the ethic of improvement in education. For the improvement advocates, teaching is a moral enterprise that demands an ethical commitment to improvement from its practitioners (Fullan, 2003b). While this may seem unexceptionable, a moment's thought will prompt us to question if this applies to all teaching. Does it apply to any teaching in any political context? Does it take into consideration some of the more questionable features of modern and contemporary educational institutions, systems and practices? The automatic universalization suggests that we must regard social change as the remit of education and that this change must be in the direction of improvement. Much of the history of education might suggest otherwise. Beyond questioning the precise effects of the 'schooled society', there is good evidence that social inequalities are regenerated through education as we know it, whether its institutions are consciously or not dedicated to that process. To suggest this would be to risk offending against a taken-for-granted truth: only the 'wayward' (Gorard, memorandum [parliament]) would suggest that the educational reforms since 1988 have done anything other than improve education in the direction of equality. But there is a wealth of literature to suggest that this is not at all the case. Inequalities remain deep-seated in a divided system, where private education supervenes in terms of success rates, and where university access is heavily socially weighted. To recognize some of the uncomfortable truths concerning contemporary education punctures the myth that education can solve social problems, that education in our world is essentially and necessarily a force for good.

To acknowledge the possibility that education is not necessarily the essential grounds for social salvation is not to abandon the idea of educational research, nor to adopt some ultimately anti-educational position. Rather, it opens education as a field of practice, as a dominant idea in modernity and as a historical force, to question. The big, ontological question seeks to understand the role of education in contemporary social life, riven as it is with persistent inequalities within and between nation–states (Martin and Peim, 2011).

For research ethics, an open approach to education, one characterized by a hospitality untempered by a commitment to the present mythology of education as salvation, seems more apposite to an interrogative approach. Such a research ethics would demand that research and researchers understand their own grounding – their own situated-ness within a nexus of ideas, historical context and institutional appara-tus. For such a grounding, practice cannot be the main arbiter of truth, although that is not to say that practice doesn't have a claim to truth. For educational research to claim a responsible form of enquiry, the responsibility must be directed towards a number questionable entities: the object of enquiry, its definition, its description and its determination as an object of enquiry; the professional context, its history, the identity and motivating force of the researcher; and the research context, includ-ing an awareness of orientation towards the world of practice, policy and the nature of – in Foucault's rich and loaded term – the apparatus ('dispositif') (Foucault, 1980b).

It is our contention here that any ethical engagement in educational research must be, at some level, directed towards fundamental ontologi-cal questions. There is, we believe, a tradition in modern Western phi-losophy making this essential link, perhaps most strongly expressed in Spinoza's *Ethics*, a treatise that proposes that everything hangs together in such a way that our understanding of how things are determines how we orient ourselves towards one another and how we engage with knowl-edge. For Spinoza, interrogating the fundamental nature of things ena-bles us to grasp both the limits and the possibilities of what freedoms we may have, including freedoms of knowledge, understanding and action. Such limited but significant freedom demands responsibility towards the question.

How things are is simply not given through any guiding theology, as Nietzsche radically declared. God is dead; there is no ethical rule-book handed down from above. Ethics for Nietzsche, like ontology, is a matter of production: it is essentially 'art' to be composed, driven by its power to enhance life. That ethics is not given – any more than the nature of things is not given, once and for all – implies that our thinking in mat-ters of research can be much more hospitable, much more open and exploratory.

5 Schooling: The Social Landscape of Modernity

Our contention in this book is that there has been an increasing conflation of education with schooling. The school, we argue, has been and remains the key social technology of modernity, an instrument of government impinging directly on the body and soul of the citizen. Our contention is that this fundamental instrument of 'governmentality' has become an inescapable feature of the social landscape. Schooling has become essential to our collective identity, providing a model for much of cultural life. Our thinking about ourselves, our world and our potential has come to be informed by the ethos of the school. Hence, we claim that the school has become the paradigmatic modern institution indispensable to the contemporary life–world.

In the social role of the contemporary school we see continuity with the form of school developed in the United Kingdom around 1870, when the installation of universal schooling began in earnest. From this period, the population, conceived as an entity to be formed and worked upon by the application of regularized processes, became the object of schooling. One of the key points about schooling, catching them young, addresses the process of person formation to produce an organized and classified population differentiated according to known attributes and dispositions. This intervention into the character of the people is essential to the business of the modern school.

An interesting vignette of the haphazard, disorganized and ineffective precedent of the modern school appears in the early chapters of Dickens's *Great Expectations* (1861). The historical setting of the novel significantly predates universal compulsory state-sponsored education. The central figure Pip, who aspires towards social advancement through education, finds the local provision, in the form of a 'dame' school, disheartening and dispiriting. Attendance is part-time and voluntary. There is no curriculum, no age-related progression. The teaching is dull and uninformed. We might contrast this small-scale disorganized village example of school with the powerful images we have inherited of the early elementary schools, many of them still dominating urban skylines and making a powerful symbolic statement about their relation to the social landscapes they inhabit. Travelling into London on the mainline train from the north, one sees Beckford School (1900) rise above the slate-roofed terraced houses it dwells among between Kilburn and West Hampstead, an artefact of considerable solidity and a touch of grandeur, a statement of civic pride and authority. In this imposing structure it is easy to see a symbol of the redefinition of urban life in terms of ordered conduct, time-management, purposeful activity and solid institutional

Mr Shoveller

management, sharing pride of place among other public spaces: parks, clinics, libraries and town halls (Hunt, 2004).

Images of relatively early elementary schools vividly represent something of the flavour of these institutions and their characteristic ways of working. In this image from 1895, we see the ambiguous gesture of the teacher figure, Mr Shoveller, signifying the dual function of the school: pastoral care for the potentially neglected and discipline for the potentially wayward. Mr Shoveller's charges belong to a poor urban context: they are clearly in the throes of being organized and form a more or less coherent collective body. The signs of their potential resistance to order and unpredictability are evident in their different postures and expressions, their varied clothing and their apparent mobility. This group has not been brought to order easily, but to a kind of order they have been brought. We may see them as quintessential subjects of the modern school: no longer legitimate subjects of labour, in need of formal training in literacy and numeracy, in need of bringing self-management into their potentially chaotic lives. They are the raw material of a new, competent and hopefully self-governing citizenry. Mr Shoveller is its agent, not too far removed in social identity from his charges, but nevertheless the much more polished social product that their educational socialization might realistically aspire towards. It seems clear that this image signifies that this still relatively new education is about more than teaching and learning. It has transformed the urban sociocultural landscape. Its scope extends into the substance of collective national social life. Contrast this image with the engravings of London life in the work of Doré and Jerrold or with Mayhew's accounts of the lives of working children in London from an earlier period (Mayhew, 1861; Doré and Jerrold, 2006).

One astonishing feature of early photographic images of schools after 1870 is the representation of age stratification as a *fait-accompli*. Although an everyday feature of our contemporary world, age stratification is an extraordinary 'event' in the history of modernity. The idea that the population as a whole should be systematically segregated on the basis of age, that this segregation should be carefully staged and ultimately that this staging should relate to specified norms of development – or ideals of being – is worthy of astonishment. Mr Shoveller's crowd of individuals provides a relatively early and dramatic instance of this event. A collection of wayward boys brought together due to social, geographic and age proximity, they can be collectively worked upon according to more or less set norms of conduct, attributes, attainment and development. As time goes by, and particularly during the latter part of the twentieth century, these norms will become more tightly specified and more carefully elaborated as national curricula take hold with elaborated programmes of study, key stage attainment targets and related levels of performance. Mr Shoveller's crowd clearly has not yet been subjected to that tight enclosure of their being with such norms that seek to define what attributes and accomplishments, forms of knowledge and competence constitute what is remorselessly defined as normal development and 'progress'.

Two further images will, we believe, enable us to give some account of what Foucault might call the transition from sovereign to capillary power and the attendant transformation of the state in relation to practices governing the body and the soul (Rose, 1990; Foucault, 1997b). These historical images enable us to feel both the distance of time and world and, at the same time, an uncanny resonance with the contemporary. No doubt, it is very important to remember that the historical version of the school we confront in these images is quite different in a number of important ways from its contemporary comparator.

Girls doing Drill

We might say that the elementary school represented here occupies a rather different position in the symbolic order from the contemporary school, given a history of transitions, shifting emphases and major changes in the nature of welfare provision and the state. Nevertheless, we are also confronted with a sometimes surprising fundamental continuity between the contemporary institution of the school and its early twentieth-century elementary ancestor.

The drill class photograph clearly depicts an urban context. We can read this from the 'low-rise' tenement constructions. The brick-built buildings, with their grimy exteriors closing off any vista, indicate an urban proletarian environment. This is echoed in the figures of the children; their clothes, their aprons, their very body styles seem to speak of a particular socio-economic stratum.

Historically speaking, we know that the school arises in that context as a special, differentiated space within which particular kinds of regulated events may occur, shaping and transforming the social environment (Jones, 1977; Mann, 1979). What we witness in the photograph

Boys knitting

is one of those well-regulated, purposeful events that signal the realization of a new era in the governance of urban proletarian populations. The girls appear to belong to that portion of the urban population for whom elementary education was designed as an array of practices in disciplined self-management, the cultivation of a limited range of literacy skills and domestic competences, and a regime of ordered management of the body (Lowe and Seaborne, 1977; Donald, 1992: 17–46). We can see too that age stratification is at work: the girls appear to be close enough in age for us to conclude that their training is heavily norm oriented. The choreography of the activity indicates this clearly. The pose is held, with inevitable differences of personal body style, but at the same time with an implied unity in the arrangement. A well-established disciplined practice is evident, as in several other images in the book it appears in (Horn, 1989). Through the organization of bodies in space, a collective disciplinary training of the person is enacted.

The meaning condensed into these images concerns the reconstruction of social space and the formation of a specific architecture that remains in force today (Lefevre, 1991). We've already noted the nineteenth-century emergence of universal state-sponsored schooling as the arrival of a far-reaching transformation of the social landscape. This change was in the direction of greater order, hygiene and control (Allen, 2008). The population – from this point on – was no longer an unpredictable agglomerate of haphazard entities but became, as Foucault indicated in relation to the soldier, something to be moulded, forged, formed and stamped with specific attributes. These attributes may have been historically specific and changing, but in general they concerned self-management. Through a varied training of the body – including sitting properly, using a pencil or italic pen correctly, moving in unison to an ordered pattern – discipline in the arts of dexterity addressed the general disposition of the person and the collective body. In addition, this newly formed population was to be – at the very least – literate, numerate and moderately aware of their world and their collective history. Values were also important. Along with the domestic virtues of husbandry and the economic use of time, the schooled population was also to be imbued with collective values, celebration of national identity and perceived cultural heritage, as we shall briefly touch on.

Schooling: The necessary supplement to learning

Much current educational research is predicated on the firm conviction that schools are primarily dedicated to learning. According to this view, learning is both necessary and good for its 'subjects'. Learning is often implicitly conceived of as good for both the individual learner and for society at large. Where individual dispositions or specific social groups cause difficulties in terms of so-called underachievement or inadequate operation of the institution, these cases should be researched, their causes dug out and remedial action taken.

This is the foundation of much educational research and the basis of the school improvement movement expressed in various contexts, including government policy offices and academic education departments in universities. There are a number of interesting, and questionable, assumptions embedded in this vision and in the ethic of school improvement. One is that learning is a significant feature of being and is in fact necessary to individual well-being, hence the recent positive value attributed to lifelong learning. In this view, the individual self is conceived of as always in process, as a continuous project. The end point of this project is rarely, if ever, addressed, but we know that even lifelong learning must terminate with death. At the other end of the life cycle, recent times have seen an increasing emphasis on learning as a staged and norm-oriented activity. Even very young children – infants in their state of almost absolute potentiality – are subject on entry to nursery to a curriculum that states what they should learn and the norms of achievement for their age/stage. The characteristic activity of such infants, hitherto known as 'play', is thus rendered meaningful within a grid of charted attainment to reveal the development of the individual child against its peers within a framework of normativity. When the Scottish government issued its *Early Years Framework* specifying the norms of attainment and development for preschool children (supported by the research of a 'professor of social change'), it did so without embarrassment in a spirit of positive necessity, as though such a move would inevitably be seen and understood as progressive (Allen, 2008).

Anyone who has spent time reading the (often daily) reports under early years curricula knows that what gets commented on and what the institution deems significant is more than the stuff of learning and formally specified attainments. Nursery reports, like school reports, frequently comment on disposition and conduct, especially in cases where either or both are deemed to be in need of improvement. When the reports do address learning activities, they include reference to social matters – to orientations towards learning, sociability, the capacity for self-management and general disposition. In this supplementary commentary, the institution emphasizes its interest in defining the child under headings that do not involve learning or the attainment of knowledge and specific skills. The fact that we take this extra-curricular concern for granted doesn't make it any the less interesting or questionable.

The concern with matters above and beyond learning – albeit in the name of learning – indicates something fundamental about the nature of the school as institution. While schools do certainly operate in the name of learning, providing occasions for learning and producing what they are pleased to call 'learners', this concern with learning cannot be separated from social processes with far-reaching consequences for individuals and for whole social groups. While the aspiration of many educational professionals and institutions may be to focus above all on learning, the extra-learning dimension of the institution cannot be side-stepped, suppressed or eradicated.

In one sense, this is an obvious truism, but it is one that even the most sophisticated advocates of school improvement hardly recognize. In fact, for ontological reasons for the school improvement movement, it is necessary not to recognize such supplementary dimensions and effects of schooling. But as Derrida has decisively demonstrated, what is supplementary often comes to dominate and determine the very nature of what it supplements, becoming an essential attribute or dimension of that thing and not a removable adjunct (Derrida, 1976). So it is with the school. The social function takes priority. This is an ontological necessity. The social function demands that subjects of the school conform to norms of conduct, values and aspirations. We can see this in the emphasis on discipline as a precondition for learning. We can see it in the simple fact of age and stage stratification.

School life is saturated with a discourse of submission to the symbolic order: adjurations to work hard; to take care of one's conduct and development; to become a model self-directing, self-motivating and self-correcting subject, synchronized to the institution's purposes, judgements and values. And what is this discourse, if not an attempt to align the individual, the group and the population to the institution's 'metaphysic', in other words, to its view of how things are with the world and how things should be for the individual – and the group – in relation to that world.

A second supplementary – but also essential – function of the modern school goes beyond matters of both learning and conduct. This is the function of social distinction. This function is regarded – especially by the advocates of school improvement as well as by all those concerned with education and 'social justice' – as scandalous. The scandal attaches to the fact that institutions that are supposed to be dedicated above all to the pursuit of learning and the inculcation of knowledge turn out to be, at the same time, instruments for defining social identities. What's more scandalous is that these definitions are, as the data reveals time and time again, rooted in social class differences. Perhaps most outrageous, though, is the misleading idea that schooling can be liberated from this social distinction function. Nothing in its history, its present functioning or its general ontology, in fact, suggests that this might be the case.

Curriculum epistemology: Governing knowledge

The school curriculum defines knowledge in its own specific way. In a sense, the school decrees that the knowledge it defines as significant is knowledge itself. Imposing its vision of what knowledge is, the school excludes other forms of knowledge from its real interests. Official knowledge expressed in the school curriculum frequently is at odds with forms of knowledge that may belong to the lifestyles and belief systems of different cultural groups (Williams, 1983; Eagleton, 2000). In fairly recent times, awareness of cultural difference and of its impact on schooling in the United States, for example, has produced quite fierce debate about the language of schooling, about the style and contents of the curriculum and about the cultural exclusion of African-American children in particular (Delpit, 1995; Smitherman, 2000). Given the structuring of national schooling systems – with their remorselessly norm-related, assessment-driven practices – it should hardly be surprising that schooling is not, in its hegemonic form, at all receptive or responsive to different orientations to language, culture and knowledge.

Some of this exclusionary force can be attributed to Enlightenment and modernist epistemology. After the domination of knowledge by religion through the medieval and even into the Renaissance period, a certain faith in progress accompanied the rise of scientific knowledge. Enlightenment epistemology supervened in post-Renaissance period in Europe, both giving rise to and feeding an attending faith in science and technology that remains, albeit problematically, influential.

The emergence of the domination of science as knowledge in modernity both puts 'man' as the author of science at the centre of things but also problematizes the grounding of knowledge. Enlightenment rationality is fraught with contradictions, aporia and a tendency to turn against itself. These awkward features are problematic, but are also strangely creative, giving rise to new and productive ways of thinking, understanding and knowing things. What Enlightenment rationality doesn't lead to, necessarily and inevitably, is the current 'technological enframing' that decrees that knowledge is progressive and that the empirical is the fundamental ground, embodied in the practice of science, for what we know and that we can attain direct access to it. The legacy of Enlightenment thinking and science are both, fortunately, much more interesting than that (Kant, 2003).

During the early classical period of the Enlightenment, one of the big questions that beset Western thought and philosophy was the certainty of knowledge. Descartes (1596–1650) is frequently cited as the first thinker of the modern period to confront the big epistemological question: how can I be sure that I know what I know? This question permeates everything for Descartes. And this question translates into a general question for European culture, a culture peculiarly intent on grounding its knowledge in absolute certainty even while it repeatedly plays out the theme of uncertainty. Descartes could only be certain of anything because he could be certain of himself as a thinking subject. For Descartes, it is self-consciousness that guarantees knowledge. Later,

Kant (1724–1804), writing with a rather more subtle legacy, was fascinated by the critique of knowledge proffered by the sceptics of the eighteenth century who pursued a line of thinking that problematized all certainty. Kant's philosophy is an elaborate attempt to confront that uncertainty and scepticism with a thoroughly logical account of human understanding and knowledge. Kant's ideas, though radical at the time of their introduction into European thought, are now so deeply embedded that they can be said to be fundamental to Western thinking. Kant expressed strong faith in the intuitive self-reflective rationality of consciousness, the very stuff of thought. But Kant couldn't argue away the recognition that there was no guarantee that humanly generated rational understanding, that essential faculty, was automatically attuned to or automatically in line with the real world of things. For Kant, there was much more to seeing than meets the eye.

Only a determined positivistic spirit could counteract Kant's sceptical line of argument. It is one that still holds sway in educational research today, but it could never answer Kant's critique and could only survive by evading it. The Enlightenment idea of knowledge pursued by Kant achieves a kind of zenith in the thought of Hegel (1770–1831), the philosopher of 'dialectics' who in turn deeply influenced Marx's progressive version of history. Kant had identified self-consciousness as a peculiarly powerful facet of thought. Hegel saw history as a kind of self-managing logic of progress. Through conflicts of difference, new forms of being and knowledge come into existence and are themselves transformed and surpassed by others. This is the logic inherent in the world – and it corresponds to the logic of self-consciousness. For Hegel, history must follow a law of progression. It is in the nature of things to do so. This idea of necessary progression applies to knowledge and thought as well as to history. In other fields of knowledge, a similar progressive rationalism came to dominate thinking. Empirical knowledge combined with powerful, testable theory produced a new age of scientific and technological advancement. Such thinking was applied to the new domains of knowledge that came to be known as the 'human sciences' or the 'humanities'. These new forms of knowledge took up a special space and frequently saw themselves as addressing fundamental questions about progress and the meaning of sociality.

Science itself had posed serious epistemological questions and had demonstrated the instability of authorized knowledge emphasizing its historical specificity. At the dawn of modern science, Copernicus's model of the universe challenged the centrality of the earth with disturbing implications for the position of man. Even as the concept of 'man' as the measure of all things arose, the idea was, at least implicitly. From its inception, the Copernican revolution continued to imply a similar revolution in the field of metaphysics. The place of man in the universe had been decentred and was to suffer further blows to any sovereignty it might have claimed. Copernicus's example also provides a useful illustration of the necessarily provisional nature of knowledge, given that the revolutionary model of the universe that he produced was itself extremely limited and was displaced by later knowledge. As the universe itself was brought within the sphere of rational human knowledge, rational enquiry would continue to produce equally modifiable models. In its mobility and its ongoing displacement activities, science raised questions about position, proclaiming both relativity and uncertainty as indispensable principles.

Enlightenment thinking brought its own, often productive, problems. Marx took Hegel's dialectic into the political sphere and produced a new epistemology, based on materialist philosophy and revolutionary action. History was not the product of destiny but was forged, according to Marx, from a great battle of ideas arising from the struggle for material power. There were no guarantees in this, however. Much nineteenth-century continental European thinking was founded in suspicion rather than certainty (Ricoeur, 1977). While Nietzsche (1844–1900) announced both the death of God and the contingency of human ideas, here was no haven of logical necessity, no great faith in science to provide answers and models for living. Life itself was rather to be celebrated and treated as an art form activating a creative approach to both life and knowledge. The death of God implied an end to the very idea of a 'master' plan. Did this not mean then, as Marx had maintained, that religion, one of the main historical forms of knowledge, was no more than a kind of drug to keep the masses in their place or, as Freud (1856–1939) would later describe it, nothing more than an illusion, the product of unconscious fears and desires? If God really was dead, it seemed there could be no ultimate grounding for belief or conduct. Nietzsche and others who came after saw this end of ultimate metaphysics potentially as a great liberation. Existentialists felt it implied great responsibility for the individual to define and live by their own ethics of action. As socialist ideas held sway, other proclaimed a new era of collective responsibility.

The events of the twentieth century, however, with its hi-tech total warfare and various genocides, have prompted greater uncertainties about human progress, the history of knowledge and Enlightenment values. From the postcolonial histories of the twentieth century, powerful voices and movements have emerged to challenge the domination of Western enlightenment (Fanon, 1967; Said, 1978; Spivak, 1990). Nietzsche, Marx and Freud are often cited as the thinkers who instigated the demise of Enlightenment thought, Nietzsche by emphasizing the correlation between truth and power, Marx by proposing a class-based rethinking of history and Freud by introducing the element of the unconscious into subjectivity (meaning that the self-present subject, the very centre of enlightenment epistemology, was nothing more than a self-deluding ruse). Heidegger's critique of all forms of ontotheology and warnings about the supremacy of technological enframing amplified these ideas (Heidegger, 1993b). After Heidegger's intensely interrogative thinking, a new generation of 'masters of suspicion' proposed new, troubling questions for hegemonic knowledge, and proposed also that knowledge itself was fraught with politics and the new dominant principle of thinking – difference (Ricouer, 1977: 6). Challenging forms of knowledge that hubristically laid claim to certainty and a sovereign authority, Foucault's (1988b) injunction to 'problematize' such pretensions has far-reaching implications for the everyday, taken-for-granted practices of schooling and of education in general.

An interesting vignette is provided by state schooling in England after World War I. The Russian revolution had engendered fears of Bolshevism as a possible new and dangerous form of working-class solidarity. The school was charged with the task of providing an antidote in the form of national culture and with nurturing the national language as a repository of accumulated knowledge and historical identity. The postwar crisis of civilization in Europe had engendered a powerful concern for the corruption of language and culture along with a fear of the newly emerging forms of popular culture. There was perceived to be a desperate need for sociocultural cohesion (Baldick, 1983; Doyle, 1989). In the early 1920s, English in schools was proposed as the mechanism that could work against the depredations of commercial culture to maintain proper standards of language and promote a culture of national unity. English in schools was to be a bulwark against cultural corrosion as well as against the dark force of Bolshevism.

There was good, if strange and hardly recognized, reason for the authors of the Newbolt Report (1921) to focus on English as this serious political linguistic-cultural project. A scandalous account of subject history traces the origins of English curriculum to India where the subject first appears as a vehicle for the enculturation of subaltern populations. Imperial rule required that sections of the native Indian population be instructed in the language, culture and values of their rulers – studies in English language and literature served that purpose (Viswanathan, 1989). English came to serve a parallel function in England and Wales after World War I, when sections of the English population seemed increasingly restless, potentially Bolshevik and in need of cultural and linguistic discipline (Peim, 2003). English has consistently been a subject freighted with anxieties and concerns about the linguistic and cultural health of the nation, always an ideologically loaded business long before national curriculum specifications occupied subject identity (Doyle, 1989). Arguments about the proper nature of subject identity have had a highly political edge. In the 1960s upstart, liberal practices were set against more traditionalist views. In the early 1980s, English was burdened with responsibility for national cultural coherence when racial tensions surfaced in urban centres. In the early 1990s, the traditionalists restored grammar to the curriculum, making a strong correlation between standards of the 'proper' in language and general behavioural standards of modern youth (Batsleer et al., 1985; Peim, 1993). The struggle that took place over English in the national curriculum concerned intensely political issues of social coherence, national culture and identity (Anderson, 1992; Cox, 1994).

We may occasionally think that real knowledge is not tied to beliefs and values and that the square of the hypotenuse is, in some incontestable way, the sum of the square of the two opposite sides. It would seem very strange now to argue that the world is really flat, after its roundness has been long established. It is the case, though, that knowledge, no matter how well established scientifically, cannot be totally fixed and absolute. It is always, in some way, relative and contingent, even though for the practical purposes of living we must behave as though certain knowledge is simply true and reliable.

Some forms of knowledge change dramatically with time and culture in significant ways. Different groups of people hold quite different views of the world. We know, for example, pretty confidently, that in order for the sun to continue to appear day after day and to give life to things that we need for our continuing earthly existence, it is not necessary to perform regular human sacrifices. But the ancient Aztecs did not share our scepticism. They believed precisely that it was necessary. And they had plenty of empirical evidence to prove that it was so. After all, it always worked. We may now have established beyond doubt that the shedding of human blood is not an essential prerequisite for the maintenance of solar energy on earth. For the Aztecs, though, it was as absolute and complete a truth as any idea we might now claim universal truth and validity for.

The collision of different forms of knowledge generated from different life–worlds can be tragically illustrated in the history of Australian Aborigines and their systematic methods of accounting for history and time. When the English first went to Australia, the Aborigines proved a deeply mysterious phenomenon. So perturbed were the English by their apparent difference that they regarded Australians as not human. They had none or hardly any of the characteristics that the white Europeans could recognize as human. This was not, as the dominant idea of the time would have it, because the Aborigines were primitive. It was because the two peoples inhabited totally different life–worlds. The difference had dramatic and tragic consequences for the Australians, whose world was largely destroyed by the invaders. And yet the 'invaders' would hardly have described themselves in those terms. Australia had been defined as 'terra nullus', a place of nothing, without identity, and the Australian peoples, for all their differences and their many different types of knowledge, were regarded as having no world-picture at all. The point here is that fundamental knowledge about truth and reality can differ critically. The most commonplace forms of knowledge – about time, history and very fundamental things – are expressions of world-creating forms of life. In the very fact that certain forms of knowledge predominate we can see the increasingly important relation between knowledge, politics and power. We can also see how knowledge has become, in modern school curricula with their strict delineations of content and their levels of attainment and lines of progression, subject to technological enframing. Even though no one now would try to justify the curriculum in terms of purely rational organization of knowledge, as some early philosophers of education seriously proposed, no one now seems able either to instigate a radical redefinition of the privileged, authorized, established forms of knowledge that are ensconced in the curriculum (Hirst and Peters, 1970).

The relative stasis of school curricula, especially national curricula with regulated testing regimes, is symptomatic of the taken-for-granted organization of school subjects and their conventional contents. The idea of the curriculum as the organization of knowledge into separate subject areas has developed powerfully through state education systems (Bowles and Gintis, 1976; Bourdieu and Passeron, 1977). As recently as the 1970s, Hirst declared (ironically in the name of the new area of philosophy of education) that the conventional school curriculum was derived from universal 'forms of knowledge' into distinct areas which have their own concepts by 'sovereignty of nature', as it were. Hirst categorized knowledge in the following schema: mathematics, physical sciences, human sciences, history, religion, literature and the fine arts, philosophy and moral knowledge (1975). This view of knowledge as a given, self-organizing system exerts powerful influence over subject divisions in schools, sixth-form colleges and universities. This is the essence of 'real' academic knowledge, it declares.

Knowledge is deemed to inhere in specific subjects with their own discrete and different sets of ideas, practices and contents. These are not just collections of facts but include ways of looking at things and modes of understanding. Each follows its own rules and practices, being a separate language game or discourse, though all fall within the general cultural and linguistic environment of the school. The national curriculum in England, for example, divides the curriculum in terms of different subjects, some defined as more central and essential than others. Thus, English, mathematics and science all have core status and are the central concerns of state schooling. In some subject areas there have been voluble disagreements between different stakeholders about what the proper contents of the subject should be. In subjects such as history, English and music, for example, the content may appear to be more contentious and open to debate. In these subject areas questions about subjectivity, perspective and ideology may appear to be more relevant and critical (Cox, 1994; Burden & Williams, 1998).

Hirst's view is thoroughly liberal, functionalist and uncritical. It accepts the dominant conception of knowledge embodied in the history of curriculum since 1902. The idea that the formal curriculum reflects an ideological history is not entertained in Hirst's account.

Against the idea that knowledge is rationally self-defining is the recognition that knowledge is, in fact, constructed through social activity. Different social practices, engaged in by socially differentiated groups of people, will necessarily give rise to different forms of knowledge and different forms of knowing. A number of commentators on education have explored alternative ideas of knowledge, challenging the forms of knowledge and pedagogy installed in contemporary state and national curricula as limited and excluding (Young, 1971; Aronowitz and Giroux, 1986; Apple, 1996). In general, twentieth-century tendencies in philosophy would argue against Hirst's position. The confidence that knowledge can be limited, defined and parcelled has been seriously challenged from many perspectives. Foucault, for example, sees knowledge systems as shifting according to the dominant 'episteme' or regime of knowledge (1977). These systems are not progressive and may differ radically from one historical period to another. This works against the confident assumption of accumulating human knowledge and argues for ideas about knowledge that are more open to the excluded and different. Postmodern and post-structuralist views generally characterize the curriculum much more as a provisional construct than as the expression of functional and intrinsically important knowledge. In the postmodern world, knowledge is at the centre and controlling it means exercising power. Knowledge is always contested and what we take for progress – the steady march of science, for instance – towards more inclusive and more powerful explanations of the world is really the victory of one set of ideas and one kind of knowledge over others (Lyotard, 1986; Harvey, 1991).

Officially sanctioned knowledge exerts power, while at the same time it requires authority for its continued sovereignty. The authority of sanctioned and official knowledge sustains education systems and institutions that are endowed with the power to grant social status, to award credentials and to authorize ideas and practices in the name of what counts as significant knowledge. Accreditation systems police such knowledge at different levels within a knowledge hierarchy.

A number of positions have challenged the assumptions of Western knowledge to totality and exclusivity, including recognizing that Western knowledge has represented 'the east' as something 'other', alien and exotic and has diminished the claims to legitimacy of other kinds and traditions of knowledge (Said, 1978; Spivak, 1990; Ahmad, 1992). In many cases, the West's own recent traditions of critique have been deployed to challenge the authority of its dominant system of knowledge and power. Postcolonial perspectives, often informed by continental philosophy, have redefined ethnicity as a radical form of difference in terms of knowledge, values, beliefs and culture. As different ways of seeing and even of being mingle and collide in contemporary urban centres, education tends to promote one dominant form of cultural practice. As individuals and populations negotiate identities in a world of mingling forms, critics have emphasized that knowledge is actually a contested field and the value of what is learned is less important than the social authority that learning in an official educational context carries with it. While there is increasing recognition that discourses of knowledge are historically 'contingent', the authority they exert is less a matter of their 'scientific' truth than the social forces that give them legitimacy. And while formal education draws its authority from the symbolic power invested in the curriculum, the promotion of social values and beliefs remains a primary function.

Schooling and social reproduction

A striking challenge to the dominant metaphysic of schooling is the extent that schools operate as sites and agents of cultural and social reproduction. Many educationists have addressed the fact of social reproduction, and many have sought to address it in terms of school reform. Successive governments in all so-called Western nation–states have implemented policies to address the inequalities that get enacted through the school system. In spite of all the thought and energy devoted to educational reform that enhances equality, including the ongoing work of university 'social justice' departments, there is little comfort in figures that consistently indicate certain social groups will likely benefit from what education has to offer and certain groups are fated to fail.

Knowledge of this persistent pattern of inequality goes back a long way, and successive waves of reform have sought to address this phenomenon. The UK example is instructive. In 1944, with the end of World War II in sight, the UK parliament passed the education act that would grant all children access to secondary education, albeit within a stratified system. When the political climate in the 1960s decreed that this 'tripartite' system was unfair, because it decided the social destinies of large numbers of young people at age 11, the comprehensive school became the vehicle on which ideals of equality through education were to be realized. Unfortunately, not all local authorities were prepared to ditch the schools that the tripartite system had sustained, as these were still regarded as providing the main route to elite education, albeit for a selected minority. Comprehensive reform – where it did happen – certainly did away with selection at age 11, but only to re-enact the inequalities that selection had promoted by allowing for the streaming and setting that guaranteed the continuation of an educational apartheid. Children of different educational status were offered different curricula and quite different sets of aspirations and possibilities. In such schools the existence of 'sink' streams and, later, 'remedial' classes was commonplace. The social profile of the inhabitants of such zones of failure was alarmingly predictable. Even in relatively rare schools where so-called mixed-ability teaching prevailed, middle-class children systematically fared better than working-class children, particularly lower-working-class children. The situation in the United States, for example, was no better, exacerbated by a very obvious racial divide. In both UK and US contexts, state-sponsored education has been always already supplemented by a privately funded super elite of schools with enormous social prestige. These schools, of course, continue to exist and to exert social, cultural and political influence. Advocates of the improvement ethic rarely mention this injustice in their appeal to equity and social justice.

At the same time, a questionable discourse of 'ability' prevailed in schools and remains alive and well today, informing much practice in mainstream schooling. The taken-for-granted assumption that intrinsic abilities of pupils can be determined – as with general intelligence tests and all the other questionable paraphernalia of such judgements – still remains a powerful assumption that informs the daily practices of schooling and has never been addressed. This essentially eugenicist thinking can be detected at work in contemporary CAT (Cognitive Ability Test) scores – and all similar testing practices – as well as in all the daily, casual comments made in staffrooms about the relative intelligence or 'ability' of school students. This discourse of ability – although not grounded in any specific knowledge – is deeply ingrained and feeds prevailing myths that contemporary schooling, with all its various inequalities, is essentially meritocratic.

During the mid-1970s, in the United Kingdom, an alleged education 'crisis' changed the balance between discourses of equity and discourses concerning education as a driver of economic efficiency. This discourse of education as essential to economic efficiency, competition and development remains globally powerful. Ultimately, global consciousness led to the development of national curricula as central governments decreed the order of school subjects, decreed the essential contents of school subjects and, what's more, defined in specific detail the levels of attainment appropriate for the various key stages (1, 2, 3 and 4) that children would pass through on their schooled journey from ages 5–16. These moves were part of a process that meant that schooling, on a global scale, would be defined predominantly in terms of testing. However, assessment outcomes remained strongly related to the social division of labour, ensuring that the reproductive function of schooling would remain powerful. A new emphasis on competition between schools and the supervention of the logic of performativity decreed that the ideals of inclusion and equality that had accompanied the ideology of comprehensive education would, as the sociologists had frequently indicated, retreat.

The classic sociology of education had long shown that schools do not innocently offer equality of opportunity to all social groups. Bernstein's pioneering work – now well over forty years in the 'archive' of educational knowledge – clearly indicates a strong correlation between the division of labour, certain strongly class-inflected 'orientations to meaning', and educational success and failure. The cultural ethos of the school, according to Bernstein, is largely at odds with the cultural ethos of significant segments of the school student population. In this, it is fair to say that for certain groups (those of lower social status) there are systematic prohibitions to achieving educational success. Recent research has confirmed similar patterns of systematic exclusion in relation to certain ethnic groups. This exclusionary effect is unrepresentable within the policy world that determines the drive towards improvement.

Studies conducted in England and Wales across several generations concluded that reforms of the education system had hardly made an impact on social inequality (Halsey, 1961; Halsey et al., 1980). Although working-class children were staying in the education system longer, their relative chances of accessing higher education and significantly enhancing their economic and social status were not much changed by post-war reforms. During the period in question changes that had been designed to produce a more meritocratic society had not had that effect. More recent studies indicate similar class differences in university attendance leading to variation in educational qualifications that are still distributed in relation to social class.

In England and Wales, the tripartite system had been founded, after the 1944 Education Act, on commitment to secondary education for all, but it made assumptions about children's innate, inherited intelligence. Tests determined progress at age 11+ to secondary modern schools or grammar schools. Grammar schools provided a more academic education essentially designed for progression to university, and secondary modern schools were more like an extension of the elementary schools they had partly been designed to replace. At least the tripartite system seemed to offer the chance for all to receive a grammar school education. All children would be sifted through the testing net. Educational psychologists of the period, though, notably the discredited Sir Cyril Burt, promoted the essentially eugenicist idea of intelligence as inherited (Silver, 1973).

In the 1960s and 1970s, symbolic interactionist and ethnomethodological studies in sociology demonstrated that social factors – especially relating to language, conduct and self-presentation – significantly defined schools' attitudes to pupils. Negative valuations were commonly attributed to pupils whose subcultural identity was perceived as different from the school's social values (Hargreaves et al., 1975). Studies in American kindergartens indicated that teachers quickly and decisively labelled and defined pupils as soon as they entered school. The crucial factor in determining positive and negative identities was social class. The labels imposed had enduring effects (Rist, 1970). Research in Chicago uncovered how teachers defined the 'ideal pupil' (most frequently, a pupil from a non-manual background) and saw 'lower-class' students as furthest from this ideal (Becker, 1952). Another American study found that factors of personal cultural, class style, such as posture, gait and speech patterns, led to pupils being defined negatively in terms of ability and academic potential (Cicourel and Kitsuse, 1971). The self-fulfilling prophecy was established as a significant factor determining academic success and failure (Rosenthal and Jacobson, 1968).

Perhaps the most insistent and remorseless form of labelling in schools is banding and streaming, the organization of pupils into populations according to supposed 'ability'. Both banding and streaming can have the rather drastic effect of producing quite different forms of education within the same institution. Anyone who has ever worked in a school knows how easily children are labelled as being 'less able' or of 'low ability' – often with much more derogatory language and invariably on questionable grounds of performance. There is a powerful and negative component of social construction at work in this process of discrimination. Streaming and banding usually have the decisive consequence of directing 'appropriate' knowledge towards 'appropriate' pupils, sealing educational fates (Keddie, 1973; Ball, 1981).

When Bernstein was commissioned to examine inequalities in education in the 1960s, his main focus was language. He explored the school as a social environment that operated through language as an indicator of 'culture' (Bernstein, 1971; 1973). The 'elaborated' and 'restricted' code distinction Bernstein deployed corresponded with middle-class and working-class speech patterns, but also indicated how these arose from different forms of life that were strongly conditioned by the social division of labour. In effect, language differences represent different 'symbolic orders' for various social groups (Bernstein, 1971; 1973). In schooling, judgements are made negatively or positively on the linguistic, symbolic legacies of sections of school populations: 'The different focusing of experience . . . creates a major problem of educability only where the school produces discontinuity between its symbolic orders and those of the child' (Bernstein, 1971: 122). Halliday amplified Bernstein's critique: 'The child who is not predisposed to this type of verbal exploration in this type of experiential and interpersonal context "is not at home in the educational world" as Bernstein puts it' (Halliday, 1979: 26).

In the United States during the 1960s and early 1970s, Labov's work offered a challenging theory questioning the 'juridical' issue of the cultural linguistic authority of the school. Labov sought to challenge the deficit theory of 'verbal deprivation': black children from the ghetto area are said to receive little verbal stimulation, to hear very little well-formed language, and as a result are impoverished in their means of verbal expression. It is said that they cannot speak complete sentences, do not know the names of common objects, cannot form concepts or convey logical thoughts (Labov, 1972: 4–5). Labov's radical departure in debates about language and education was to insist that 'the logic of non-standard English' was, in terms of expressive power, utterly comparable with the standard, dominant and educationally privileged forms (Labov, 1972). The effect of Labov's thesis was to deflate the myth of linguistic deprivation, while also insisting that the domination of standard English was both arbitrary and essential to inequalities of access.

In the United States, language has been at the cutting edge of educational controversy, especially in relation to the underachievement of large sectors of the population, particularly African Americans, who have consistently fared less well through state-funded schooling than any other sizeable ethnic group. Rather than see their children and pupils suffer cultural negation, some black communities and educators have chosen to use the language of black Americans, called 'ebonics', as a medium of instruction. They decided to celebrate their linguistic heritage and teach the distinguishing features of ebonics, drawing comparisons with the characteristics of so-called standard English. The need to make schools more friendly cultural and linguistic environments for African-American pupils has driven the ebonics movement to strive to change the success rates for African-American children in state schools (Delpit, 1995; Smitherman, 2000). Results of such programmes are uncertain. At the same time, in the United Kingdom, the depressing realization that children of some ethnic minorities who were entering school with high 'threshold' scores for literacy were leaving with low attainment in public examinations seemed to indicate that the school must have been penalizing such children. Some commentators even cried 'conspiracy' while continuing to argue for the reform of the very system that was perpetrating inequalities on the grounds of ethnic, cultural bias (Gillborn and Mirza, 2000; Gillborn, 2008a)

Social reproduction and correspondence theory

That class culture is a major factor in determining educational success and failure in contemporary Western contexts has been argued consistently since the 1970s. The Marxist-influenced concept of 'cultural capital' has been deployed to explain how the cultural dice are loaded in favour of the dominant culture and the culturally dominant (Bourdieu and Passeron, 1977). The failure of working-class children in education relates to the systematic bias of the system, rooted in culture. In schools, working-class culture is either not recognized or is denigrated as an inferior form of culture, a kind of anti-knowledge. Success in schooling is a matter of adopting a certain 'style' of being. The school reward system recognizes certain styles positively and others negatively. Cultural capital is visible in social habits, styles of speech and modes of conduct and being that belong to the general way of existence known as *habitus*, that is, the durable dispositions engendered by the class/cultural environment of your upbringing. Through the various gradations of the education system cultural capital translates into wealth and power. Academic success can be exchanged for economic success (Bourdieu and Passeron, 1977). In a later work, when Bourdieu addressed questions of culture in relation to the social division of labour, he found that cultural practices, habits and preferences were largely expressions of the choices strongly influenced by social stratification. Cultural practices followed patterns of economic division of labour. Similarly, linguistic differences can be seen as expressions of different class orientations. Language habits and attitudes are differentiated in line with social class, economic and ethnic differences (Bourdieu, 1991). Education is strongly attuned to this patterning.

When the infamous phrase 'hidden curriculum' was coined it expressed the scandalous idea that going to school is less about learning mathematics or literacy and more about learning how to behave, how to conform and how to accept your position in the order of things (Bowles and Gintis, 1976). Their book, *Schooling in Capitalist America*, was initially an account of the failure of wave after wave of school reform legislation to alter the deep-seated, class-based patterns of achievement in American state schools. Bowles and Gintis brought attention to the regulatory practices of the school: uniforms, time keeping, rowed seating in classrooms, rules for corridor movement, countless injunctions to maintain order and so on. They pointed out the training in boredom represented by the majority of school time spent passively being instructed or actively performing tasks with no obvious meaning or visible use. They highlighted the training in accepting relations of subordination. In all this, the school forms a sound preparation for working life.

Willis's (1979) refinement of the position expressed by Bowles and Gintis offers an entertaining though not always comfortable account of school failure as a deliberately chosen class-based option. Willis posits that certain groups of pupils with strong class or cultural affiliation weigh their realistic chances of school success and make a more or less conscious decision in adolescence to eschew the value system of the school. They prefer to dedicate their energies to the varied practices of 'having a laff' and 'mucking about'. Willis's study of Hammertown School, based on an ethnographic research case study, provides a graphic illustration of how a segment of the school population makes active decisions and constructs resistant practices in the face of Bowles and Gintis's grimly deterministic, controlling school. The social consequences of the two positions are the same – 'working class kids get working class jobs', as Willis's subtitle memorably puts it. But Willis's account is at least enlivened by a sense of working class 'lads' exerting agency and being anything but passive dupes of an all-controlling system. They make good use of their time in their own terms; nevertheless, the 'lads' fail at school and certainly fail to achieve the possibilities for social advancement that liberal educators claim is at the heart of the comprehensive ideal of state schooling (Willis, 1979).

Given all this, it is hard to represent education as a gift that is offered freely for those who would apply themselves, as the liberal rhetoric would have it. The above accounts conspire to conclude that for certain social groups, education makes you an offer you can't accept.

Supplementary supplements: Governmentality and performativity

The governmental perspective represents the school as a relatively recent invention that alters the nature of government from visible, sovereign power to a more pervasive form of capillary power that takes both the population and the individual 'self' as units of address and transformation. Within the governmental perspective, the school is actually the dominant mechanism for the production of a certain type of self-governing citizen. According to this view, the function of the school is to organize and work upon mass populations, to order and rank the performances and acquired competences of individuals within a normative grid. The very architecture of the school – with its division of spaces into communal hall, playground and classroom – clearly indicates its complex social technology. The communal hall acts as an arena for the public dissemination of values and ethos: school assemblies remain occasions for moral exhortation and promotion of the values of self-construction and self-improvement. The school playground is the more remotely supervised space where the culture of the child meets the (gently) corrective supervision of the institution – in the figure of the teacher or carer that watches over the conduct of the group (Stow, 1850; Foucault, 1977; Donald, 1992; Hunter, 1994; Peim, 2001). The classroom is the space where relations of proximity between pupil and teacher enable a more close, personalized supervision that encourages the self-regarding gaze of the pupil to function as a kind of ongoing corrective principle, hence assuring the production of the self-regulating citizen.

According to the sociological perspective, the curriculum – rather than furnishing a model of universally valued knowledge – provides the occasion for the social relations that prevail in the school. These two dimensions – curriculum and social relations – are constantly in a dynamic relation with one another, systematically interacting as, in Bernstein's descriptive system, 'classification and framing', generating modalities of practice and identity. Current practices in schooling distribute identities in intricate ways, charting the progress of individuals and defining their being within the normative, hierarchical grid of attainment – ensuring that identities are 'properly' distributed to meet the perceived needs of the social division of labour and to constantly validate the order of knowledge and the social practices that the school maintains.

Recent times have seen schools dominated by a shift towards the 'logic of performativity', in which the measurement of specified outcomes determines legitimacy, failure or success – even the right to exist. Performativity is a key feature in Lyotard's account of the postmodern condition: in the absence of an overarching system of values – or grand narrative – that might lend meaning to education and give significance to learning, efficiency becomes the key (1985). We can see how the logic of performativity now lends an unquestioned force to the idea of ever-increasing efficiency. In the present context in England, for example, performativity is represented as an indispensable condition of social efficiency. We can see this as a kind of nihilism. Along with the appearance of CAT scores – a contemporary version of the IQ test – it is evident that a disturbing new element of labelling has appeared. Individual pupils carry with them a CAT score that is supposed to represent their intrinsic academic ability or 'general transferable abilities'. It is common practice for these scores to accompany pupils into every class in the form of electronic registration data. This is surely the triumph of technological enframing. And, is it not a thoroughly disturbing development?

While knowledge is defined in terms of curriculum contents, intuition determines how that knowledge is to be deployed and delivered. The process and context of delivery in turn define how the acquisition of that knowledge is to be judged in relation to individual and institutional performance. Judgements are about institutions in terms of a logic of performativity concerned with driving them towards improvement and keeping them ever self-conscious about their current performance. CAT scores provide data about the 'nature' of the raw material schools work on. Schools can then indicate 'added value' by achieving attainment levels above the norms for the average CAT scores for any given 'year group' or age-stratified segment of the school population. Success and improvement can thus be achieved and demonstrated. Nothing in this process has any necessary connection with or relation to education. And yet, the system decrees that this essentially is what education is.

The enframing operates insistently through the significant dimensions of the school. It exerts a powerful kind of agency. This agency, for all its power and its ubiquitous reach, has the strange property of operating independently of the individuals who manage it and who administer its implementation. It is essentially an embedded agency. The power it exerts is likewise embedded in the educational order of things. It is possible to see interpret this agency and to describe its ontological status in terms of Weber's account of modernity and Bauman's troubling expansion of it (Weber, 1958; Bauman, 2000). The work of teaching has become the subject of the enframing in the demands of the national curriculum, the regime of inspection and the competition that holds sway between schools. The general logic of performativity is particularly strong in the secondary sector, where schools are judged in relation to performance in public examination results, but operates now throughout the school system. However, the contemporary control– and delimitation– of teaching extends beyond curriculum specifications and levels of attainment that accompany assessment.

The acquisition of professional teacher status is closely regulated and delimited. One of the main effects of changes that were made in 1992 in the United Kingdom was to give emphasis to classroom practice. The balance between time spent in the university and time spent in the classroom was changed in favour of time spent in the classroom. Subjects that had been given some importance in Initial Teacher Education (ITE), such as psychology, philosophy, sociology and history, were banished. 'Whole School Issues' supplemented curriculum knowledge in their stead. Trainee teachers were to spend much more time in schools acclimatizing themselves to 'real world' of practice. Their recontextualized subject knowledge – learning the contents of the national curriculum – and quick induction in the context of the university could then be realized in relation to existing schemes of work and lesson plans. More importantly, the governmental regime of the school was to be understood as necessary and inevitable.

In line with the shift in emphasis in teacher education, special attention has been given to planning schemes of work for the delivery of the national curriculum. These schemes of work are conceived of a series of lesson plans. Lesson planning, therefore, came to be central to the business of learning to teach and be a teacher in a contemporary school. The teacher in training now must produce lesson plans, which form an important element of professional proficiency. Innumerable guides exist that provide templates for an effective approach to lesson planning. Government agencies provide exemplar lessons. At the very heart of a 'good' lesson plan, according to the accepted specifications, is the determination of the 'learning outcomes' for the class in question. It is essential, according to this now powerfully ensconced rhetoric, that the learning be specified in advance. Time has to be – just as Foucault indicated in his account of 'discipline' – utilized to the maximum. The lesson has to be carefully staged according to the given logic of learning, and the plenary session (every lesson must have one) must reinforce consciousness of precisely what has been covered and learnt. Thus the curriculum can be delivered according to a carefully staged, step-by-step, stage-managed, developmental procedure. The different dispositions of various groups of pupils – known thoroughly in advance by the teacher, who has vital information such as CAT scores and previous histories of performance, conduct and disposition – will have been catered for. Pupils will thus understand themselves and will have taken on, in their learning, the identities ascribed to them by the process of schooling.

Our argument has been that the school is a key governmental instrument in modernity. This governmental function has intensified, if anything, as education has become the key vehicle for governmental management of identities and dispositions among the population at large. In this, the school follows a consistent sociocultural architecture: spaces, identities and social process combine to produce a complex activity system with its own specific technologies. School design works to differentiate symbolic spaces with the classic model of classroom, playground and hall being subject to variations that retain cellular context for more or less formal activities of learning, the open space for 'play' where the culture of the pupil is allowed to express itself under the gaze of the institution and the 'public' space for the expression and reinforcement of values and codes of conduct. All of these activities fall within what Bernstein's sociology referred to as 'framing' – a series of contexts, practices and relations that organize the identities of things within the institution. There is some variation in the modalities of these elements – as with the emergence in the 1960s and 1970s of 'progressive' state schools. But their impact, in the long run, is similar.

The patterned institutional structuring of the school, in spite of the enframing, gives rise to 'improper' identities and practices that the symbolic order of the school cannot formally acknowledge, except as cases of deviance. The power exerted by the institution can be both resisted and thwarted – as in the case of Willis's 'lads', but the price paid is rejection from the symbolic order or the ascription of negative identity. Schools are culturally dynamic spaces for the meeting of cultures and identities, but schools are imbued with formal and informal kinds of power. They act as the vehicles for the realization of social processes such as 'reproduction' that sociologists have suggested takes logical precedence over learning.

Contemporary schooling both borrows and intensifies the historical governmental role of the school, inherited from the period of the installation of state education systems. The process of population management that such systems introduced and gradually refined is now realized through high-tech registrations systems and extensive, subtle and long-developed techniques of the self. Schools themselves are being refashioned as multi-agency nodes that will more effectively ensure that social exclusion is not an option for the wayward or the deviant. The borders of social exclusion are now to be managed by agencies working in partnership to ensure maximum participation among those in danger of social exclusion.

We seriously propose the idea that in the operations of the school we can see a more general governmental function for education, as education has become a 'master' concept in our time, an ontotheological principle. If we take the critique of the school and schooling offered above seriously, what then becomes of the high value placed on education among 'we contemporaries'? Does this ontotheological inflation of education, as the supreme principle of being, become highly questionable?

What if the school is unredeemable? What happens to the whole apparatus of school improvement with its research statistics, analyses, projections and projects when that question gets taken seriously? What happens to the whole movement of alternative schooling, alternative education even, when the very sovereignty of education as a ruling concept for social life is seriously called into question? It is difficult, if not impossible, to envisage our world without the school. It is an unlikely prospect, given the absolutely central governmental role the school now occupies, given the weight of political rhetoric thrust upon it and given the extent it has taken root as an essential feature of our social landscape.

What is being proposed here is not a formula for the redemption of that institution from its fallen past to a reborn future. That, it seems to us, is the dream of the school improvement ethic and its adherents. It is a dream in the phantasmic sense, although it often presents itself as a hard-headed, statistically verified, scientifico-bureaucratic possibility on the horizon of the present. What is being proposed here is an understanding of what schooling and education are in their contemporary manifestation. This implies a further understanding of what they might be. Our proposal here is that any serious thinking of the future must include the possibility that the school, schooling and education be displaced from their present sovereignty.

Initial Teacher Education: Practice, Performativity and Identity

---

Chapter Outline

Performativity and the enframing

This chapter addresses the performativity of that familiar identity we have come to know as the practicing teacher. In borrowing from J. L. Austin's (1975) account *How to Do Things with Words,* the distinction is made between 'performative' statements signifying the promise of events enacted in practice, and 'constative' statements of facts. In thinking about practice, the feminist writer Butler (2004) has developed an understanding of 'performativity' as part of a wider project of what it means to be human and to be recognized by others as human.

Butler's argument suggests that the regulatory practices and norms of Initial Teacher Education (ITE) produce bodies, selves and identities of practicing teachers by demarking, differentiating and circulating entities as appropriate in the field of ITE, these being regarded as real and significant (1993: 1). In Butler's argument, the performativity of the practicing teacher can be conceived as a 'reiteration of a norm or set of norms' that in acquiring 'an act-like status in the present . . . conceals or dissimulates the conventions of which it is a repetition' (1993: 12). What is concealed by repetitions of norms in discourses of ITE and Initial Teacher Training (ITT) is the subject of this chapter.

In England, as one extreme case, Butler's thesis does not provide an entirely plausible rationale for the hard-wiring of disciplinary space for ITE and ITT, except at points where training becomes an issue. Rather than being governed and administered by universities, each with their own awarding powers, from 1992 onwards the governance of ITE has become a state matter, incorporating a large disciplinary apparatus for training, setting standards and monitoring how well the system is functioning against established benchmarks of performance. Valerie Brooks, director of taught postgraduate courses at Warwick, reflecting on ITE in the previous decade, spoke of a 'quiet revolution' regarding the 'impact of training schools on initial teacher training partnerships' (Brooks, 2006: 379), following the implementation of the Department for Education (DfE, 1992) 'Circular 9/92'. This had invested secondary schools and HEIs with joint responsibility for the planning and management of ITT courses and the selection of candidates. The government circular had required a significant proportion of ITT to be completed in schools – 24 weeks per annum for PGCE students and 32 weeks for BEd students, compared to the earlier 15 weeks in schools required by Circular 24/89. It also established a framework of 27 competencies for ITT, which had placed emphasis on the development of subject knowledge in the light of the earlier implementation of the national curriculum in 1988. When coupled with the Office for Standards in Education (OfSTED) inspection service, which had been set up as part of the

Education Act in 1992, the full scale of the changes in ITT became apparent. Drawing from Foucault (1977), in the then newly emerging state apparatus of ITT, the subject and object of the system – the body of ITT students – became conscious of its own visibility on the basis of continual surveillance in what can be seen as a disciplinary system. For the first time in ITE this body was the subject of on-going observation and monitoring of its performativity and the requirement to raise its performance on grounds of the 'principle of assessment' against nationally authenticated benchmarks for competence (Peim and Flint, 2009). The unfolding history of governmentality in this system, narrated in this chapter, also provides one more example of the dispersion of state power, in this case in a whole system of ITE.

In the English system of ITE, the installation of this disciplinary apparatus has tended to move debate away from issues of teacher expertise and teacher education found among many teacher educators in the United States. Similarly, questions concerning the divorce of theory and practice taken up in Australia have moved towards the privileging of development of practice in England. While adding to our understandings of ITE in the developed world, the foregoing histories and debates do not provide a satisfactory explanation for the coordination of disciplinary space currently found in the English system of ITE (Pierides, 2006: 1; Zeichner, 2008: 17; O'Donoghue and Whitehead, 2008).

Butler's implicit challenge, asks us to consider matters that are ordinarily inexplicit, not least the newly emerging performativity arising from the continued surveillance of the body in ITE – the individual teacher and the population of those being trained – which enacts what is spoken in the present. In Derrida's (1988) re-reading of Austin's performativity, even 'facts' are found to be performative and the performative is understood to be always open to the possibility of its own failure. For Derrida such performativity is necessarily inhabited by the existential possibility of its own death. This way of thinking at least provides an explanation for the growing reach of the instruments of performativity in our state institutions such as ITE that are ineluctably called upon to avoid the possibility of failure. One particular form of instrument that serves to reduce any ambiguity about what is required of trainees and of teacher educators in this system is that of assessment based on tightly defined criteria that provide the basis for measurable outcomes for the body of new trainee teachers. This instrumental drive to reduce ambiguity about the standards of ITE and, in so doing, raise standards on grounds of measurable outcomes, itself colonizes stakeholders around this issue. But the question of what actually structures this ever-growing colonization around instrumental reason in ITE is only mentioned in passing by Derrida. This chapter seeks to address this issue by returning once more to the matter of the enframing.

In doing so we open consideration of the 'standing reserve': this can be seen as the surplus energy and resources possessed by the body of ITE students. The energy and resources of this body are there to be optimally and efficiently directed or ordered in the enframing. Such ordering of the standing reserve in ITE is subject to a directional constraining force – inscribed in the system of assessment and surveillance. This ordering of the standing reserve then mediates teacher identity; those stories that teachers tell about their own experiences in education. It is our position that in the most general sense the possibilities in being a teacher arise from the play of difference in our essential home – language. In this chapter, we examine these possibilities both as a locus of resistance in a range of professional discourses and a place where popular culture assimilates the identity of the teacher as hero through the medium of film.

Disciplines to practice in ITE: Performativity and the enframing

In England, the moves in ITE to the performativity of practice with the concomitant excision of the traditional disciplines supporting ITE is by no means regarded as a universal enduring good. The recent response of the Association of Teachers and Lecturers to the inspection of ITE by OfSTED in England and Wales for the period 2008–2011 expressed concerns that 'instead of being taught practical skills', suggested as grounds for a variety of knowledges and understandings, 'increasingly teachers are being trained instead to implement the decisions of others', defined by the standards agenda. This organization, though it attributes value to 'trainee teachers', who have the capacity 'to recognize standards and levels', also identifies with the importance of 'developing teachers to engage with academic disciplines, including philosophy, psychology, sociology, and the politics of education' (ATL, 2008: 1).

With the implementation of the national curriculum in the late 1980s in England – structured around those aforementioned foundational subjects – the break-up of the former ITE organization was decisive, and rapid. Within discourses of the philosophy of education, issues remain regarding the demise of the disciplinary languages of philosophy, sociology and history which historically were used to lay the foundations for initial teacher education. In the emerging focus in the language on 'training' to develop practice, most departments of education within higher education institutions (HEIs) still retain distinct elements of the former disciplines depending on local interests. Moreover, in practice, as Ball and Bowe also suggest, 'practitioners do not confront texts' naively – they have their own histories and values, they also work within their own particular institutional constraints (1992:22). 'They have vested interests in the meaning of policy' and so policy makers 'cannot control meaning' (Ball and Bowe, 1992: 22). It seems important to ask, what are the benefits and the costs of this focus upon the performativity of practice in ITE?

In terms of an evolving 'professionalizing agenda' (Furlong, 2002: 24) over the past two decades, the immersion of 'trainee' teachers in the classroom, working alongside experienced teacher-mentors and university tutors, has sometimes presented difficulties, but has undoubtedly provided the foundation for trainees to develop a range of knowledge and skills. 'Knowledge-in-practice' (Cochran-Smith and Lytle, 2001: 45), that is, the knowledge developed by trainees that is embedded in their practice, is arguably indispensable, the *sine qua non* of their professionalism and their work. In the same vein, thanks to the guidance of their mentors and university tutors, trainees are assisted in the development of their 'knowledge-of-practice' (Cochran-Smith and Lytle, 2001: 45). For example, it has been argued that embedding-in-practice provides pre-service teachers with grounds to develop their understandings and knowledge of teaching as an essentially moral activity (Hargreaves, 1995; Villegas-Reimers, 2003: 45).

It is always easy to accept positive evaluations of what is done in practice. What could be better from an educationalist's perspective than helping students further their understandings and knowledge of practice? But what is the measure of the knowledge and understandings they variously gain from experience?

The value ascribed by many in ITE to the immersion of pre-service teachers in practice also has significant but variable implications for their learning and development as part of the wider community of a school, as suggested by Lave and Wenger's (1991) model of participation in a community of practice, a learning that 'develops around things that matter to people' (Wenger, 1998: 2). In diverse ways, trainees expand the horizons of their changing identities as members of their school communities (Wenger, 1998: 4). In England, the 'Every Child Matters' (DfES, 2003a) agenda provides another driver for widening horizons. However, the foregoing essentially reflective models (Schön, 1983; 1990) of pre-service teacher development, themselves the subject of critical evaluation (Tennant, 1997; Moon, 1999), are always in danger of falling short: where is the space for more reflexively structured thinking?

In the UK, the latter may be seen as characteristic of what many regard as high level undergraduate work and is likely to be given further impetus with the development of M-level provision in ITE programmes. For example, reflexively structured learning and development of knowledge can help pre-service teachers to understand more fully, and to place in context, their understandings of the limits of their work with school-based mentors and their own learning and teaching (Muijs and Reynolds, 2005). It may also be useful for examining some of the limitations of discourses exploring the notion of 'communities of practice' (Hughes et al., 2007).

But even the latter collection of essays by leaders in that field makes no mention of the considerable extension of governmental instruments and the microphysics of power that the state now controls. It is our contention that the machinery of the state in education has been greatly extended following the inception of ITT (DfEE, 1998a).

What for some (Durkheim, 1956; Daine and Foster, 1977) might be in danger of being lost in the pre-eminence given to the multi-disciplinary forms of 'mode 2' knowledge (Gibbons et al., 1994), – that is problem focused and intradisciplinary forms of knowledge grounding practice is firstly and most significantly students' induction into, and development of, new languages (in contrast, Mode 1 knowledge for Gibbons et al., (1994) is discipline-based academic knowledge that privileges the discourses of investigators). New 'languages' then, also include the traditional disciplines of psychology, sociology, philosophy, history and – not least – linguistics. One could argue that engagement in any of these discourses has the potential to provide pre-service teachers with appropriate grammatical and conceptual structures that ground different ways of thinking and open them to lively debates that problematize many aspects of the education project. In the words of Boix-Mansilla and Gardner, academic disciplines 'constitute the most sophisticated ways yet developed for thinking about and investigating issues that have long fascinated and perplexed thoughtful individuals' (1994: 15). In the privileging of practice in ITE, some argue that pre-service teachers are in danger of being cut off from fully engaging with traditional groundings and challenges that these disciplines can bring to discourses of education.

The 'shepherd–flock' metaphor has its roots in the power of pastoral discipline, where the 'relationship between God and his people is conceived as the relation between shepherd and flock' (Dean, 2010: 90). It is this relationship that is played out in many subtle ways in the academic disciplines, the latter certainly constituting no panacea as grounds for ITE. As Foucault suggested in his genealogical study of 'the birth of a prison', there are also 'polymorphous and polyvalent' (Foucault, 1994b: 82–3) political forces at work in the disciplines that tend to have the effect of creating 'docile bodies' (Foucault, 1977: 135–69). Moreover, it is clear that the political relationship of these disciplines with education continues to change. As Biggs concluded from his *Vernon-Wall Lecture*, which surveyed the 'changing role of psychology in educational practice', there has been 'an interesting change from' a 'hierarchical to co-existent' relationship over the past forty years (2002: 18). In *Re-Thinking Science*, Nowotny et al. also 'highlight' concomitant shifts over a similar period from 'certainty to uncertainty and from 'linearity to complexity' in practice-based knowledge, giving rise in place of planning to 'a pervasive sense of volatility and ambiguity' (2001: 47).

One obvious response to this emergent complexity, having not escaped the practice of ITE, has been the insinuation by 'powerful interest groups' of 'a particular model of teaching into the national consciousness in some countries including Britain, Australia and New Zealand' (Snook, 1999: 5). We argue that Snook's 'model' is, in fact, an outward manifestation of the enframing that emerges in the world of education. The case study that follows seeks to reveal aspects of the modus operandi of one apparent 'sovereign power' (Foucault, 1980a: 103; Dean, 2010: 34–6), the British Government, and the capilliarity of governmental powers unfolding in the changes made in ITE in England over the past two decades.

The English system of ITE: Standing reserve in the enframing

Rather than concentrating on the agency of the government in this matter, our argument draws attention to the enframing unfolding in discursive practices of ITE and ITT that preoccupy governmental apparatus. It will also consider ways in which the teacher can be rendered, as Snook (1999: 5) suggested, 'as a functionary' given to the accomplishment of 'relatively narrow technical tasks' in accordance with what can be measured on the basis of the 'principle of assessment' (Peim and Flint, 2009). It is no accident that in England ITE is now officially identified as 'training' (DfEE, 1998a). In fact, involvement in training does not by itself provide an exclusive indication of the presence of standing reserve. Foucault's (1977: 135–94) 'docile bodies', both teachers and government agencies, are themselves always in danger of becoming available for use in the enframing in education (Peim and Flint, 2009). Pivotal to enframing is Nietzsche's doctrine of 'eternal recurrence' of the 'will-to-power', manifest in the perhaps more familiar positing of values in ITE – is seen by many as grounds for developing the current system (Nietzsche, 1989: 5).

In the seemingly interminable issue of change in education the enframing has until now generally been recognized only within specialist discourses of philosophy and the philosophy of education in accord with only one true way of revealing the world on the basis of the principle of reason. Nevertheless, as Hargreaves noted in his opening reflections on devices and desires in 'The Process of Change':

> People are always wanting teachers to change. Rarely has this been more true than in recent years. These times of global competitiveness, like all moments of economic crisis, are producing immense moral panics about

> how we are preparing the generations of the future in our respective
> nations . . . Few people want to do much about the economy, but every-
> one – politicians, the media and the public alike – wants to do something
> about education. (1994: 5)

In considering changes in teacher education outside specialist discourses of the philosophy of education, and even within many of them,
the enframing is simply not recognized as a driving force. This re-reading of Heidegger's (1977b) ontology of the enframing attemps to address
this issue within this deconstruction of ITE (Peim and Flint, 2009).

Since the introduction of a national curriculum in England, primary and secondary level education has been explicitly aligned with
the structures of the state as a means of the sovereign power 'seizing
control' of ITE (Furlong, 2002: 24). The discourses presented in a series
of circulars (DES, 1984, 1989; DfE, 1992, 1993; DfEE, 1997) finally provided a formal statement for a national curriculum for ITT and gave
it the official seal of the incoming New Labour administration (DfEE,
1998a).

The enframing (Peim and Flint, 2009) in this case is extolled in what
can be seen as dry, juridical and veridical forms of language. This law-
like language establishes normative truths for a population within the
ITT economy identified as 'teachers'. This does not mean that teachers have no freedom; to the contrary, they are granted freedom to work
within a tightly specified national framework structured by criteria and
principles of procedure. For example, Circular 9/92 (DfE, 1992) regarding 'ITT (Secondary Phase)' opens with the following words:

> This circular introduces new criteria and procedures in England and Wales
> for the accreditation of courses of initial teacher training (ITT).

The language presupposes not only a level of formality and compliance
among a designated population involved with the implementation of
ITT, it is also tacitly predicated on the assumption that the agencies
involved will have the energy to put into place the bureaucratic measures
instituted by the government. It does so because the enframing (Peim
and Flint, 2009) in ITE has already rendered these agencies as no more
than a standing reserve (*Bestand*) of energy that is optimally available
for use in essentially technological structures of state.

For example, in regard to ITT in England, soon after the New Labour government came to office in 1997, the behaviours of the subject or object of this political economy – the pre-service teacher – were precisely delimited by the juridical powers inscribed by the 'standards for the award of qualified teacher status' (DfEE, 1998a: 7–133). In being rendered (*zustellen*) as standing reserve, in the enframing (*das Gestell*), teachers are assumed to have sufficient energy for the demands placed upon them. Here we have included the German terms in parenthesis, in order to make obvious the semantic connections with the verb *stellen* (connoting 'to place something') that are possible in the German language. Of course, in the many possible identities assumed by the teacher, Dasein has many more possibilities and more energy available than is required for the object (or subject) of the ITT economy. These possibilities and the reserves of energy that this particular population of Dasein have constitute the standing reserve (*Bestand*) in the enframing found in formal education discourse (Peim and Flint, 2009).

Furlong's lament concerning the curtailment of 'agency' in England almost misses the point completely (2002: 24; Furlong et al., 2000). Although there has been the opportunity for more professional debate in the context of ITE in the United States (Zeichner, 2003; 2008) than in England (Furlong, 2002: 24), the dominant 'habitus' or disposition of governmental agencies and professional researchers on both sides of the Atlantic currently appears to be locked into simply not recognizing the enframing. This is not just a measure of the characteristic rendering (*zustellen*) constituted in the enframing; it is also a product of the enframing in discursive practices that separate each of them into particular specialisms, each with their own 'regimes of truth' that constitute a particular 'picture of the world' (Heidegger, 1977a: 129). As Heidegger suggested, 'specialization is not the consequence, but the foundation of the progress of all research' and the development of knowledge concerning ITE (1977a: 123).

It would appear that the enframing unfolding in the institution of ITT has not been left to chance, arising instead from a multiplicity of possible readings of government documents. In practical terms, technological enframing is not something produced by humankind; it is, as Heidegger (1977b: 4) once remarked, 'nothing technological', but simply one way of revealing the world in accord with the principle of assessment that now governs ITE. In the English system, the world of ITE is now structured by the disciplinary apparatus of the panopticon, directed towards ensuring the performative enactment of policy across all HEIs and schools. However, it is significant and as yet largely unrecognized, that in this disciplinary system, the enframing (*das Gestell*) is not something imposed upon ITE from central government. Government agencies themselves are also unwittingly immersed in the enframing that is almost completely disguised (*verstellen*) behind the current agenda for 'raising standards'. In their evaluations of 'performance' and in their comparisons with each other on a global stage, governmental agencies are often caught up in the nihilism of the very same enframing. They too are always in danger of being constituted as standing reserve (Heidegger, 1977b: 17).

The English system of ITE: The regime of truth as further grounds for the enframing

The very functioning of the system of ITE in England was made to be dependent upon 'a system of ordered procedures for the production, regulation, distribution, circulation and operation of statements' (Foucault, 1994c: 152) concerning training and education. Here, then, are the institutional grounds for the reproduction of a 'regime of truth'. In this reading of Foucault (1994c: 152), 'truth is linked in a circular relation' not only with the obvious surface technology mediating governmental powers (Foucault, 1994a: 201–22; Dean, 2010). Essentially, it is also grounded in the principle of assessment as the officially legitimatized way of benchmarking authentic forms of knowledge in the world of ITE in accordance with the enframing (Peim and Flint, 2009).

The governmental administration of ITE first began its development in the Thatcher Administration in 1984. Government Circular 9/92 (DfE, 1992) made clear that the 'criteria and procedures' that it had identified were to be governed by 'the Council for the Accreditation of Teacher Education, CATE' which 'was established in 1984 and reconstituted in 1990 with greater terms of reference'.

In the language used in Circular 9/92 there is an implicit challenge, it sets in order (*bestellen*) what is required by each HEI in the training of teachers. In Heidegger's earlier deconstruction of our essential relationship with technology as a 'challenging forth' (*herausfordung*) can still be heard the driving force for the standing reserve within the economy of ITE (Heidegger, 1977b: 15). Circular 9/92 imputed a duty and functionality for HEIs and schools, which were immediately challenged with managing ITE in accordance with their accountability to the government of the day. This accountability was enforced through the agency of government. This accountability and its modalities of surveillance was reflected in the former title of the government agency which oversaw ITT, namely, the Department for Children, Schools and Families (DCSF). Its former identity as governmental apparatus had been instituted to ensure it worked in accordance with principles inscribed in practice.

In the English system, perhaps, some measure of the management of the space ITT has freedom to operate in is reflected in the range of agencies now controlling this process. In one sense the freedom for agencies within the education service to operate autonomously in accordance with the overarching governmental system reflects what we might see as a contemporary variation on the ancient 'city–citizen game'. As Dean suggests, this imputes 'the careful cultivation of a set of attributes and a form of moral personality' on the part of the ruling class (2010: 96). With the infusion of the powers of governmentality into every classroom in the land, morality is now inscribed in the language of ITE and the professionality of the various agencies involved (Hargreaves, 1995).

As we recognized earlier, all performatives in practice are always open to failure. In the new bureaucratic technology governing ITE in England, almost nothing is left to chance: there are a number of agencies involved that constitute the abstract contemporary panoptic architecture in ITT (Foucault, 1977).

In addition to CATE, as the dominant mode of prescribing ITT in England, the enframing is inscribed in a number of agencies that work closely with the government Department for Education (DfE, 2011). These include the Teacher Development Agency (TDA, formerly the Teacher Training Agency, 2010a), the Qualifications and Curriculum

Development Agency (QCDA, 2010) and the Office for Standards in Education (OfSTED, 2010a). The latter governs an inspection regime for all schools and HEIs involved in ITE.

The English system of ITE: The principle of assessment grounding the enframing

Each of these agencies would not be able to function in concert as the institution for this mythological object or subject of the ITE economy, the teacher, without the arbitrary and tacit imposition of the 'principle of assessment': nothing of educational value (measured in accordance with laws inscribed by current professional protocols) is without assessment. 'It is our contention' that the currency of assessment 'is not something that accompanies' initial teacher education or training 'as an additional – sometimes lamented, but somehow necessary – supplement' (Peim and Flint, 2009: 343). Its value as a currency lies in now assuming the status of a foundational principle for all formal systems of ITE that 'organizes the thinking, the material practices and the structures of contemporary' education in much of the Western world (Heidegger, 1996; Peim and Flint, 2009: 343).

In the principle of assessment lies the basis for regimes of truth continually unfolding as circular economies of signs – juridical and veridical structures that determine what has to be done in the name of ITT.

The website of the Training and Development Agency, TDA (2010a) clearly indicates the issue of the principle of assessment. What can be found beneath the glossy headline rhetoric of 'developing people: improving young lives'? Most obviously, the website includes very well-organized and clear definitions of standards for different levels ascribed to teachers – 'qualified teacher status', 'core teacher', 'post-threshold teacher', 'excellent teacher', 'advanced skills teacher'. Each of these levels represent (*vorstellen*) the 'teacher's performance' in practice, measured on the basis of assessment against three complementary dimensions of 'professional standards'. Standards are further differentiated in terms of 'attributes', 'knowledge and understanding' and 'skills' for this object or subject of the economy of education in England.

The English system of ITE: Ontical concerns eliding the enframing

We use the terms *object* or *subject* advisedly. Our deconstruction of these terms found in ITE is based on indications drawn from the philosophical term – Dasein – referring to human beings as individuals or collectives as a body. 'To say that Dasein exists' in ITE 'is to say that Dasein *is* in such a way that it understands being – its own being but also the being of things other than itself' (Heidegger, 1962; Gorner, 2007:4). Despite the fact that teachers variously take up the challenge of educating with an understanding of what it is to be a teacher and some understanding of 'being', all of which is integral to Dasein, it is significant that the 'meaning of being' (Heidegger, 1962: 370–1{324}) and its relationship with the temporality of being is noticeable for its absence on the both TDA and Department for Education websites (Publications.education, 2010). The reason for this elision is simple. For the most part, the concerns of the structures of state, set up in the name of ITE, are 'ontical' in their focus, that is, the whole structuration of structure is primarily concerned with the ever more detailed characterization of objects of ITE in the enframing. It has already inscribed much of the officially authenticated language with structures that make it almost impossible to do otherwise; the very professionalism of teachers depends upon the outcome of performativity (in the sense used by Butler, 1993, 2004). For example, officially sanctioned observations of teaching and learning of pre-service teachers in classrooms is almost invariably structured by a set of criteria or benchmarks against which practice is observed.

It is relatively straightforward to make observations of interactions that are themselves structured on grounds of our own temporality. For example, a simple question posed by one ITE student: 'What are you doing today?' contains within in it a tacit understanding of our relationship with the future that can never be known, in having been up to this point a trainee teacher. Such observations begin to open questions concerning what it means to be a student, a lecturer, a teacher, a teaching assistant and an agent, at the workplace. A recent study of interactions illustrates that, although the temporal unfolding of the future and past events in the classroom are essential to Dasein, as possibilities of being they tend to be completely elided by modern methods of observation and assessment of classroom behaviours (Flint, 2011a).

The force of inscription in the language of ITE is enhanced by the inspection regime within the state apparatus, which is again currently structured entirely by its ontical focus on particular objects in the workplace. Moreover, the focus is not confined to OfSTED inspections. Sultana (2005), an experienced researcher, has produced an incisive review of the 'issues and trends' in 'Initial Education of High School Teachers', concentrating the force of its critical faculties upon the characterization and delineation of concerns, rather than considering the meaning of being a teacher involved in 'education'. The leading reviews of teacher education around the globe (e.g. O'Donoghue and Whitehead, 2008) follow a similar course. The focus of the argument is almost exclusively ontic, and concerned with what *is*, rather than the being of what is. It would seem that the reality of being human reflected as it is, in a multiplicity of often unspoken concerns about the question of being, is certainly not foregrounded in the OfSTED organization or in much research concerning ITE. It points to the scandalous possibility that these agencies have been already rendered as standing reserve.

What we have yet to consider in the reproduction of a regime of truth structuring the formal system of education in England on grounds of the 'principle of assessment' is the inspection service, in the form of OfSTED. It is in the OfSTED inspection that the regime of surveillance characteristic of modern disciplined practices reaches its acme in a 'highly ritualised' (Foucault, 1977: 184) form of public examination for an institution. The benchmarks it uses for its examination of institutions and individual performance tend to privilege particular forms of observation and assessment in accord with the very same benchmarks. The public examination by OfSTED of an institution for ITT is one of its 'key mechanisms of discipline':

> The examination combines the techniques of an observing hierarchy and those of a normalising judgement. It is a normalising gaze, a surveillance that makes it possible to qualify, to classify and to punish. It establishes over individuals a visibility to differentiate them and to judge them. (Foucault, 1977: 184)

In fact, in standing over training institutions, OfSTED not only provides a framework for the inspection of ITT provision in England, it has the power to assign grades regarding an institution's performance and to close down underperforming institutions. Here, then, are the grounds for the performativity of pre-service teachers in classroom practice.

What is also clear from the foregoing deconstruction of the enframing in ITT in England is that in concert with the central policy-making machinery of government – the DfE, its aligned national TDA and the OfSTED inspection service – the system only makes sense as a regime of truth if it has a common grounding. A common grounding has already been uncovered as the 'principle of assessment' (Peim and Flint, 2009). As a national system of ITT focused upon improvements in practice of teaching on grounds of public standards, the principle of assessment has effectively foreclosed other modalities of professional induction.

It has become apparent, then, that the ever-present danger of the technological enframing, seen in ITE in England, is not simply a national phenomenon. Although there are many complexities at the local level, the current global reach of the principle of assessment seems to be almost unlimited. What is equally apparent is that governmental agencies are always in danger of being caught up in the enframing. Given the competitive global milieu in which governments are now situated, it is perhaps no surprise that the particular regime for ITT in England has emerged in response to the will-to-power, reflecting the value-positing of government (Heidegger, 1977c; Dean, 2010).

The global reach of the enframing: The saving power in the standing reserve

The will-to-power of the governmental apparatus in engineering a system of ITT is intimately intertwined with the globalization of the enframing. For Heidegger this intertwining marks a significant point of danger where humankind is 'taken as standing reserve' and becomes 'the orderer of the standing reserve' (1977b: 27). The application of Heidegger's thesis to the world of ITE, sees the enframing as a means – ends way of revealing this world of education in accord with the 'principle of assessment'. It is then pertinent to look at what Heidegger draws from the poet Hölderlin as the 'saving power' of the enframing. For Heidegger 'the verb, to save, says more' than simply to seize hold of and to keep from ruin. He sees this saving power as the possibility of opening questions concerning our essential relationship with the enframing (1977b: 28). It means opening questions, in this case in ITE, about the way in which the enframing has the character of revealing the world of ITE in accordance with the principle of assessment and blocking all other ways of revealing the world (Heidegger, 1977b: 1–35; 1991; Peim and Flint, 2009).

In developing such understanding we might also enquire how the unfolding of the standing reserve over time works in practice in ITE. Most obviously, there is a requirement for institutions involved in educating and training pre-service teachers to make explicit the standards for Qualified Teacher Status that are delineated by the TDA (2010b). Helping students gain purportedly meaningful understandings of these standards forms a distinct element in the induction of pre-service teachers before they even enter their practices. In planning work with their children in primary schools or young people in secondary schools, student teachers learn to structure their episodes of teaching using 'objectives' as a way of structuring young people's learning.

In the classroom, the stepwise hierarchy of standards inscribed on the TDA website provides benchmarks for planning lesson objectives and observing lessons by teacher-mentors and tutors from university institutions. These constitute the constraining forces for the reservoir of energy contained within the body of trainees. As apparently good subjects in the disciplinary 'panopticon' of education practice, all of the actors are continuously aware of the OfSTED-like public examinations of their work.

Trainees and their tutors and mentors, however, are not mechanistic objects in an engineered system; Dasein interacts and learns from the other (Heidegger, 1962; Dreyfus and Wrathall, 2007b). There is among everyone involved an at least tacit awareness that what is given in official assessments falls short of what is learned from engagement in practice. In two recent studies of practice in a university classroom and in a secondary English classroom (Flint, 2010a, b, c; 2011b) of the play of temporality and of the ways in which moods had revealed particular understandings, both the lecturer and the teacher expressed their surprise at what was uncovered. Here was an indication of the sometimes hidden possibilities within a reservoir of energy, the standing reserve, constituted in this case by the body of people involved in education.

The notion of teacher identity that unfolds in this chapter is not an essentialist one but rather, as we have already witnessed, it is continuously repositioned in the play of difference, open to dislocation and deconstruction. Teacher identity, in its relationship with the forces of education, is never unified, perfected and totalized, but rather traces of it can be seen continually unfolding in the ongoing struggle between the multiplicities of, in some cases, antagonistic discourses, practices and positions where only its cinders remain.

But, we have yet to examine further our claim that the whole system is grounded in the assessment of what is happening in the classroom, assuming the position of an organizing principle for the modern system of ITT in England that, until now, has tended to be taken as a given.

What is given in assessment?: The enframing in the CPD of teachers

In addressing the question of what is given in assessment, there is, however, a significant issue within the metaphysical circular economy of giving and receiving that may not ordinarily be perceived by teachers to be the somewhat unilateral 'gift' of assessment, requiring 'the security of an apparent origin and the purity of memory' (Flint, 2011b: 14). In one decisive move, Derrida (1995b), in his re-reading of the traditions of philosophy, challenges and also breaks irretrievably the security of the metaphoric circular economy of the giving and receiving of a gift with the catastrophe of memory:

> I would say that what I suffer from inconsolably always has the form, not only of loss, which is often! – but of the loss of memory: that what I am living cannot be kept, thus repeated, and – how to put it? – decipherable, as if an appeal for a witness had no witness, in some way, not even the witness that I could be for what I have lived. This is for me the very experience of death, of catastrophe. (Derrida, 1995b: 207)

What Derrida has called the 'catastrophe' of memory renders the identity of what is thought to be known as impossible; in the English system of ITT, this provides some explanation of why there is so much institutional apparatus that focuses attention on the assessment of particular objectives for learning.

In his book, *Given Time*, Derrida (1991) posits that 'the pure gift can never be presented' (Dooley and Kavanagh, 2007: 9). The giving of a gift always imputes a requirement for the recipient to respond in some way, including the possibility of not responding. The gift always draws people into an 'economy of exchange'. But, the possibility of giving a pure unconditional gift – here the time, space and language in which assessment is embedded – is the very impossibility of a pure unconditional gift:

> If the gift is annulled in the economic odyssey of the circle as soon as it appears as a gift or as soon as it signifies itself as a gift, there is no longer any logic of the gift and one may safely say that a consistent discourse on the gift becomes impossible: it misses its object and always speaks, finally of something else. (Derrida, 1991: 24; Dooley and Kavanagh, 2007: 9)

The circular economy is hence broken with the gift leaving only its 'trace' behind. In so doing, what is given in time and space and in the language of the 'principle of assessment' is at last brought into question.

Paradoxically, in ITE it is the trace of the gift that creates an ineluctable driving force for ever more sophisticated measures of performance in ITE that, in effect, attempt to make good what has been lost, but in generating further technologies only create their own *lacunæ*.

Raising the question of the principle of assessment in this way also points to why so much energy is being invested in continuing with the mythological circular economic journey of what is given in the principle of assessment, which has until now seemed beyond question in the field of education. Here is the tacit rationale for teachers being trained to structure their teaching with objectives for learning. In the ordering of the standing reserve, based as it is on the principle of assessment within the English system of teacher education, seemingly nothing is left to chance in maintaining this circular economy. The regimes of truth, continuing to hold on to such mythology when faced with the ever-present forces of reiteration, have instituted a hierarchically structured programme of 'continued professional development' from Qualified Teacher Status (QTS) through to 'advanced skills teacher' (TDA, 2010a).

For the TDA, continuous professional development (CPD), arising from 'many sources', 'consists of reflective activity designed to improve an individual's attributes, knowledge, understanding and skills'. But clearly, in the 'enframing' in CPD, the 'individual' is always in danger of being reduced to a series of characteristics that can be 'improved', just as an engine might be upgraded before a race. While CPD opens exciting new possibilities for many, as standing reserve the body of 'teachers' is always directed towards specific and relatively circumscribed professional roles and trajectories.

Much of the CPD in support of teachers in England is no longer a series of events reflecting local interests and policies; it has become a strategic initiative reflecting the will of the sovereign state. The new version of the shepherd–flock language game, reflecting the will-to-power of governmental agencies, identified three categories as national priorities for CPD between 2007–2010 in terms of 'pedagogy', 'personalisation' and 'people'. In a remarkable essay, 'The Word of Nietzsche', Heidegger reminds his readers that 'the will' of governmental agencies has a sense of an 'empowering to power' and that 'truth', in this system of ITT, 'is the condition of the preservation' of 'power' (1977c: 79, 84).

Interestingly, in concert with established forms of 'governmentality', the latter two governmental 'priorities' – concerning 'personalisation' and 'people' – open further scope in some subcultures for the 'citizen–city game' (Dean, 2010: 93–6). Played out within this particular language game, inherited from the Greek model of the *polis*, is a 'careful cultivation of a set of attributes and a form of moral personality on the part of the ruling classes' (Dean, 2010: 96). As might be expected, the shepherd–flock game already played by the governmental agency has also colonized a series of networked professional agencies supporting particular stakeholder groups within the curriculum (TDA, 2010a).

The enframing and CPD

Although policy rhetoric on the government website regarding 'lifelong learning' is somewhat dated, in the enframing in 'training and development' for teachers there still remains a law-like structure extolled in the language of 'standards' expected at each stage of a teacher's career. This imputes for teachers an obligation to engage in the circumscribed forms of CPD throughout their careers. It also ascribes and benchmarks 'teacher development' according to 'standards' negotiated within each school but based on national standards for teaching (www.tda.gov, 2010e). It is interesting to note that for some practicing teachers, their performance management targets become the drivers for their work, while others doubt the relevance of targets to their relationship with their students.

What has been revealed in the national system of ITE is a series of 'regulatory' and discursive performative 'practices' for the normative production of 'bodies' and 'identities' as distinctly circumscribed entities that are regarded as real and significant. Lyotard's (1984) essentially Heideggarian account, *The Postmodern Condition*, underlines the nihilistic logic of performativity. Ironically, the foregoing deconstruction shows that performativity constitutes the ethos of policy and practice within ITE in England. But there is a double irony here. It follows from the deconstruction of the enframing that governmental agencies are always in danger of being rendered as puppets of the enframing, when, in fact, agencies tacitly view themselves as leaders in the system of ITE.

Performativity of identity: Enframing in pedagogized societies

At this point, we would like to take the reader back to Kay-Shuttleworth's mid-nineteenth-century vision of the coming teacher, contrasting the then existing monitorial pedagogy with that modelled at the inception of state-sponsored mass formal education in England. Again, even at this early stage in the unfolding history of education, the focus of interest in terms of the requirements of teacher identity had been ontical, that is to say, it is concerned with characterizing teacher identity, rather than opening questions about the being of a teacher.

An archive (Kay-Shuttleworth, 2007) detailing 'four periods of public education' provides a remarkable account of Kay-Shuttleworth's contributions, particularly in his ten-year secretaryship of the 'Committee of the Privy Council on Education' that came into being in 1839. As McCann noted, in his review of R. J. W. Selleck's (1994) account, 'Journey of an Outsider', 'Kay-Shuttleworth had applied himself to the difficult task of beginning to develop the system of national, popular education with the same zeal that he had brought to his Poor Law duties' (McCann, 1996: 124).

What had been in place in the 'workhouses' and the 'Schools of Industry for Pauper Children' had been 'Dr Bell's monitorial system' of education in a number of schools 'that had taken the first steps towards the pupil–teacher system' in what later emerged as 'model' and 'normal schools' (Kay-Shuttleworth, 2007: 106, 287–92). In Kay-Shuttleworth's picture of education, instruction in cognitive matters 'depends for its efficacy on the fact that by simultaneous method, the mind of the teacher may be more constantly in contact with that of every child under his care' (Kay-Shuttleworth, 2007: 253). He made the remarkable observation that 'in the early steps towards the formation of correct habits, it is necessary that (until the power of self-guidance is obtained) the pupil should be constantly under the eye of a master, not disposed to exercise authority so much as to give assistance and advice' (Kay-Shuttleworth, 2007: 253).

We return once more to the moral groundings of ITE and the dimensions of this relationship that very much reflect integral parts of the teachings of Christianity. As Dean observes (2010: 90), in the Christian tradition, 'the relation between God', the pastor (his representative) and his people (the pastorate) 'is conceived . . . as a relationship between the shepherd and the flock ("The Lord is my shepherd")'. Here, then, in Kay-Shuttleworth's vision was the advent of the 'pastoral care' of young people. Teacher identity variously began to unfold in the interplay of emergent discourses regarding what Kay-Shuttleworth had called 'intellectual and moral aims' (Dean, 2010: 337) of education.

There is an astonishing consonance of Kay-Shuttleworth's vision in the contemporary ethic of pastoral discipline (Best, 2002). It now grounds the practice of teaching in every school in the land. In the modern practice of teaching it opens many possible variations in both the city–citizen metaphor and the shepherd–flock metaphor inherited from Christian tradition. Moreover, from the foregoing deconstruction, it is clear that both of these images continue to be played out in modern government. It points also to the inexorable transformations of modern society within dominant pedagogic structures (Bernstein, 1996: 1–39). The pedagogy of ITE, Bernstein suggests to his readers, is a process of 'recontextualisation' (2000: 33) – the selective appropriation, relocation and refocusing on the salient features of ITE practice in accordance with the 'principle of assessment', along with defined benchmarks for performance and measurable qualities of our student teachers. By definition and of necessity such ontical structuring elides completely any difficult questions concerning what it means *to be* a teacher. Ironically, however, in the extreme it is the being of the principle of assessment that provides the basis for the pedagogic recontextualizing and ordering of ITE in the enframing in the first place. While Bernstein's schema recognizes that pedagogic recontextualization 'has a crucial function in creating the fundamental autonomy of education' (Bernstein, 2000: 33), it remains located in the ontical structuring of education and misses the enframing completely.

There is, then, a double irony, because the government of the day in England, in its reiteration of the 'citizen–city game' as the democratically elected 'shepherd' of this society within pedagogic structures, is already completely immersed in and continues unwittingly to reiterate the challenging demands placed upon its own agency in the enframing. The body of the student teacher, whose identity as the mythological object or subject of the ITT economy as circumscribed by the enframing, is also always in danger of being reduced to a mere functionary of government apparatus.

The enframing: Possibilities open to the standing reserve

Let us for one moment stop to consider whether development of centralized powers in ITT on the mythological grounds of the enframing is inevitable – indeed, inescapable – or whether there is a potential for resistance to contemporary strictures on professional identity. In fact, in the spirit of Derrida, it is safe to say that when faced with that 'monster', the always unknowable future, every discourse and practice of initial teacher education is contingent. While the capacity of every discourse to repress and exclude appears to know no bounds, everything, including the claims to authority that inhere in the system of ITE in England and the many institutions of ITE around the globe, remain reformable.

The reason is straightforward if we look a little more closely at the metaphysical language of what is present in ITE, that is, of what is known at present to be the best available knowledge. In fact, applying Derrida's incisive reading of Husserl to the discursive practices of ITE, 'the presence of the present is derived from the repetition of signs and not the reverse' (1973: 52). For example, the presence of what is known to be best practice in ITE takes on the unity of subject or object to the extent that it is brought forth by repetition (Caputo, 1987: 123). Being or identity in this reading of pedagogic practice is 'proportionate to reiteration' (Caputo, 1987: 123). Reiteration is repetition with the inflection of difference. Difference within institutional systems is no accident; it is not something external to the correct institutions of ITE, but has inhabited every discourse and practice of ITE right from the start.

This is why so much has been invested in the English system of ITE in developing what is essentially a metaphysical regime of truth regarding the best knowledge available at present. As Caputo reminds his readers, 'in metaphysics', the mirror image of Derrida's position has always prevailed, 'something is "repeatable" to the extent that it "is"' (1987: 123; emphasis added). Essentially, it is this standpoint that constitutes the primary drive in science developed from ITE to generate valid, reliable and trustworthy knowledge of what 'is'. Representing knowledge of what 'is' in ITE is really no more than building so many bridges over the flux of time, in which everyday events are constituted in what Derrida calls the play of '*différance*'. In fact, teachers make sense of the present in their practice by drawing on the temporal movement of future possibilities against what has been happening (Flint, 2011a).

In the unfolding and disjointed history of the professional self over the last two decades, Derrida's post-structuralist explorations undoubtedly open many possibilities and radical questions for the dominant 'modernist project'. There would appear to remain very little space for exploration of what post-structuralism means in terms of the contemporary strictures on professional identity in ITE. One notable exception is the work of Grenfell and James (1998). In their reading of Bourdieu, a teacher's 'objective knowledge' is always regarded as 'provisional', 'subject to ongoing test and reformulation'. Some of the possible implications of this standpoint for what might be seen quite literally as a source for the revitalization of teacher identity within ITE are explored in Grenfell's

'Bourdieu and Initial Teacher Education – a post-structuralist approach' (1996: 287–303).

There are also are number of practices that emerged in the late nineteenth and early twentieth centuries that offer alternatives to both the possible *telos* of the enframing and final closure in the modernist vision of the professional self as a perfectible entity in readings of the history of ITE.

For Montessori, teacher's assessments of children's learning were not seen as a technological revealing of the world, but rather an ongoing process of observing how children work and adapt to their ever-changing world. In fact, in her pedagogy, young people are first and foremost encouraged to self-assess their progress in learning derived from their own projects. Teaching, for her, is about continually changing the environment in which children learn and about teachers observing how children's work adapts to those new environments (Montessori, 1988: 79–81). It also is concerned with how their new sense of being unfolds (Montessori, 1972: 46), teacher identity again being open to the possibility of regeneration and growth.

Another alternative to the current strictures on the professional identity of teachers came into being with the work of Freinet, whose philosophy of education became prominent in France in the early 1920s. In concert with Montessori, he had worked within the Romantic tradition that viewed the child as innocent and full of potential. His pedagogy was also essentially experiential. In fact, in Germany, Hellmich and Teigler (1992) have argued that the works by Montessori, Freinet and particularly Steiner have been very influential in terms of developing alternative forms of understanding of achievement in student's work outside of the principle of assessment.

The 'Dalton Plan' takes its name from a high school in Massachusetts, where it was first enacted in 1920 (Parkhurst, 1922). It provides another alternative to the current technological enframing in relation to teacher identity. Parkhurst, its originator, took as her first principle of pedagogy not 'the principle of assessment' but that of the freedom of 'the pupil', who 'must be made free to continue his work, on any subject in which he is absorbed, without interruption' (2010: 19). In working in 'laboratories' as places where teachers investigated their children (Parkhurst 2010: 11), the teacher is continually challenged to 'be on the look-out for inter-relations which would stir the minds of the children' (Parkhurst 2010: 53), opening, once more, possibilities for the continual renewal of teacher identity.

Of all the alternatives located in the ancient history of Greek civilization, Heidegger's understanding of '*paitheia*', from his reading of Plato's allegory of the cave in the seventh book of *The Republic*, creates space for a truly radical opening for teacher identity (1998a: 155–82; 2002: 67–84). For Heidegger, '*paitheia* is not education' in the sense of '*Bildung*', that is, it is not 'self-cultivation' in any of its multiplicity of forms (2002: 83). In his view, *paitheia* is a position taken in questioning and thinking, which concerns 'our essential being' (Heidegger, 1998a: 167). It is a questioning and thinking which 'precedes all pedagogy, psychology, anthropology', indeed, every 'form of humanism' (Heidegger, 1998a: 83). It is 'real education', which, as a questioning and thinking, concerns our relationship with truth that challenges the 'superficiality of ideas as values and *paithiea* as culture and education' (Heidegger, 1998a: 167). What this ontic structuring of questioning and thinking means for the identity of teachers within the context of contemporary ITE still remains to be examined.

The enframing: Other pedagogic models of teacher identity

In this dislocated and sometimes fragmented history of the professional self, a group of pedagogic models derived from social psychology also opens possibility of regeneration within a multiplicity of identities. Among this group, Bandura's (1986; 1997) model of the 'social foundations of thought and action' theorizes learning being based on the reciprocal interplay of 'the person', 'the behaviour' and 'the environment'. It was first animated by the realization of just how much people learn by simply observing the actions of others. It is premised on the assumption of the efficacy of the self, which is more than simply a belief in one's capability to do particular actions. Bandura's technical conception of 'self-efficacy' incorporates four dimensions of learning, which he defines as 'mastery learning', 'imitation', 'modeling' and 'social persuasion'. Each in turn opens the possibility of continual renewal of the identities of the lead professionals within a community setting (Bandura, 1986: 18).

In a Derridean reading of Vygotsky's model of mediated learning, Flint (2009) explores the possibilities of the ever-changing identities of lead professionals in the 'zone of proximal development'. They are seen to unfold continually in the play of *différance*, that remarkable interplay of presence and absence that makes possible identity and play and everything else we have touched upon in this chapter. Flint's (2009) reading is the first to take seriously Vygotsky's standpoint that 'play is a leading activity' and turns upside down many contemporary readings of Vygotsky in modern 'activity theory', which all tend to view play at the lowest rung on a hierarchy leading to higher forms of learning.

Hierarchy – indeed, the hierarchical structure of most organizations – is no accident. This structure is homologous with the metaphysics of repetition, which, as we have seen, holds with the illusion that something is repeatable to the extent that it 'is'. In foregrounding the significance of language, we believe, to the contrary, that something 'is' to the extent that it is brought forward by repetition. The full implications of this new reading for the ever-changing identity of professionals have yet to be explored.

Lave and Wenger's (1991) and Wenger's (1997) model of 'peripheral participation' in a 'community' was first inspired by observations made of apprenticeships within a range of seemingly unrelated settings. Although in each of the cases they had studied there had been no formal teaching, the pair was genuinely surprised by the levels of understanding and knowledge new participants developed and generated within each of the communities.

A case in point to illustrate the application of these foregoing various social psychological models in an attempt to reconceptualize the modus operandi of a state school is that of Countesthorpe College in Leicestershire in England in the 1970s. Here again was an alternative to the endless moves towards an illusory closure of the modernist project of formal ITE in England, where the professional self is always in danger of being rendered as a functionary, its very being reduced to standing reserve. At Countesthorpe, the identity of the professional self was open to continual renewal within a community setting for a 'democratically' run school organization. All internal decisions were made (Watts, 1977: 28–32) in the weekly school 'moot', where every member of the teaching community had one vote.

In England, following the changes wrought during the 1980s, the fight for justice in society and for localized forms of democratic organization as had been exemplified at Countesthorpe, is no longer possible. But, in turning to the relationship between formal education and society, it is now time to consider yet more powerful forces at work in the ideological representation and positioning of teacher identity in the public mind in the myth of the hero.

In *Mythologies*, Barthes (2000 [1972]) uncovers how myth takes hold of a historical object, in this case the myth of the hero in a local drama, and turns it into a trope of universal value: the individualized spirit yet universalized heroic figure as a context for the identity in the public mind of effective and high-performing teachers. In fact, the powerful yet contradictory form of public rhetoric invested in this identity provides an almost perfect *trompe-l'œil* for the ever present danger of it being rendered as standing reserve in the enframing in educational systems.

Here we will concentrate briefly on two films, illustrative of a wider genre that paints what almost emerges as the epochal hero in dramatic relief: 'To Sir with Love', both the title of the film and the earlier book by Braithwaite on which it was based and 'Dangerous Minds', also based on an autobiography, 'My Posse Don't Do Homework', by former US Marine journalist Johnson.

In 'To Sir with Love', Braithwaite is played by the character Mark Thackaray who, as an out-of-work communications engineer, takes up a job in a tough school in the East End of London. Led by the characters Denham and Dare, Thackeray's new class surpasses even his expectations. As the rising hero of the piece, he begins to win over the youngsters by respecting them as adults, only to fall from their favour in his handling of an incident within another class. Finally, in the spirit of the illustrious warrior, Thackeray wins the class back once again in handling a staged boxing match with a show of remarkable strength of character, courage and true nobility of soul.

As a retired US Marine, Johnson, the heroine of the film 'Dangerous Minds', is surprised to gain a teaching job working with a group of tough-minded, sullen and underprivileged teenagers, all from lower-working-class backgrounds, at Parkmont High School in California. She finds favour with the class by her fortitude, courage and bravery in the face of adversity; however, she resorted to a range of idiosyncratic

and eccentric techniques that also place her in conflict with bureaucratic norms.

In these films' representations of the hero, there is no question of
the misrepresentation of character; mythical representation 'operates' as
myths do, in transforming 'a meaning into form' or as Barthes puts it,
there is a 'language robbery' where myth has the task of giving an historical intention a natural justification, and making contingency appear
eternal' (Barthes, 2000 [1972]: 131, 142). In the unfolding postcolonial
discursive interplay between education and spirit, this genre of film
illuminates how the complex subjectivities experienced by young people and other stakeholders in systems of education can be mobilized.
The films bring to the public imagination another emergent theme of
contemporary postcolonial discourse: the interplay of dominance and
resistance. Interestingly, there is an elegant ambiguity in the power practices of the mythical heroes, who both position themselves in the order
of domination in accord with the enframing of education in the classroom and resist extant bureaucratic norms.

It is interesting, then, to view this complex postcolonial stage set for
our mythological hero in formal education against the contemporary
configuration of technique, as exemplified in the paradigmatic text
Models of Learning – Tools for Teaching (Joyce et al., 2009). In the seemingly familiar and cosy rhetoric of 'families of models of teaching' (Joyce
et al., 2009: 33) and the various familiar 'scenarios' drawn from classrooms, the reader is provided with exemplars of what all 'students' are
purported to 'need'. Beneath 'needs' represented as a 'range of instructional approaches drawn from the information processing, social, personal and behavioural families', there is a hard-edged technological
rationalism (Joyce et al., 2009: 34).

It is no accident that the standpoint adopted in this text is entirely
consonant with what can be seen as the post-1988 colonizing 'episteme'
in ITE. This 'episteme' can be understood as a 'strategic apparatus' that
the state implemented following the introduction of the national curriculum in England in 1988. This apparatus comprises a 'field of scien-
tificity', gathering and then distinguishing statements that accord with
this field from those which do not (Foucault, 1980b: 197). The 'episteme' in question, this study has shown continues the reprogramming

of teacher identity in its multiplicity of forms under the sway of its instrumental rationality.

Being a teacher: Reflections on the enframing

In being positioned in this post-1998 episteme, induction into teaching is formally structured as a form of *techne*. The episteme of ITE in England refers to the pre-cognitive space, determining 'on what historical *a priori*, and in the element of what positivity, ideas could appear'; 'the science' of ITE could be established, 'experience be reflected in philosophies, rationalities be formed', only, as we have seen already, 'to dissolve and vanish soon afterwards' (Foucault, 1970: xxii). The *Models for Learning – Tools for Teachers*, as the affirmation of an intellectual groundwork for the current episteme structuring ITE in England, is also the re-affirmation of the enframing.

In this view of ITE in England, teacher induction is a form of techne. This word is often translated as 'craft', but this is misleading. In fact, *techne* refers to the gathering together and the revealing of the intellectual resources, including the foregoing paradigmatic text (Joyce et al., 1997), so informing and shaping teacher induction in advance of the technological enframing in the discursive apparatus of ITE.

In two recent phenomenological studies of 'know how' and 'tacit knowledge' in both higher education and secondary classrooms, Flint (2010a, b) has demonstrated how much is elided in standard observation protocols. Against this will-to-power of governmental agencies in ITE, the capacity for creativity and both the desire and fact of being otherwise, expressed by practicing teachers, remains undimmed.

The Enframing in the Leadership and Management of Education

Introduction

The last fifty years have seen a significant reconfiguration in the leadership and management of education in England and elsewhere in the world. Education as an apparatus of the state has been extended from a hierarchical to more distributed model of leadership through the opening of new space for the subjects and objects of the enframing: the leaders and managers of education. OfSTED self-assessment procedures for schools in England provide a case in point.

In contrast to the dominant discourses of leadership and management, placing the leader at the centre of debate, our argument will be decentred to uncover the ways discourses shape practices. At issue is the role of the discursive practices of managerialism. We regard managerialism in the broadest terms as educational practice that draws upon management techniques. In the colonizing of space by managerialism within the apparatus of education we contend that the enframing creates the coding for the extension of governmentality. This expansion of state apparatus is most obviously reflected in a multiplicity of competing forms of distributed leadership. In seeking a modus operandi for the development of governmentality we uncover how practitioners are variously positioned as leaders and managers in the enframing through a deconstruction against indications drawn from a critical review of democratic participation in education.

The standing reserve of leaders, managers, practitioners and other agencies is examined as a means of effecting the realignment of the professional environment. We question too discursive representations of leaders and managers, and the concept of improvement as an organic discourse of change. Our argument also considers 'emotivist' culture and the 'character of the manager', drawing from MacIntyre's (2007) incisive critique.

Contrary to the prevailing ideological commitment of education to reducing inequality, the argument in this chapter will explore how organizational hierarchies within formal education are merely reiterated as homologous social distinctions. For example, a case study of the academy as an attempt to re-engineer the institution of the school makes concrete the complex relationship between performativity and social progress in the name of social justice. Here the enframing in such managerialist practice is elaborated through a Lacanian perspective that connects the active rhetorics, aspirations, identities and practices of professionals with the desire to improve practice.

Finally we are concerned with both the constraints imposed upon the standing reserve of that body involved in the leadership of formal education and the various possibilities that such a standing reserve of energy creates for the system of education.

Emerging managerialisms: From hierarchical to distributed forms of leadership

Our argument draws once more on Brecht's approach in 'making strange the familiar', which is our translation of Brecht's original term, 'Verfremdungseffekt'. In 'The Theatre of Bertolt Brecht' Willett indicates this is a 'matter of detachment, of reorientation: exactly what Shelley meant when he wrote that poetry 'makes familiar objects to be as if they were not familiar' (1977: 177). By deconstructing the terms *managerialism*, *leadership*, *leader* and *manager* against indications drawn from the phenomenological ontology of Dasein, we hope to examine the unfolding discourses of leadership in different ways, reflecting what until now has tended to remain concealed within such practices, namely, the enframing (Heidegger, 1962; Willett, 1977: 177–8).

At issue is what is signified by managerialism and its relationship with discourses of leadership. Our concern are places and language where Dasein and organizations are variously 'thrown'. It is our contention that the practice of managerialism in education is one surface manifestation of the enframing. In such discourses the means–ends ordering and the continual challenging of individuals in accordance with the 'principle of reason' and its analogical counterpart in the field of education, the 'principle of assessment', is already apparent from contemporary conceptions of leadership and of leaders represented in the literature. Cuban, for example, provides an incisive distinction between leadership, signifying 'the influencing of others' actions' – the means – 'to achieve desired ends' and management, connoting the efficient and effective 'maintenance (the means) of organisational arrangements' (ends) (1988: xx). While in schematic terms we have underlined the means–ends logic of the enframing in managerialist discourse, in practice ends become means and vice versa; there is always a blurring of any such distinctions. Rather than approaching Cuban's conception of leadership with the prejudice of already placing ourselves at the centre of things, we might ask – as only one way among many of revealing the world of education – what, not who, is the source that 'influences' the actions of others? In speaking about the work of teachers or lecturers, for example, we sometimes will say '"they" are involved in the education of . . .'. In each case, of course, in managerialist discourses the designation of the 'others', like the 'they', refers to an amorphous body of people. Is it not the case that what 'they' suggest gives expression to what 'one' should do in any given circumstances?

The question of the precise locus of the structure that is shaping discursive practices of leadership, however, still remains unanswered. It is, of course, the 'principle of reason' and, in contemporary education, the principle of assessment. The precise locus for both principles is the subject and object constituted in the very grammar of managerialist discourses. In fact, at least intuitively, as Dasein, all of us are also intimately aware in our everyday professional interactions that it is not some abstract connection between subject and object that animates our existence: it is the fact that we are all essentially temporal beings. In our daily interactions with 'others', the sense we variously make of what is happening to us at this point in time – now – derives from our possible understandings and projections of what might happen in the future – in the next minute, hour, week and so on – on the basis of what has been happening. Temporality is one of Heidegger's big ideas, it arose from his deconstruction of Aristotle's notion of clock time as a sequence of now-now-now ... In *Being and Time* Heidegger shows more formally that Dasein's very being is grounded in temporality. For Heidegger (1962: 401 [350]) 'temporality temporalises as a future which makes present in the process of having been'.

Temporal possibilities of being are always far beyond the machine-like connection between subject–object in the grammar of managerialism. As Dasein, it is the endless play of such temporality that is always already at work mediating all interactions in the workplace. In defining schematically within the logic of managerialism the function of the subject (the leader) is that of bending 'the motivations and actions of others to achieve certain goals' (Cuban, 1988: 193), it is apparent that the leader is there in the workplace to build up and guide the standing reserve of energy constituted by this amorphous gathering of the 'others'. From this perspective in the hegemony of managerialism, the function of the leader is that of giving shape to the standing reserve involved in education. There is, of course, always the need to maintain order within the standing reserve. This is the role of another subject of the managerialist economy, the manager. Within the standing reserve, the manager has the job of 'maintaining, efficiently and effectively, the current organisational arrangements' (Bush, 2007: 392). In other words, the manager is the object of any ideological 'change strategy' in education and 'the subject through which' such ideological 'change is delivered' in this field (Clarke and Newman, 1997: 68).

Since it is grounded more broadly in 'the principle of reason' and its counterpart in education, the principle of assessment is not constrained by the contingent boundaries of any organization, district or country. Rather, the standing reserve in the enframing has a tendency to colonize other discursive practices and to generate new possibilities in building up an ever larger reserve of energy.

Such colonization of the standing reserve is evident in the systematic shift from hierarchical to distributive forms of leadership and management in managerialist discourse in the post-war years in the English-speaking world (Harris, 2002; Spillane, 2006; Leithwood et al., 2008). Changes in leadership research in education reflect dominant themes of the prevailing zeitgeist. Much of the significance for this chapter arises from the completely unconscious concealment of the enframing. The latter emerges as managerialist practice from its associated standing reserve and also from the powerful, seemingly almost beyond question, principle of assessment 'upon which'[1] managerialist discourse is being shaped and is shaping practices of leadership in education. The enframing instituted as managerialist practice tends to have become dissembled in the 'endemic ambiguity' of its own cultures (Hoyle and Wallace, 2005: 21–48, 111–28). The obfuscation of the enframing is only further strengthened by the ontical structuring of forms of discourse, concerned primarily, not with questions of what it means to be a leader, but with the characterizations of objects (or subjects) within managerialist economies.

The archaeology of managerialisms: From Fordism to neoliberal ideologies

The enframing in the order of things does not simply impose itself. Examining how it emerges requires an archaeological approach in exploring the space for the transformation of public research concerned

---

1 The 'upon which' is a translation of Heidegger's term, Woraufhin, which refers to the structure – in this case the principle of assessment – on the basis of which 'things are intelligible' in managerialist discourse (Dreyfus, 1991: xii). .

with leadership in the post-war years. It began with 'bureau-professional' regimes of practice and has now unfolded into the exploration of distributed and sustainable forms of leadership within what are represented as forms of managerialist practice.

One strand of research informing the management of organizations, 'Fordism', emerged from the management of the American Ford Motor company. Fordism has its roots in the work of F. W. Taylor. Taylor had worked as a foreman in the 'machine shop of the Midvale Steel Company' in the 1920s (Kanigel, 1997b: 1). Taylor was interested in finding out how to make the work processes more efficient. The series of experiments he conducted over twenty-six years in his ceaseless quest for 'The One Best Way' changed the former craft know-how of workers into scientific data; the factory came to be ruled with 'time and motion' studies based on measurements of the stopwatch (Kanigel, 1997a) It is significant that the principle of rationalization built into the science of Fordism that followed Taylor's work provided the basis for the possibilities open to a foreman who accepted the responsibility of working with others in order to achieve particular goals in the factory. In Taylor's biographical narrative the behaviour in practice (the means) of the foreman had been circumscribed by the goals (the ends) identified within the existing factory system. Measures of organizational performance (the object) determined efficient behaviour (the subject) and not reverse. The grammar of performativity of practice connecting subject and object on the basis of reason enacted in the foreman's efficient practice was always already determined in the enframing – it was made tangible in the essential means–ends structure of the technology of production in the factory. Here was the basis for a significant logic of practice (Kanigel, 1997b: 1–5).

Such bureaucratic and scientific modes of coordination, which were hierarchically structured and concerned with stability and uniformity (Weber, 1947), were also found in the 1950s in most school organizations in various leading economies in the world such as England, Canada, Australia and the United States. They were combined with forms of 'professionalism' that stressed the indeterminacy of the social world and so necessitated the intervention of 'expert judgment' (Metz, 1978; Grant, 1988; Pace, 2003). Again, the principle of rationalization of the art of 'running' such schools, requiring the intervention of professional judgement, arose from the behaviours of those governed in schools. As James (later Lord James) is reported to have recalled in the 1960s, when High Master of Manchester Grammar School: 'In drinking his morning coffee in the staff room' and in 'being approached by teachers with requests and proposals . . . he would generally reply "Why not?" thereby inviting them to go ahead'. (Hoyle and Wallace, 2005: 79). As Headteacher, 'James advocated a pure meritocracy'. One commentator in James' obituary in the Telegraph noted: 'Selection at Manchester Grammar School was by competitive examination, with no marks added for wealth or family connections. It was the essence of his philosophy that grammar schools should serve as ladders, giving all levels of society access to the highest places in the land' (18 May 1992). His moral credo, which he held onto 'unflinchingly', was that of 'academic standards'.

In educational discourse before the 1960s, schools were 'run' by head teachers who were 'defined by their moral qualities and their capacity for giving moral leadership' (Grace, 1995: 5–25). As Hoyle and Wallace note, in the earlier times 'running a school was about keeping things on track – the mere routine of school management' (2005: 79). With the emergence of discourses in leadership, running a school has come to have quite different connotations.

Research into workplace leadership was initially concerned with eliciting particular 'traits' that could be used to distinguish leaders from other individuals. Surveys of studies concerned with the characteristic traits of leaders (Stogdill, 1948; Mann, 1959) appeared to differentiate leaders from their followers, though others had found no such differences (Wright, 1996: 34). For some, the rationality of the characteristic traits of leaders remained undiminished. Other researchers shifted their analysis to another strand of research of various 'situations' in which leadership is practiced. In taking the notion of styles with them, yet another group of researchers, who focused on what emerged as a 'contingency theory', sought to find what constituted 'effective leadership'. Once again, in the field of leadership research, reason connecting the grammar of the individual is derived from practice. The research had been animated by the continual play of differences, but it remained ontically structured as a basis for characterizing behaviours: ontological explorations concerning what it means to be a leader or manager have simply remained separated and removed from questions concerning how to manage change. Rather than supplanting former research, each of the emergent, distinct strands of enquiry continued to run parallel to each other.

In the context of the mid-1970s international oil crisis, Prime Minister Callaghan's speech at Ruskin College Oxford provided a focus for raising 'professional standards' in education. At this time, Burns's (1978) work on political leaders had distinguished between ordinary (transactional) leaders, who exchanged tangible rewards for the work and loyalty of followers, and extraordinary (transformational) leaders, who engaged with followers. It brought to life a distinction between transactional and transformational forms of leadership that Downton had made earlier (1973). In the hegemony of managerialism the issue of transformational leadership had focused on specific educational outcomes and how to achieve these with various apparatuses of the state (Barnett et al., 2001). In England, for example, in practice, the rationality of transformational leadership mediated moves from sometimes 'charismatic', 'individual, hierarchical and patriarchal' forms of leadership of the head teacher, to leadership that could be shared within 'communities of leaders' (Grace, 1995: 54–5). In the practice of contemporary education, there had been 'huge variations in focus and quality', a 'lottery of leadership' reflecting the play of difference, which largely determined 'whether a school was traditional or innovative, excellent or awful, creative or bland' (Hargreaves and Shirley, 2009: 5).

For Derrida (1982), this play of difference in language is the very basis for our making sense of anything. In the field of leadership and management research, it tends to be manifest in the continued examination of the differences (Bass, 1985; 1990; Bennis and Nanus, 1985). Others, including Foster (1989), drawing on critical social science, sought to challenge the managerialist structuring of transformational leadership with the notion of 'educational leaders'. Research had shown that charisma alone, while a 'necessary ingredient', 'was not sufficient to account for the transformational process' (Bass, 1985: 31).

More recently, in examining what is actually done in practice by teachers and head teachers involved in attempts to transform their schools, Hoyle and Wallace (2005: 153, 185–98) have theorized what they call 'temperate leadership and management'. Their research recognizes that the actions of teachers and head teachers in response to reform 'does not take the form of "outright rejection" but constitutes a principled effort to make unrealistic reforms viable in contingent conditions'. Their work illuminates the ways the rationalities of practice differ from those of the research-based managerialist agendas for educational reform. The former essentially represent the unfolding possibilities of Dasein situated in particular professional roles; the latter constitute discourses for those objects (or subjects) of the economy of education – the teacher and the head teacher.

The mid-1970s to the late 1980s marked a time in which 'market principles' infused welfare states with new pressures from governments on performance in New Zealand, the Canadian province of Alberta and the Australian state of Victoria. In England, for example, following the 'winter of discontent' and the 1979 election of Margaret Thatcher's Government, market principles suffused the emerging agenda for reforming the welfare state: privatization of services gave new emphasis to the dynamics of competition and 'placed new pressures on professionals to perform' (Hargreaves and Shirley, 2009: 7) in accord with officially identified benchmarks of improvement. Politically also, within discourses of research, management had repositioned itself away from 'Taylorism' and re-presented itself as 'regenerative', that is, results oriented, strategic and enabling.

The coded space for these unfolding transformations is constituted in the enframing. Its effects at each place of work are graphically illuminated by the Office for Standards in Education (OfSTED).

OfSTED and the rationalization of place

Many continue to preserve the uniqueness of each place for education – the school, the college, the community, the town, the city, the country and so on – against the forces of global commodification (Davies, 1998). The enframing in the institutionalization of OfSTED therefore comes under threat with one stroke in the field of education. In the ontically structured rationalization of OfSTED inspection as integral to the machinery of improvement, each place of education is 'represented' by its own context on grounds of the same coding of space used for each unique organization. Although OfSTED assiduously reports the context of each place, their structuring is ontical; the significance of being in a place has not yet been given the focus it deserves.

The challenge for neoliberal ideology is perhaps best reflected in a case study of more recent OfSTED self-assessment procedures that have been in place since 2009. These procedures epitomize governmental will to redefine the ethics of school management and what is deemed good practice. In England, OfSTED provide one of the disciplinary arms of the improvement nexus. In accord with the regime of truth, the OfSTED 'self-evaluation form for all-through mainstream schools' makes a statutory demand for all such institutions in England to complete a detailed annual self-assessment of their performance against national benchmarks, ascribing categoric values to each of their assessments – 'outstanding', 'good', 'satisfactory' or 'inadequate' (OfSTED, 2011)

The language of self-evaluation imputes a tacit promise that each school is, indeed, 'embedding ambition and driving improvement'. Such performativity, witnessed in many different contexts of formal education, is here elevated to a statutory requirement. Again, we have already observed how the troubling discourses of 'governmentality' (Foucault, 1991) represent the leadership of schools as a means for 'improving' the performance. The driving force for such improvement, as Lyotard (1984) had recognized more than three decades ago, is that of performativity.

However, as Butler's argument suggests, once such performativity, conceived as 'the reiteration of . . . a set of norms', acquires the position of a statutory obligation, it serves to 'conceal or dissimulate' and almost completely block any critical discussions regarding 'the conventions of which it is a repetition' (1993: 12). For example, here we could point to philosophical arguments regarding the enframing, to the ontology of 'place', or to the ethic of using data – signifying what is 'given' – for such evaluations, so concealing as much as it reveals in its 'gift' to busy schools.

At issue is the concealment in such data collected about formal education, representing for Fullan (2007: 173) a 'key to high yield capacities' of change, where education has been constituted as our relationship with the enframing. We can see what this means in phenomenological terms when Giddens pictures the enframing in the late modern world in terms of the 'juggernaut of modernity' (1990: 139). Within the regime of truth constituted by the closed circle of OfSTED and governmental apparatuses there is always the danger, as we have seen before, of reducing all agents and agencies in education to objects and subjects of these economies, constituting individuals as standing reserve.

Paradoxically, in the coded space produced by OfSTED and the principle of assessment, the possibilities of being and our very energy as a body of objects–subjects involved in education is reduced to being in reserve, available for use and driven in the enframing.

By the 1990s, there had been a noticeable concomitant conflation of the rationalities of leadership emerging from government and those of research communities centring on 'improvement'. In *School Improvement for Real*, Hopkins indicated that 'systemic reform had lasted throughout the 1990s', combining a series of 'strategies' for 'centralization and decentralization' (2001: 37). Here within discourses of improvement were further clear indications of the diffusion of 'governmentality'.

Systemic change gathers together whole systems of formal education as standing reserve in the enframing. Ironically, and with almost unsurpassed ambiguity, discourses of systemic change appear to speak to Dasein in the role of teachers, head teachers and so on. In fact, the focus for such discourses constitutes such identities as objects and subjects of the economies of state education.

The standing reserve both closes down some possibilities and opens others (Peim and Flint, 2009). As Hargreaves and Shirley note, education 'markets were overlaid by growing government centralization and standardization of educational goals'; in 'England, the energy' and drive for 'innovation had been lost'; 'in US schools teachers bemoaned the taking away of professional judgement and autonomy' and in Canada one teacher in the 'Change over Time Study' said that 'the creativity is gone' (2009: 8, 9, 11). Although, within such discourses of improvement, *The Fate of Place* (Casey, 1998) has yet to be thematized and the ways in which identities with the particularities of 'place' mediate the creativities and energies of people involved have yet to be examined more fully.

Systemic leadership and standing reserve

Systemic forms of leadership have now emerged in ever extending governmental apparatuses on the international stage, with the potential to constitute much larger standing reserves in the enframing. Currently, these remain largely confined by national and regional boundaries. From this perspective it is, therefore, ironic that Fullan (2005: ix) conceives of such leadership 'as the capacity of the system to engage in the complexities of continuous improvement consistent with the deep values of human purpose', with no consideration for the standing reserve or to Fullan's own will-to-power in his value-positing. Given the driving force of the enframing at work in this discourse and its associated practices, it is even more ironic that two leaders within the international field, Hargreaves and Fink (2006: 17), conceive of such leadership as 'sustainable'. The full implications of the enframing within practices of improvement have yet to be debated.

The extension of governmentality constituted in the enframing is also apparent in 'distributed' forms of organizational and institutional forms of administration, conceived as a 'continuum of leadership from the chief executive to the practitioner' (Bartlett, 2007: 4). For Harris (2002; 2003), such distributed leadership is an important element in a school's capacity for improvement. This capacity arises, of course, from the standing reserve.

Tacitly, sustainable leadership as conceived by Hargreaves and Fink (2006) is entirely in harmony with such possibilities of the standing reserve, although there is yet no explicit recognition of the enframing within this discourse. According to Hargreaves and Shirley, the principles of sustainable leadership have been constituted to 'preserve and develop deep learning for all characterised by its breadth, justice, resourcefulness and endurance: a compelling form of leadership that does no harm to others' in 'surrounding' environments (2009: 97). Indeed, in being reflexive there is always the possibility that such learning may also question the very 'enframing' itself.

Narratives of leadership and management

Rather than beginning with the individual and particular actions, our decentring foregrounds the language of improvement into which agencies are variously thrown. It opens questions concerning how people attempt to make sense of their worlds in and through the language of educational improvement. Here we are not arbitrarily decentring agencies within formal education. It is apparent that what has been uncovered from the decentring that follows underlines the commonality of narrative structures used to position agencies within the remaking of the welfare state more generally (Clarke and Newman, 1997).

The official account of change in formal education draws on a multiplicity of powerful images and is constructed around a number of typical narratives that draw out different sets of associations and oppositions to underline the urgency of what is represented as an almost unquestionably essential need for improvement in formal education.

Two typical texts – *School Improvement for Real* (SIR) and *The New Meaning of Educational Change* (NMEC) – by two leading figures within the international field of school improvement, Hopkins (2001) and Fullan (2007), provide an illustration of how such language represents continued attempts to reposition 'leaders' and 'managers' within the enframing.

Narrating change as natural

Both texts create images which seek to position leaders in a discourse of change conceived as 'natural'. Presenting again managerialist discourses of change as natural produces powerful metaphors. For example, SIR makes a number of references to 'school growth', 'school growth states' and 'professional growth'; NMEC talks of the 'evolution of reform' and 'mutual adaptation' in relation to training in leadership. Indeed, SIR uses similar language of 'adaptation vis-à-vis the environment'. The narrative structures in both texts premise 'growth' on the 'capacity' for particular forms of development, again positioning leaders with particular imperatives for improvement. SIR speaks of the 'capacity to change', itself dependent upon 'leadership capacity', 'capacity for development' and 'capacity building'.

Similarly, NMEC also emphasizes 'capacity building and the focus on results' and 'school capacity'; in NMEC, it is clear these 'cannot be developed in the absence of quality leadership'. In speaking of the 'evolution of reform', NMEC attempts to constitute improvement as obvious 'in the relationship between the text and its audience'. The absence of an active subject in relation to the object, 'improvement', further reinforces this message. Neither text references 'we' who argue/think this, which only establishes the imperative for improvement with ever 'greater clarity'. As suggested earlier, although the details are different, there are broadly similar narratives of change as natural that have been used to reposition stakeholders in the state apparatus as a whole. In our deconstructive reading of these discourses, these capacity-building measures reflect the positioning of the body involved in education as standing reserve in the enframing.

Narrating change as hopeful struggle

For Hopkins, 'there's no hope of creating a better world without deeper scientific insight into the function of leadership and culture' (2001: 26). Fullan also makes a personal statement regarding his hope 'that it is obvious that leadership comes from many sources'. Certainly, in that same edition and in SIR, such aspirations are mixed with a sense of battle; there are a number of references in each to 'struggle'. This narrative positions teachers and their support agencies to see improvement as a military campaign. NMEC uses the military imagery of a 'strategic orientation' to confer upon leaders the imperative of 'using school improvement plans and an instructional focus to attack incoherence'. SIR speaks much of 'strategy' in relation to 'school improvement', 'educational change', 'developing literacy', the 'offsetting' of 'underachievement', 'self-evaluation' and developing curriculum change, which are used to place leaders in positions seen as advantageous to the advance of improvement.

Certainly, within discourses of improvement, both texts have rendered leaders with numerous insights on the basis of re-presentations of what has been done in practice. In accord with the enframing, of course, they also constitute a significant disguise in our relationship with being. Hopefully, what should now be obvious is that it is the unfolding of such a relationship that always constitutes the possible danger of the enframing. The enframing is never circumscribed by any one particular narrative structure; it is grounded in the principle of reason and, more narrowly in formal education, in the 'principle of assessment'.

This is why in particular texts, such as SIR or NMEC, there are many different narrative structures that variously complement and contradict each other. In these two narratives, leaders have been positioned variously within essentially managerialist discourses; as standing reserve, of course, there is always the possibility that such leaders may become authentically involved.

Narrating change as transformation

The narrative structure of transformative change situates 'effective leaders' in not only 'thinking about' what they have done, but 'thinking in order to . . . foster success in others'. The NMEC text also makes reference to 'Perkins', for whom 'the work of transformation . . . is done by developmental leaders'. Within this hegemony, change is represented as a progressive force for transformation; 'this is a much more expansive view of change' represented in the improvement literature as moving towards a 'new order'. For example, NMEC cites Mintzberg, for whom leadership 'has to be learned not just by doing but by being able to gain conceptual insight whilst doing it' (2004: 200). The text indicates that the 'goal . . . is not just to develop better leaders, but also to develop the organisation and to improve the larger system'. For NMEC, therefore, 'changing and developing individuals, and changing and developing cultures suited to the 21st century *is the same work*' (Fullan, 2007: 297; emphasis as in the original). What seems 'absolutely crucial' from this particular perspective is not so much that 'professional learning' should provide the basis for 'designing policies and practices', but that it should take full cognizance of the enframing.

'Transformative change' requires much 'more than a cognitive shift' in the way subjects and objects of managerialist discourses understand the world of education; as the text of SIR makes clear, it opens leaders to particular challenges in terms of what are re-presented as personal, organizational and institutional system-wide transformations.

Narrating change as turbulence

In fact, NMEC links such transformational imagery used in positioning leaders with an even more comprehensive representation of change, drawing on the 'metaphors of discontinuity, instability, fluidity and chaos'. Again, this narrative structure for change is not limited to positioning leaders within the field of improvement.

In considering some of the issues raised by complexity and chaos theory for improvement in formal systems of education, NMEC makes particular references to the works of Stacey (1996a: 7–8; 1996b: 349) and Senge and his colleagues (2000: 5). In NMEC, the challenge to the extant order of the world of education brought into this discourse is much quieter in tone than the loud siren calls made for a complete rethinking of organizational change in Fullan's (1993; 1999; 2003a) trilogy of *Change Forces*. In those texts, the narrative of change as uncertainty and turbulence is represented as no less than a series of 'lessons', giving every appearance of being a new bible of change. This particular narrative structure is there to position leaders with the imperative to rethink completely the complexities of the very idea of change itself.

Democratic improvement and governmentality

Each of the former three forms of leadership – distributed, systemic and sustainable – together with the discursive apparatus of improvement, also serves to embed leaders, managers, teachers and other agents and agencies in the language of governmentality. Ordinarily, of course, in discourses of improvement, the leadership and management of school organizations is viewed almost atomistically, as though they were each discrete agencies, or even regionally based networks. But, in terms of the governance of education, the distributed model of leadership actually extends the very mentalities of government from the centre throughout the body of education, constituting a clear extension of the state apparatus.

Given such an extension of 'governmentality' within discourses of improvement on an international stage, we should stop to consider, critically, the impact of democratic participation on practice. As Gutmann (1999: 11) suggests, 'a democratic theory is no substitute for a moral ideal in education', the latter providing the all-important grounding for democratic practice. Gutmann argues that 'there is no morally acceptable way to achieve social agreement on a moral ideal of education, at least in our lifetimes'. To her, 'we can do better to try instead to find the fairest ways of reconciling our differences and for enriching our collective life by debating them' (1999: 12). For example, we hope that this book may open further discussions regarding the enframing. Given the implementation of a state-wide reform programme in England aligned with the extension of governmental apparatus, we must also stop to ask whether education itself remains democratic. Is it still creating the space for the modification of ideals concerning the improvement of education through the process of engaging in democratic debates and reconciling our differences? Certainly, in England, where the organization of schooling has never enjoyed democratic forms of practice – with a few notable exceptions – the new 'coalition government' (Institute of Government, 2010) is seeking to institute 'mechanisms of local accountability' in its new reform agenda (Number10, 2010) despite the contradictions of the coded space in governmental institutions identified earlier in this chapter.

Perhaps, a good benchmark for reform is Gutmann's notion of 'political education' as the 'cultivation of the virtues, knowledge and skills necessary for political participation' (1999: 287). For her, such education 'has moral primacy over other purposes of public education in a democratic society' (1999: 287). Within the context of an ever growing international agenda for improvement in public education and its aligned extensions of governmentality, there remain significant questions regarding whether continued reform will be based on the principle of the 'moral primacy of public education', which 'supports a presumption in favour of participatory over more disciplinary methods of teaching', as grounds for 'democratic education'. For Gutmann, a benchmark of education is 'a shared trust of parents, citizens, teachers and other public officials' (1999: 287–8).

The challenge of realizing democratic education in practice, however, is that it would stand in a contradictory relationship with extant dominant forms of organization of schools, despite the ideological rhetoric of 'distributed leadership'. In England, for example, as Grace has noted, as leaders 'are expected to be *accountable to school governing bodies* (only partially representative of local communities) and to a *constituency of parents* rather than to a *constituency of citizens*' (1995: 200; emphasis added). Grace suggests that 'the culture of accountability' that still remains 'empowered within English schooling is corporatist and consumerist rather than democratic' (1995: 200). For Grace, the corporate model of education in England is currently constructed as analogous to a large-scale commercial enterprise, with the secretary of state of the day (as managing director) delegating responsibilities to school governors (as directors of schools), with head teachers (as delegated directors) delegating powers to many other leaders and managers who are responsible for managing 'teams' of practitioners – the teachers, teaching assistants, pupils and their various support agencies. It remains to be seen, therefore, whether the current order of formal education in England moves out of its system of 'market accountability' to embrace a true form of 'democratic accountability'. It might be tempting to connect 'local mechanisms of accountability' with 'competition, choice and social action' (School System, 2010), but there is yet no critical account of the enframing that is already shaping and driving the reform agenda.

There are, of course, models for democratic accountability that have been explored in practice. Grace (1995; 1990), for example, draws our attention to 'the notion of the Community Forum', as articulated in the education reforms of the Fourth Labour government in New Zealand in 1988, which for him provided a 'model for realizing . . . wider democratic accountability in education' (Grace, 1995: 201. However, in the context of neoliberal regimes of governmentality and the marketization of education in the United Kingdom, United States, Australia, New Zealand and Alberta, there currently seems to be little space remaining for 'democratic accountability' on the scale of national education systems. What such systems of accountability would look like still remains open to question. In the name of educational improvement, these systems in many countries variously continue to be busily engaged in producing docile, 'compliant, technical[ly] proficient and skilled' individuals in the enframing – as standing reserve.

It is important to keep in mind that it is not just the practitioners who are variously constituted as standing reserve; the enframing knows no distinction between the 'ruling class' and 'the proletariat' or between the corporatist world and the world of public education. Any possible developments in the practice of democratic education, therefore, need not only to take account of the enframing in the ordering of beings more generally, but must also consider one particular aspect of such social technology, namely, the education market and its alignment with what is represented as social progress. Schematically, within improvement discourses it should also now be obvious that the market constitutes a mechanism, opening the possibility of further stimulation of the standing reserve. Social progress, on the other hand, has been largely reduced within the enframing to being benchmarked by measures of student performance on public examinations. In many localities, the interplay of the market and social progress, constituted within managerialist discourse, establishes synergy.

Standing reserve within narratives of change

Of course, there are complications, complexities and contradictions on both sides. Most obviously, there is the complication that Dasein exerts its will in making sense of, and in taking action in response to such interplay. Woods and his colleagues (1998: 206) suggest that in their identities as professionals there is a sense of 'expertise' reflecting 'commitments' to learning at the level of the 'self', 'society' and the 'polity', regarding moves to develop a more 'inclusive' system of education. Such tendencies obviously run counter to any possible 'self-seeking individualism'. An obvious source of complexity is that, as we have seen, there are a number of discourses of improvement that variously position parents and students as customers and consumers, and teachers and others as producers having to meet specified performance targets. One of the obvious contradictions created by the so-called quasi-market of public education is that practitioners can find themselves both in collaboration and in competition with each other. Certainly, from Bagley's (2006) study, in the English system both competition and rivalry among schools and their various support agencies had intensified over the previous 30 years.

However, the complications, complexities and contradictions inherent in the standing reserve are given a sharp focus in the measures of progress made in the system. There remains here a continued debate regarding examination results as the outcome measure of the system of education (see Chapter 9). Indeed, most professionals and school organizations make much of other qualitative outcomes that are of significance for children, students and others involved in education. However, it is examination results that are currently deemed to provide benchmarks of professional standards. It is public examination results that bring together both the 'facework commitments' 'in which indicators of the integrity of others' – both parents and professionals – 'are sought' and 'faceless commitment where faith in the abstract workings of the education system is maintained. For Giddens (1990: 88) both of these forms of commitment are there to maintain trust in the system of education. The fact is that trust creates the basis for the enframing in this current system and it is trust placed in reason. Being has not been missed but is, for the most part, glossed over in the docile reiteration of public mantra concerning how the education system works.

A similar mantra is enshrined in the narrative structure of 'change as natural', drawing on the metaphors of the 'organic' and 'evolutionary'. Working within the empirical tradition that dominates research into improvement (see Chapter 5), we might ask what sense is made of 'change as natural'. Ultimately, the science grounding discourses of improvement is represented as providing a rigorous foundation for the generation of knowledge in this field on the basis of our sensual experiences. But, here in the science and in making sense of 'change as natural', we are in danger of missing another much more significant question. We can ask, 'How can such 'subjective egological evidence of sense become(s) objective and intersubjective?' In response to such a question, Derrida (1989a {1978}) showed formally that the truth of what is meant by change as natural cannot be constituted 'without language in general'. Speech is not something on the outside of the completed object, 'change as natural'; it is constitutive of the 'concrete, juridical condition of truth', here concerning a number of re-presentations of 'change' (see Chapter 2). More broadly, Derrida's response to this question turns on the distinction between two kinds of repetition of signs in language, which, for Caputo, correspond closely to two kinds of interpretation, the poetic and the rabbinical:

> There is a repetition which comes later, which is reproductive of prior presence – let us say a metaphysical idea of repetition, which moves backward. This is opposed to the repetition that moves forward, which is prior to presence and productive of it, and which, as a kind of reading, is therefore free to produce as it reads – let us say a critical idea of repetition. (1987: 121)

In moving back into the science of improvement, re-presented by the metaphor of change as natural, the original locus of change are transformations involving Dasein. Formally, Heidegger uncovered a number of ways the historicity of Dasein can unfold over time, including for being variously caught up in an amorphous body of humanity mediating a continual repetition of the same rather than any transformation. Ontologically, this is far removed from the symbolic reality constituted in discourses of improvement, purporting to represent natural change as 'organic' and 'evolutionary'. The rhetoric of metonym, dissimulated as metaphor, has substituted the identity of natural for the multiplicity of ways Dasein can unfold over time, including the repetition of the same (Heidegger, 1962). In this way, the seemingly familiar rhetorics of organic growth and so on are projected in order to arrive at a common consensus regarding particular ways of making sense of re-presentations of change.

Essentially, such discursive practices constitute the very means of structuring work in helping young children and students achieve higher-order achievement outcomes than were anticipated on the basis of past experience: the truth of such experience is revealed on the basis of the principle of assessment. Ontologically, within the discursive practices of improvement, in making sense of the truth of the world of education, people are positioned to rely almost exclusively on their senses through 'formative' and 'summative' assessments, rather than invited to explore the 'empire of signs' (Trifonas, 2001) that variously mediate our lives in the modern world.

Alternatives to emotivist morality

There is another side to Fullan's ironic aside that there has been little change, in concluding his fourth edition of *The New Meaning of Educational Change*. The continued repetition and reiteration of improvement would appear to be caught up in a largely metaphysical repetition of signs, returning to those familiar narrative structures for change represented as: 'natural', 'struggle', 'transformation', 'uncertainty' and even 're-engineering' (see Chapter 2). These narrative structures project an understanding of what is re-presented as 'change' in the same way.

Morally, within the managerialism of improvement, MacIntyre sees it as a function of such 'emotivist' cultures to interpellate others; 'emotivism entails the obliteration of any genuine distinction between manipulative relations and non-manipulative social relations (1984: 23). In MacIntyre's understanding of emotivism, the 'sole reality of this distinctively moral discourse is the attempt of' the will of the manager 'to align the attitudes, feelings, preference and choices of another with its own' (1984: 24).

Here is an indication of why Fullan's *The Moral Imperative for School Leadership* currently makes no response to MacIntyre and instead talks of the 'combined forces of shared leadership' (2003b: xv). Being constituted within managerialist discourse of improvement it already speaks from the 'realm of means, the realm of fact and the realm of measurable effectiveness' (Fullan, 2003b: 30).

MacIntyre's thesis suggests that the 'character of the managerial role' provides cultures of improvement with their own moral definitions (1984: 31). In fact, these are the focal points for disagreement in both of the aforementioned texts, providing evidence of the very function of the character of the manager. Managers in schools are primarily concerned with technique and effectively helping young people to transform themselves, in accordance with the directives of the principle of assessment, so to raise their achievement levels in examinations. In the structuring of schools and their associated networks, those ends are always the cause of raising the official examination results. Such ends become the 'very means there to be served'; 'they cannot escape service to power' (Reiff, 1975: 22), meaning that emotivism always inserts a question about organizations' capacities to provide a service. Power and the authority derived from it, embedded in the enframing in formal systems of education, can appeal to no other rational criteria for vindication, except that of the principle of assessment, 'which appeals precisely to its own effectiveness' (MacIntyre, 1984: 26). The enframing has emerged as a very successful power within practices of education.

Of course, there is an alternative to emotivism; it is to take up Kant's moral kingdom of ends. From a neo-Kantian perspective, emotivist culture has no morality; in Kant's thesis, a person informed by morality 'treats the other as an end' (MacIntyre, 1984: 23). As MacIntyre notes, 'To treat someone else as an end is to offer them what I take to be good reasons for acting in one way or another, but to leave it to them to evaluate those reasons' (1984: 23). Here lies the moral foundation for democratic education considered earlier.

However, the grounds for emotivist cultures are perhaps far reaching, as reflected in one recommendation by the European Parliament in 2001 for continuous improvement in education. The growing use of quality assurance and evaluation (QAE), inscribed in policy across the European Union, has 'adopted neo-liberal design principles of efficiency and competitiveness' (Ozga and Lingard, 2007; Croxford, 2010: 5). Scotland is one of the few countries in the European Union where there are readily available published findings of studies showing trends in student attainment in relation to social class (Croxford, 2010: 12–17). Social class is viewed as a 'major source of inequality'. Empirically, the evidence of the effects of social class on attainment at ages 16 and 18 points to 'slight' reductions (Croxford, 2010: 3). The architecture of social stratification constituted by schooling identified earlier in this book has itself become a specialist form of practice, a product in the enframing. Nevertheless, the policy of continuous improvement became a statutory requirement of the Scottish Executive in 2004 and is reflected in the current demands placed on managers, according to a recent case study of 'equity and equality' in Scottish schools (Croxford, 2010: 11). It has been noted that policy has placed 'tremendous pressure on schools' (Croxford, 2010: 11). It was found to lead 'managers to behave in ways that raise outcome measures in the short-term, but do little to improve teaching and learning' (Croxford, 2010: 11).

The architecture of social stratification

Indeed, the Centre for Educational Sociology (CES) in Edinburgh has provided an indication of the trends over the past decade in the relationship between social class and levels of attainment in examinations. CES reported that the 'past two decades have witnessed major changes in the context of secondary schooling and substantial increases in attainment. However, social inequalities in the system remain as powerful as ever' (Croxford, 2009: paragraph 7.6). While graphical representations of the changes in the achievements of students in Scotland from 1980 to 2002 show a clear increase in each of the four social classes, the differential achievement of social classes remains. In a House of Commons report it was also noted that in England 'there remained a clear correlation between pupil achievement and social class' (HCESC, 2003: 4). The report quotes Gillborn – who remains wedded to ontologies of improvement, as we saw earlier (see Chapter 6) – for whom 'the best predictor of achievement' remains 'social class' (HCESC, 2003: 19).

It would seem that hierarchical systems of education, in priding themselves on ideals of working towards equality of opportunity, are in fact homologous with systematic social stratification and do not contain within them the potential to enact social equality. In metaphysical terms, both hierarchical organization and social stratification arise out of the questionable ontotheological structuring of the enframing (Thomson, 2000; 2005). The ontology provides the grounds and the theology for the ever rising ceiling of possibilities available to Dasein. As we noted in the last chapter, an error of metaphysical thinking is to suggest that 'something is repeatable to the extent that it *is*' (Thomson, 2005: 123; emphasis added), carrying with it the need for hierarchical forms of organization in order to ensure the apparent rigour and integrity of the iteration, conferring differential stratifications of social status.

Perhaps this should not be any surprise. The enframing has been in the architectural business for sometime. As the line of force in drawing up proposals for that ever present horizon of being in education and in shaping the multiplicity of beings projected as understandings of improvement, it is always metaphorically creating blueprints for the relationship between being and beings, as the basis for improving education. The enframing is there in drawing out the ontological grids of managerialism, in constructing hierarchies of organization, networks for improvement, and in the maintenance and development activities of leaders and managers. The line of force constituted by the principles of reason and of assessment in education is there providing security for people, shaping a balance between capacity-building measures and activities designed to enhance teaching, learning and organizing the standing reserve around an apparently 'solid centre' – those very principles of assessment and of reason – grounding systems of education on what seem to be clear foundations.

What is 'there' in each case is that very same hierarchical and ontotheological structuring of metaphysics as the very grounds for the enframing. The enframing is not something that can be overcome; that would only be more of the same. At issue from a philosophical perspective is how we might come to understand our relationship with being when so much of our language has become branded with ontical structures.

It is the metaphysics of the enframing that holds something is repeatable to the extent that it *is*: objects within discourses of improvement are spoken of as though the truth of what an object *is* will eventually be revealed, given sufficient thought and research. Indeed, in England, objectives purport to constitute the truth of what *is* to be learned in the classroom. Despite efforts to examine and even to counter notions of authority and power in relation to the production and dissemination of knowledge, it is this classical metaphysical enframing in forms of repetition that constitutes grounds for the centralization of power in our increasingly 'pedagogized' societies. Currently, it is simply reiterated in different ways in our everyday world.

Fortunately, there are other possibilities. Derrida suggests that the 'presence of the present' managerialist ideology is derived from the 'repetition' of signs and not the reverse' (1973: 52). Something is – for example, 'the managerialist hegemony of improvement' in the various discourses we have uncovered – takes on the unity of a subject or object to the extent that it is brought forth by repetition: being (or identity) in this reading of improvement is proportionate to repetition. Improvement is always vulnerable and filled with lacunae, always open to reiteration and quite different possibilities. Ironically, however, there is always a danger that overcoming such lacunae, too, can become another driving force for the enframing (Flint, 2011a).

The policy of 'engineering change' in opening academies in England came to fruition in 2000 and is a case in point. It was launched by the education secretary (Friedman, 2010: 2), and was represented as the administration's targeting of 'seriously failing schools' and their attempt to 'break the cycle of underperformance and low expectations'. It has been said that the policy had been 'inspired by the old Labour values of education as emancipation, the ideal of a good school on every door-step' (Friedman, 2010: 4). It was embedded in the former New Labour Government's attempt to engineer social progress through education. The policy has been recently given a new focus with the election of a new Coalition Government. In the political rhetoric, this will turn '150 top schools' into academies almost immediately, and opens the prospect of an apparently ready-made political solution of turning currently 'failing' schools into academies in 2011 (BBC, 2010).

Unconscious drives and desires within improvement

There is now a renewed momentum with the change of government (Friedman, 2010). What has so far elided attention in any of these debates is not the multiplicity of events, of which we are variously conscious. Borrowing a metaphor from Freud, if for one moment we can regard our world as an iceberg, what has so far remained hidden from view has been the great mass of the iceberg, some 90 per cent of it, that remains hidden beneath the surface in our unconscious. Yet, for a number of psychoanalysts following Freud, including Lacan and Zizek, the unconscious is seen to structure our very existence.

From Lacan's (2006) perspective on the unconscious, which some may feel places too much emphasis on something that is largely intangible, what is it that connects and drives the reiteration of aspirations, rhetorics, identities and practices of professionals in the desire to improve the social world through education? In Lacan's readings of Freud, he distinguishes three orders of the unconscious that he likened to language: 'the real', 'the imaginary' and 'the symbolic'. Indeed, Fink (1995: 1–31) has suggested this is language. In identifying the subject as constituted by the symbolic order, Lacan followed Heidegger in argueing that 'language speaks the subject'. So, rather than placing the individual at the centre of debate that has been always the case in managerialist discourse, Lacan's decentring of his analysis suggests a way of examining how the continually shifting symbolic order of improvement discourses affects the subjective experience of individuals. Lacan identifies and capitalizes the symbolic order as 'the Other' that in its totality can never be assimilated into our subjectivity. Lacan distinguishes 'the Other' from 'the other'. For him, the imaginary others have their roots in the 'mirror stage', when the infant sees an other that it thinks will fulfill its desires. Desire in Lacan's way of thinking originates from something lacking in the subject and the 'the Other' (Fink, 1995: 3-70) – as Fink (1995: xi) notes, 'otherness runs the unlikely gamut from the unconscious (Other as language), and the Other as desire (ego ideal) to the Freudian superego (Other as jouissance). Improvement carries with it the presumption of such a lack, both in the subject – including its professional rhetoric, aspirations, practice and identity – and the various symbolic orders of narratives mediating such practices we have seen being constituted as 'the Other'.

Desire, Lacan suggests, 'moves from one signifier to another' in discourses of improvement in its continual attempts to satisfy itself; desire's purpose is insatiably directed towards desire. Unconscious desire becomes manifest through fantasy. For example, one particular fantasy has set the scene for engineering social justice through the building of academies. Indeed, what structures and constitutes such imperatives of desire for Lacan is *jouissance* (Fink, 1995: 98-122; Lacan, 2006). Misleadingly, this is ordinarily translated as 'enjoyment', but in Lacanian discourse it carries the certainty of pleasure in pain and, in the original French, has obvious resonances with sexuality and sexual pleasure. In such light it would seem that the practices of improvement have yet to be subjected to any such psychoanalytical examination.

In fact, what is real in the unconscious, for Lacan, can only become manifest through trauma; it is the unknowable *objet a* – Lacan's unobtainable object of desire – that is implicated in each of his three orders and cannot be absorbed into symbolic reality. 'In Lacanian terms, fantasy defines a subject's impossible relation to the *objet a*' that was always there from the earliest writings of the Ancient Greeks, in Homer's *Odyssey* (2005: 88), for example, always constituted as an excess beyond words. Here, the *objet a*, as the object cause of desire for improvement is a void, a gap, the lack around which such discourses are structured so that such an abyss is completely masked. The unconscious imperative for the principle of assessment as the basis for the enframing in formal education now becomes clear. It is the ever unfailing jouissance that structures our desire and the impossibility of our encounter with the real. Fink puts it as follows:

> 'It insists as an ideal, an idea, a possibility thought permits us to envision. In (Lacan's) terminology, it ex-ists: it persists and makes its claim felt with a certain insistence from the outside, as it were. Outside in the sense that it is not a wish (desire), 'Let's do that again!' but, rather, 'Isn't there something else that you could do, something else that you could try?' (2002: 35)

As a structure for desire, jouissance does not exist; it is sustained through fantasies, including those of our ever improving schools. In England, for example, at the time of writing this book, it can be seen in the building of academies in accord with the fantasy of engineering social justice in the name of improvement. It is through fantasies that we construct our social reality in the improvement of education in answer to the intractability of the real.

Concluding remarks

The orientation of ways of thinking in this chapter has been ontological. The enframing only becomes an issue in discourses and practices of improvement when viewed in such a way. Rather than being constrained by the rationality of ontically structured discourses of improvement, the writing in this chapter is premised on the assumption that being human has its own particular and complex rationalities that are grounded in our ever unfolding temporality.

Although there is rarely any explicit mention of metaphysics within managerialist agendas for change, it is our contention that existing discourses and practices structured by improvement that are in play in so many formal systems of education around the globe are themselves constituted by an ontotheological metaphysics, to which we will return in Chapter 9. As we have seen repeatedly, the ontology of improvement has been, until now, almost exclusively structured by factual forms of discourse and practice. In ontical terms we might suggest that being – that which is – has been reduced to matters of fact. However, in considering the ever unfolding temporality of being, it is apparent that such movement is always in danger of 'setting upon' Dasein, reducing it to calculable individuals that can be optimized within the various economies of education found in the world. Here is the movement of the enframing or its historicity.

In metaphysical terms, the theological aspect of the enframing in improvement is another form of a largely empirically based belief system that continues to extol the virtues of moving people to ever higher levels of attainment measured by officially ratified systems of assessment. Indeed, we have illuminated in moral terms a deep contradiction at work in the metaphysics of improvement. Managerialisms of improvement, which structure various forms of leadership and management in our organizations of education, are simply the outward and more tangible manifestations of the same metaphysics.

In this book, and particularly this chapter, we are concerned that issues of managerialisms are opened to further debate. Is there no place for debate regarding not only on the enframing, but also the many psychoanalytically grounded questions regarding improvement that emerge from the brief foray into the Lacanian ontology of jouissance and desire? Perhaps one challenge of this text is to bring to public attention a number of issues that continue to be debated within specialist discourses of philosophy and the philosophy of education.

Our deconstruction of discourses and practices involving debates concerning the leadership and management of improvement has been undertaken entirely in the spirit of attempting to revitalize debate. We hope that such discussions and their associated practices of improvement will begin to take more account of the rationalities of being human and of the play of *différance* in language (Flint, 2009; 2011b) that always have the capacity to produce significant space for education in different localities.

The Enframing and Lifelong Learning

In opening this chapter we agree with the general tenor of Coffield's (1999) thesis, critically examining 'lifelong learning' as a form of 'social control'. But, we contend that the modus operandi of control mediated by managerialist discourse, while evident in the practice, arises in the enframing. In thinking about what this means in practice, we should keep in mind that for Dasein the temporal movement evident in modalities of control also quite literally vitalizes its everyday world in the workplace. Our experiences in the workplace, each in our own unique 'lifeworlds', reflect different moods and anxieties that are variously expressed in our solicitude and concerns towards others, and are structured within an ontology of care. (Heidegger, 1962; Flint, 2011b). In everyday practice, however, in such a structure we are always in danger of being reduced to mere standing reserve of energy, where our drives and dispositions become available for use in the enframing, in this case variously unfolding in discourses and practices of lifelong learning.

It is our contention that, in the extreme, the enframing in lifelong learning greatly extends the capacity of standing reserves for the global extension of bio-power and discipline in their multiplicity of forms. Again, this is not to suggest that somehow the enframing is consciously enacted by individuals who are possessed by some higher order strategic intent (borrowing from the language of managerialism). In the practice of lifelong learning, the principle of assessment (along with the principle of reason) have come to provide grounds for the rationalization of what counts as learning. These principles are not confined by any arbitrary boundaries constituted by current identities that are instituted within formal state systems of education. This is apparent from the institutionalization and coordination of practices that now extend formal and informal learning outside the academic classroom to an ever growing multiplicity of practices identified with lifelong learning in the workplace.

The focus in this chapter provides an opportunity to explore from a philosophical perspective the complex and ever expanding locus of the enframing in managerialist practices of lifelong learning. Although many discourses are centred upon the individual 'learner', in decentring debate and concerning ourselves with the ways lifelong learning shapes and open possibilities for large populations of individuals so engaged, it is clear also that the locus of the enframing is here in the sense of both the body of the individual and the body as a population of individuals that have been incorporated into these institutions.

In considering various manifestations of lifelong learning affecting specific populations, our approach is necessarily polemical. As a focus for 'confrontation', it is apparent that almost all of the international discourses concerned with lifelong learning have been largely structured around ontic concerns, directed towards gaining understandings of, and characterizing, particular beings, including learning, lifelong learning, knowledge, organizations and sectors of the economy. Although the literature contains suggestions regarding the meaning of being in lifelong learning, it is difficult to find any consideration of the forces at work in unfolding the meaning of being itself. These forces tend to emerge within every noun and verb in our lexicon, colonizing and defining particular forms of professional care.

More concretely, forces in the enframing that emerge in discourses of lifelong learning will be revealed from the colonization of specific domains of professional care within social work, medicine and education. In illuminating a managerial relation between lifelong learning and population, we seek to show how colonization creates a symbiosis in the enframing in discourses of policy, academic-professional discourses and emerging practices.

We also wish to show how the conflation of higher education with government in the development and implementation of lifelong learning practices is a particular form of the enframing in the relationship between education and population. In a similar vein, we uncover the ethic of self-improvement through learning (individualization) as a human technology revealed in discourses of self-improvement, where self-development emerges as the seemingly endless project of the self. In deconstructing the practices of power involved in this technology, we draw on Bernstein's (2000) idea of a pedagogized society and Bauman's (2000) assertion of the uncertainty of self and world within the condition of liquid modernity. In these contexts it will become apparent how lifelong learning may be considered as a means to assuage anxieties at the individual and the collective levels.

In bringing this chapter to a close and returning once more to the emergent theme of governmentality, we examine the significance of lifelong learning in a case study drawn from the Children's Fund. This case study, which addresses problematic identities at the level of the individual, family and community, will illuminate the positioning and repositioning of the self within discourses as a product of technology enacted through a regime of care and improvement. In so doing we will examine key terms, including *partnership*, *prevention* and *participation*, for their role in enabling a subtle and complex technology. The argument will demonstrate how the multi-agency practitioner has emerged as the new invention of this regime of practice. Contrary to the ideologies of education, emphasizing inclusivity as an overarching goal, we show that this new multifaceted professional contributes to the management of social exclusion (or poverty), working within problem communities to effect inclusion (or compliance).

We posit, then, that the enframing manifest as lifelong learning starts at the point when the conception of a neonate first enters the public domain. Our approach deconstructs against indications drawn from Heidegger's (1962) *Being and Time*. Its intent is archaeological, attempting to uncover the historicity of the enframing unfolding in discourses and their associated practices of lifelong learning.

Conception enters the public domain

In understanding how the enframing unfolds in institutions of lifelong learning, perhaps one obvious starting point might be an agreed common conception of the term used. In practice, however, this proves to be unfruitful, although the many different understandings of lifelong learning undoubtedly point to the complexities of this subject (Aspin and Chapman, 2000). In fact, what connects the multiplicity of approaches and ideas concerning lifelong learning are not unifying conceptions, but both the 'principle of assessment' and its parent, 'the principle of reason'. It is interesting that in an otherwise wide-ranging paper on conceptions of lifelong learning, the significance of the latter in terms of the enframing had been completely missed by Aspin and Chapman (2000). At issue here is the historicity of the colonization of practices around the grounding principles of lifelong learning in the enframing.

On the surface, the possibility of learning throughout life that was perhaps first brought into the Western public arena by Plato, may seem far removed from any modern technological enframing – yet another almost perfect disguise. Until now it has certainly been very difficult to find any reference to the enframing in the many discourses and practices of lifelong learning. In terms of government policy, the term *lifelong learning* has been taken, practically speaking, to mean any form of learning by individuals who are over the school-leaving age, currently 16 in England (Teachernet, 2010).

To understand how the enframing in learning throughout life unfolds, it is important to acknowledge from the start that learning is not the sole province of formal systems of education. The reiteration of discourses from the professions of medicine, psychology and sociology prove to be instrumental in the socialization of the individual as a productive agent. From the point at which conception is first identified, Foucault (1977: 306) suggests this process may be seen in terms of the 'mechanisms of normalization' and of 'ordering' that body of future parents and their offspring. But what Foucault also left unsaid had been the enframing that continues to unfold as an essential phenomenon. His writing elicits the historicity of 'normalization' and of the 'ordering' of the body, rather than focusing on the essence of the principle of reason 'upon which' various practices of medicine, psychology, sociology and other related disciplines are grounded.

On more general grounds of 'preventive care' – specifically in the 'prenatal preparation for pregnancy, labour and birth' (Koehn, 2002: 10) – the medical profession provides a basis for the ordering of 'multiplicities of human beings' (Foucault, 1977: 205). For example, in an article presented in *American Family Physician*, Kirkham et al., (2005) speak of the need to offer 'screening' for a number of diseases to 'all pregnant women'. In clinical observation begins the fabrication of each individual as an object and subject in its own space; observation makes visible aspects of the individual who is in turn conscious of its own visibility. Observation of the mother continually accounts for the developing stages of the fetus; medicine has, of course, invested much in prenatal care. The manufacture of the individual, reflected in the individual's medical record, is also a marker of the disciplinary power invested in medicine to make visible observations and recordings.

In fact, as institutions, both the medical record and the categoric practice of medicine itself presuppose that the individual body already risks being deficient in some way. The enframing in the prenatal stage also colonizes many professional discourses and associated practices such as 'blood typing', 'genetic screening', 'nutritional counselling' and education about risks associated with 'smoking', 'use of alcohol' and 'use of other drugs' (Kendall, 2009: 493). In pointing to the historicity of the enframing in these particular contexts, it is also clear that medicine and other related professional activities have served to open many possibilities of care in practice. Care tends to be almost always grounded in specialist research underpinning a range of developments having significant implications for the well-being of the growing fetus and its mother, while at the same time reducing them both to objects and subjects of professional economies.

At birth, it is now common practice to subject the neonate to a number of possible tests, including the APGAR test devised by Virginia Apgar. This simple test evaluates the neonate's appearance, pulse and grimace (reflex) activity, along with muscle tone and respiration, one minute and five minutes after birth. Here is the first official observation of the newborn individual. The assessment provides a ready measure on a numeric scale, with scores from 8–10 signifying good health and those below 5 signalling the need for immediate medical care.

On an international stage, mothers too have become socialized as agents of surveillance; they are strongly advised to generate their own official record of the neonate on what has now emerged as a 'personal child health care record' (PCHR). Here there is a remarkably ambivalent double play in the enframing, concealing once more the logic of the unfolding process: the official fabrication of an individual in the PCHR. In the manifest temporal play of love shown by those caring for a baby, where they all learn to adapt to new ways of 'being-in-the-world', what tends to be concealed is the construction of an individual as a defined object and subject in the form of a PCHR.

A measure of the normalization of the individual in 'parent-held child health care records' (PHCHR), identified as 'passports', is perhaps given by a form of antipodean practice in New South Wales, where a 'non probability sample' of one hundred women were seen to show moderate to high levels of use of and satisfaction with the passport. There, 'maternal and child health providers require pregnant women and parents of young children to keep track of health and medical information about themselves and their children' (Stacy et al., 2008: 138) regarding their growing baby at specified intervals, reducing in frequency with age until the young child reaches 4 years. For example, parents and their professional support agencies can check progress against official charts recording measures as percentiles against age. Measures of progress made by professionals are checked against standard charts recording the expected growth patterns for individuals in the whole range from the 3rd percentile to the 97th percentile of the population. Parents can assess where their own child is situated in relation to the population of individuals at the same age.

Similarly, in England, normal stages of development are characterized by qualitative descriptions of what the baby and young child should be able to do at each stage of the growth. As an example of the unfolding of the enframing, the use of the PHCHR indicates only one official way of revealing the world, authenticated and legitimated by official records on grounds of the principle of reason.

The Early Years Foundation Stage

The emergence of the Early Years Foundation Stage (EYFS) of the national curriculum for children from birth to the age of 5 years is a further illustration of the complexities of the enframing. This was instituted in England in 2008. In practice, the obvious commitment of practitioners to the happiness and well-being of infants and their carers tends to turn attention away from any issues regarding the obvious extension and expansion of governmental apparatus. Elision is further reinforced in the context of post-industrial and post-Fordist economies. With the demands made on flexible forms of working affecting the complex multiplicities of social groupings where the neonate is variously thrown from birth, many parents welcome the possibility of a professionally organized safe, secure and stimulating nursery environment.

The unconscious dissimulation of managerialist discourse in the enframing in EYFS is apparent from the provision made by one leading local authority (LA) – Leicester – in England. In their introduction to 'nursery education' in the district, the LA places emphasis on 'the responsibility for learning and development in babies and young children under 5' – the telos inscribed in the value positing of this one particular will-to-power. They indicate this 'rests with the adults', themselves constituted as the very means. The LA's managerialist discourse, asserting as it does that adults 'provide the experiences, resources and environments for learning' (Marshall and Hoare, 2009: 3), tends to be dissimulated in practice by the many obviously stimulating nursery environments created for babies and young children. On the surface, caring, thought provoking and creative environments that appear to place the individual child at the centre are represented as grounds for the individual needs of babies and young children. Visually, grounds are also reflected in the numerous images presented on nearly every page of the EYFS literature.

Discourses represent the 'foundations' for what amounts to be an order of domination inscribed in state apparatus, a disciplinary structure for the 'normalization' of the preschool individual as a creative and productive, yet docile and submissive agent. England has built on the earlier 'Birth to Three Matters' (DCSF, 2005) framework that was introduced in 2005, following the arrival of the New Labour Government's 'Every Child Matters' agenda.

The 'Birth to Three Matters' schema, developed by a number of leading practitioners in the field, placed much emphasis on the language of 'being' in which the individual is 'thrown': 'being together', 'being with others', 'being acknowledged' and affirmed and finding a voice, 'being social and effective', 'being a communicator'. Here are many officially categorized facets of the productive individual in the officially legitimated discourses, but it would seem that these make no reference at all to the philosophical complexities of how we make sense of being.

There are a number of ways in which we variously make sense of being. How this works can be seen in Heidegger's (1962) discourse, *Being and Time*. Heidegger's text suggests that preliminary understanding of childhood learning is projected upon children's horizon of being: for example, 'in the young child being able to continue to secure relationships'. In Heidegger's terms the identity of particular beings itself presupposes a prior disclosure of being. In practice this obscure claim is perhaps clarified by Haugland's (1998, cited by Rouse, 2005: 175) analogy 'to chess'. For example, a meaningful encounter between a knight and a bishop is pivotally dependent on some understanding of the game of chess. The 'being' of knights and bishops is their place within the game, conferring their 'intelligibility' as the particular beings they are. The 'being' of young children grants their capacity to be understood as the particular beings they are. What has been apparent is that in the violence of professional observation, the many possibilities opened by a horizon of being tend to become reduced to reason connecting subject and object. The precise basis for a reduction is apparent from the early Heidegger's innovation in his interpretation of the meaning of being. His writings suggest that meaning is that which constitutes what is understood in terms of lifelong learning, 'giving it an axis around which it can organize itself' (Heidegger, 1962: 193 {152}). It is possible to distinguish a number of lines of force, or what Heidegger calls the 'upon which', referring to the background that variously shapes and constitutes the primary projection so that it can be conceived in its possibility as that which it is (Heidegger, 1962: 371 {324}).

Tacitly, for practitioners in this field and in the visual imagery of babies and young children in actions in nursery settings, one line of force in the background is constituted by the essential unfolding temporality of Dasein. It is most obvious in the solicitude shown by Dasein, reflecting those future oriented hopes and past concerns based on experience that focus upon what has been happening in the ever unfolding world of the young baby.

It is these and other forms of temporality and associated moods that quite literally vitalize practice, constituting, as we have seen already, the basis of possibilities in the standing reserve in the enframing. On the other hand, in the very same practices, managerialist discourses formally determine what has come to be valued professionally. As the Leicester LA makes clear, 'progress' (the telos – itself, always open to multiplicity of interpretations) depends on the 'quality' of. . . 'provision (means and end) and how it responds to the needs of the child (means)' (Marshall and Hoare, 2009: 3). The enframing in the EYFS is, perhaps, more apparent from the 'statutary framework' (DCSF, 2008: 6). As a 'foundation for future learning through learning' this is 'informed by the use of ongoing observational assessment' on the basis of planning, represented as being 'around the individual needs and interests of the child' (DCSF, 2008: paragraph 1.2).

In its most extreme form, apparent in some nations even before the onset of formal education, the enframing constitutes the very grounds for the production of populations of submissive, self-directed and productive individuals. Moreover, the instrumental means–ends logic as a way of revealing the world of managerialism tends to be completely disguised by a rich multiplicity of human interactions. These interactions variously show solicitude, concern and care, not as mental states but as ways of human comportment to each other. Heidegger's interpretation of 'the world accords a constitutive role to others as somehow determining what possibilities are available' for each individual to pursue (Dreyfus and Wrathall, 2007a: 6).

The standing reserve constituted in the enframing in discourses of managerialism is always open to possibilities, including that of conformity to norms and the possibility of being otherwise. Indeed, analytical to the concept of agency is the possibility of doing otherwise (Giddens, 1976: 75). Moreover, the energy and possibilities in the standing reserve is obviously greatly enhanced through colonization. Again, in borrowing from the language of managerialism, this is not to suggest some form of higher-order strategic intent. The enlargement of standing reserves is a consequence of the unbridled power of the principle of reason, not of any human agency per se. The practice of lifelong learning, now beginning in England from the point at which conception becomes public knowledge, tends to create a symbiosis between government policy, professional discourse and practice.

In practice, symbiosis is a reflection of the ontology of 'care', not as a mental state but as a structure of human dispositions to each other, mediated by specialist discourses of lifelong learning. In the activity of everyday life it manifests itself in the rich multilayered array of human interactions that may often seem far removed from discourses of life-long learning. The very fact that there is no account of the enframing and its associated standing reserve within the literature on 'early years' education arises once more from specialization, itself a measure of the enframing. The same regime in the enframing in lifelong learning is also apparent in moving beyond the official school-leaving age in almost all developed countries around the globe.

Beyond the official school-leaving age

In regimes of truth constituted in specialist discursive practices in the world beyond the official school-leaving age, the foregoing symbiosis is also apparent in a number of institutions, including the sixth form, further education (FE), higher education (HE), work-based learning (WBL), Adult and Community Learning (ACL), community learning and development (CLD), and libraries, archives and information services (LAIS) (LLUK, 2010). Together, as we have seen, these institutions con-stitute what has become the 'learning and skills sector' of the economy. Historically, on a political stage, the imperatives to influence others in efforts to improve the competitiveness of particular nations in the world would appear to be obvious. Against the backdrop of the international oil crisis that began in 1973 and the emergence of neoliberal regimes of practice involving competitive markets aligned to the rapid expan-sion of post-industrial and post-Fordist economies, there were obvious demands made upon governments. These demands were to ensure that education systems – the means – were ever more effective at produc-ing greater numbers of students with higher levels of skills as demanded by the commercial sector – the desired telos (*telos* being always open to contestation). Here is the locus of the standing reserve in the enframing: people with the skills, knowledge and experience society demands.

In practice, of course, with their numbers largely determined by con-tingencies of population demographics on a national scale, education systems alone – even with increased efficiencies – could never meet the almost insatiable demand placed upon them. Indeed, in 1972, Fauer (a former French prime minister) and his associates on an international commission set up by United Nations Educational, Scientific and Cultural Organization (UNESCO) presented a report: 'Learning to be'. The title signified for this group that 'we should no longer assiduously acquire knowledge once and for all, but learn how to build up a continually evolving body of knowledge all through life' (Fauer, 1972: 9): in fact, their concept of 'lifelong education' (Fauer, 1972:.182) had no appeal on the political stage.

Despite the many limitations of human capital theory (Coffield, 1999: 4–10), politicians in the 1980s became wedded to expropriating a crude version of it, from which they made connections with investments in human capital. This particular wedding presupposes energy in the standing reserve specifically directed towards learning and generating skills, craft and expertise – aligned with what politicians saw as the development of sustainable competitive advantage (Coffield, 1999). Bentley describes 'Labour's learning revolution' in typically florid terms:

> It requires a shift in our thinking about the fundamental organizational unit of education, from the school, an institution where learning is organized, defined and contained, to the learner, an intelligent agent with the potential to learn from any and all of her encounters with the world around her. (1999: 42)

In the microphysics of power constituted by this managerialist discourse, itself reflecting the desire of the ego, in gifting the individual body so that it is touched with the potential for learning and agency, its capacity to take action and to engage with activities and their associated discourses can be never fulfilled. Capacity becomes inserted into it as the locus of the very means of developing productivity. This power practice has simply continued to invest the body of the individual with the same imperative for learning and productivity that had started from its birth; its compliance and docility have been already the locus of normalization in the nursery and in formal systems of education. Under these circumstances in England (since the publication of the government's green paper, 'The Learning Age' [DfEE, 1998b]), despite a number of criticisms, it is not surprising that the body of the individual has tacitly become the locus of colonization of academic and other professional discourses. The driver for the colonization of all such discourses is that this body involved in lifelong learning can never entirely fulfill such investments directed towards enhancing its capacity for learning, skills and productivity. As Dasein, unconscious drives are directed towards overcoming a lack (Flint, 2011b).

Here is the impulse for the contemporary 'language games' of many academics and other professional agencies alike. For the moment let us simply mention the continued reiterations of the ancient citizen–city game (Dean, 2010: 93–6), currently reflected in the silent power of being as the enframing. We will return to this point a little later to uncover how this ancient game has been given a distinctly modern twist, arising in the enframing in pedagogic practices in society.

For the moment let us remain with the tenor of ancient games where ontologically, 'care' was seen as the possibility of granting freedom to pursue the play. In *Supporting Lifelong Learning*, for example, Reeve and her colleagues have brought together a collection of papers demonstrating a shift of concern away from 'certain groups of educators' to 'research' that has become a 'focus for debate with those concerned with business, management and organisational studies' (2002: 1). In the first paper of their collection, Barnett speaks of how the 'globalization' of the economy, 'the rise of the audit state' and the 'information technology revolution' have inserted themselves in 'conditions of uncertainty' and 'supercomplexity' in the workplace (2002: 12). Barnett represents 'work' as not just requiring new learning but demanding it at the most 'exacting standards' (2002: 19–20). Similarly, on the basis of two case studies of organizational change in the United Kingdom and south-east Asia, Ashton concludes that learning (the means) is central to the achievement of business objectives (the telos) (2002: 31). He also draws on Eraut's (1997) emerging agenda to point to the range and complexity of learning that takes place at the workplace as capacity-building measures for companies both moving towards 'transforming cultures' and being 'learning organizations' (2002: 25, 28, 31–2).

Although never acknowledged, Ashton's research begins to highlight some of the issues regarding the standing reserve in the enframing. But, it is clear that in the various representations of research in this collection the issue of the enframing and its associated standing reserve remains silent and effectively silenced (Reeve et al., 2002). It would appear that discourses of research focus attention largely upon what the body of the individual is doing, rather than more reflexively on the power of their own language in inserting itself into the body, investing it with the capacity for actions in the first place.

In attempting to meet the demands placed on a body to enhance its capacity for learning – its telos as standing reserve – in the United Kingdom, for example, the 'learning and skills sector' of the economy has colonized a range of national, regional and local organizations focused on an 'improvement strategy' (LSIS, 2009). In these political discourses the ontology of care is directed towards the reproduction of policy and its associated infrastructures. For example, unconscious of the enframing, LLUK indicates that it has a 'key role in supporting employers delivering lifelong learning' (2010: i). The historicity of the unfolding enframing is not, however, driven by any one national system of lifelong learning per se; it reflects cultures of performativity and international pressures on performance at the very highest levels. For example, in the United Kingdom in February 2007, in a foreword to 'Building for Skills', Rammell, former Minister of State for Lifelong Learning Further and Higher Education, indicated that the New Labour Administration was 'fully committed to developing a world leading FE system' (Rammell, 2006:1). In terms of policy in the European Union, this is already reflected in 'the central role of lifelong learning in achieving the goal of the Lisbon Strategy: to make the European Union the world's most competitive and dynamic knowledge economy in the world' (Europe, 2010).

It is also clear that the standing reserve of the enframing in lifelong learning on a global scale is distinctly polarized, although this is not a contradiction in terms of the human care structure. Care in this sense reflects our ontological structure as temporal beings, not any psychological representation of care. The points of view adopted as their 'mantra' in the Leitch *Review of Skills* in fact indicate that 'economically valuable skills' in the value-positing of the 'will-to-power' as yet another modality unfolding in the historicity of the enframing (2006: 2). Value positing has arisen in these managerialist discourses from what might be seen as 'hyperbolic naïveté' of humankind, positing itself as the meaning maker and measure of all things in attempts to overcome nihilism, where value-thinking becomes elevated to a principle. As Heidegger has shown in his reading of Nietzsche, 'value is essentially use-value' and must be 'equated with the condition of the preservation of power' that is itself always conditioned by 'the enhancement of power' (1982: 66–7). One inexorable consequence is that of the 'polarization' of more and less valued standing reserve. What is missed by Coffield and his colleagues (2008: 23) is very close to home in the enframing constituted by the language of values: in its place they gloss globalization as a ready-made culprit from their reading of Castells's neo-Marxist sociological account of the 'Rise of the Network Society' (2010).

Once more we can see what might prove to be a possibly short-lived positive outcome in the enframing: it points towards being as care structuring the possibility of 'authentic' modalities of learning throughout life. Coffield and his colleagues note how protection against polarization is becoming increasingly difficult for 'FE colleges and ACL centres' who 'perceived themselves to have some public duty in respect of those people' represented as 'valuable learners with learning difficulties and disabilities' (Coffield et al., 2008: 23).

In fact, as we uncovered earlier in the modalities of the enframing in preschool experience for young children, a number of studies have illuminated the potential of the standing reserve to be and to do otherwise than is indicated by those ego-centred desires inscribed in managerialist discourse. For example, both a briefing presented by the 'Teaching and Learning Research Programme' and Coffield et al.'s (2008) recent study, have illuminated the central importance to 'learners' of a positive relationship with their tutors against the government policy's focus on the individual 'learner'. Indeed, although Coffield (2008) devotes a complete chapter to the subject of enhancing the relationship between tutor and learner, drawing on the work of Alexander (2006 a, b) to illuminate the significance of dialogue, the language in which his study is structured remains that of managerialism, rooted in the enframing, albeit in what is represented as moves towards a 'democratic model of change' (Coffield, 2008: 11).

Similarly, at the upper end of the official scale of accreditation for learning in the EU, in considering the *Changing Practices of Doctoral Education*, Boud and Lee (2009) draw on the language of managerialism in conceptualizing 'practice' in relation to 'doctoral work'. In making sense of Schatzki's (2001: 283) 'teleo-affective structures', these authors remark that 'people always invest themselves in practice' (Boud and

Lee, 2009: 13). Again their insight points to possibilities in the standing reserve of bodies disciplined in practices that are not identified in the managerialist discourse. Unfortunately, in this case, as in the foregoing studies (Coffield, 2008; Coffield et al., 2008), there is no account taken of the language of the enframing, where actors are always already disposed to each other within particular structures of care.

Disciplined bodies, personal development planning and the self

We have now uncovered a multiplicity of populations of that docile, disciplined and productive individual body that has been inserted with the ego-centred language of managerialism through discourses of lifelong learning. But we have yet to consider the individual self hidden behind the ego. The repetition and reiteration of managerialist discourses and highly competitive practices in the workplace projects understandings of the individual as in some way deficient. The identification 'learner' casts the individual as continually having to develop its skills and knowledge. In fact, in 2008, Marketdata Enterprises, Inc. reported that in the United States alone, technologies of 'self-improvement' had a market value of $11.2 billion (Market, 2010). Similarly, in the United Kingdom, self-development structured through 'personal development planning' (PDP), variations of which in the ideological language of lifelong learning purport to support students and professionals alike in recording and reviewing their achievements, has become a feature of formal education and much professional practice. PDP turns out to be consonant with a number of initiatives around the globe, including the e-portfolio project (AeP) in Australia, the work of the SURF network in the Netherlands and the recently formed Association for Authentic, Experiential and Evidence-Based Learning (AAEEBL) in the United States. At the 2010 AAEEBL conference, Barratt spoke of 'the e-portfolio' as 'the central and common point (of) student experience'. In drawing on the work of Rebbeck, an 'e-learning coordinator at Thanet College', Barratt emphasized that issue is 'a reflection of the student as a person undergoing continuous personal development, not just a store of evidence' (2011: 1).

In the context of global economies, as Edwards and Usher (2007) have suggested, these developments represent one tangible strand in a much broader employability agenda, which is replacing the identity of the enlightened student with that of 'autonomous, self-directed and flexible lifelong learners' (Edwards and Usher, 2007: 55). Barnett (2003), at the Institute of Education, has similarly observed the emergence of new technologies of performance. His observation reflects a shift towards the self-generational capacities of the individual and away from more hierarchically structured rationalities of 'government' that seek 'to shape conduct, working through the desires, aspirations, interests and beliefs of various actors for definite but shifting ends and with a diverse set of relatively unpredictable consequences, effects and outcomes' (Dean, 2010: 18). Self-improvement would appear to be the unfolding of one contemporary manifestation of Foucault's (2008) notion of 'governmentality' in the context of highly competitive, market-driven economies overlaid with standardization. Standardization places much emphasis on performance and performativity in neoliberal forms of government. In Dean's (2010: 63) words, 'Foucault's immense discovery . . . that "what characterises liberal rationality" is the attempt to found the principle of rationalisation of the art of government on the rational behaviour of the governed' (Foucault, 2008: 312). At issue here, therefore, is the historicity of the unfolding rationality of the seemingly endless project of the self as a human technology (Foucault, 1988b).

In stepping back for one moment into Heidegger's (1962) seminal *Being and Time* – dedicated in its original form to his mentor and the father of modern phenomenology, Husserl – it is clear that the human subject – Descartes' stable selfhood identified in the *ego cogito*, the 'thinking "I"' – was displaced by the fluid and temporal understanding of the self. In *Being and Time*, the play of the flux of time is obvious from the self's state of mind, which for Heidegger (1962: 390[340] emphasis as in the original) 'temporalises itself *primarily* as *having been*. Its understanding, however, is grounded primarily in the future' (Heidegger, 390[340]). There is a further complication, because in my ordinary everyday being, according to Heidegger, I am not myself at all. Rather 'I am' for the most part what he calls '*das Man*', 'the one, not this one or that one, not oneself, not some people, and not the sum of them all' (Heidegger, 1962: 164[126]). For the most part, largely unthinkingly, I do as 'one' would do in any situation, and here again we note the ontical structuring of the grammar. 'The "who" is the neuter' (Heidegger,

1962: 164[126]): 'one' that is reiterated in discourses of lifelong learning. The 'one', we have already uncovered, has come to represent both a singular entity and a population.

For the most part for Heidegger, Dasein is continually falling – the 'inauthentic self' manifest as the oneself is just one such possibility. It is, in fact, the precise locus of that passive, docile voice of the productive individual constituted by discourses of lifelong learning – that is, it is the language of '*das Man*' – that speaks what the 'I' purports to say in forms of 'idle talk' that Heidegger characterized ontologically in terms of 'curiosity' and 'ambiguity' (1962: 211–19 {167–75}). Indeed, such ordering of 'man' by language may seem to be in error: after all does not humankind behave as though it were possible to gain mastery over language – as we have seen in all of the chapters in this book representing much of the field of education? In fact, Heidegger challenges all of his readers from the standpoint that 'language remains the master of man' (Heidegger, 2001[1971]: 213).

What may sometimes appear misleading is the lumbering and perhaps ambiguous bifurcation of this foregoing 'inauthentic self' from the 'authentic self' that becomes resolute and takes responsibility for its own being-in-the-world. Dasein's being-in-the-world is the ground for both modalities of the self or indeed the possibility of Dasein being modally undistinguished. Though the play of difference in Heidegger is palpable and is explored in his later work in relation to identity (Heidegger, 2002 [1957]), the locus of his examination falls short of grappling more concretely with the way history unfolds in everyday practices. In appropriating Derrida's reading of Husserl and Heidegger there remains for education the possibility of taking up the challenge of the play of *différance* in professional practices. Certainly, this is suggested in a 'Derridean reading' of Vygotsky, for whom play was a leading activity, but was never fully developed in relation to his notion of the 'zone of proximal development' (Flint, 2009). *Différance* is not a concept or an idea, but is always already at play giving expression to the fluidity of our relationship as Dasein, itself mediated by differences in space and deferrals in time between ourselves as Dasein – here more concretely identified as you the reader – and the continually changing empire of signs in which we live. As the basis for the constitution of the self in life or, more specifically, in the workplace, the play of *différance* is a humbling reminder that language is always open to reiteration; in the play of dissemination of ideas it always opens the possibility of a wealth of readings of any given phenomenon.

Seigel's (2005) historical account of the changing 'idea of the self' is a case in point, providing a reading of many philosophical interpretations of the self from the ancient world through to the present. Indeed, in another pedagogic reiteration in sociology to which we will return shortly, Giddens (2001) speaks of the self as an ongoing project, a continually changing narrative. At the workplace there are, perhaps, almost innumerable versions of such projects; indeed, an ethic of self-improvement or personal development inscribes these projects into the reality of the individual. This ethic may be directed towards particular concrete outcomes: raising levels of 'peak performance', developing 'positive thinking', improving 'personal and business effectiveness', creating and building wealth and so on. So when viewed against the multiplicity of possibilities open to Dasein as illuminated by Heidegger, Derrida, Lacan and Foucault, these take the form of means–ends structured technologies, offering just one way of revealing the world on the basis of 'the principle of reason' (Heidegger, 1991: 5-9; 117–29). Essentially they are examples of the enframing, rendering and ordering the lives of Dasein in accordance with only one way of revealing their world on the basis of the principle of reason. The ethic of self-improvement constitutes Dasein as a technology. In structuring the shaping of particular forms of 'conduct' and given the ethic is self-selected, 'working through the desires, aspirations, interests and beliefs' of the individual for definite but continuously unfolding and 'shifting ends', technologies of self-improvement also constitute the very mentalities of government (Dean, 2010: 18).

But forms of improvement have no defined ends; demands are forever made within the context of other seminal discourses shaping the behaviours of Dasein. What is the source of jouissance? It is easy to think that we have answers to questions concerning what drives the ethics of improvement. What exactly are the precise loci of demands for improvement? There are, of course, no simple answers to these questions.

The individual and the citizen

In response, we should not lose sight of the polemic that has structured this chapter, which indicates a disputatious and combative standpoint (from the ancient Greek *polemikos*, signifying 'war-like' or 'hostile'). But these understandings have already foregrounded the individual speaker rather than language itself. Rather, it seems that in foregrounding the composition of language per se, we should not forget that polemikos connotes a fugue-like polyphony that opens flight in or out of reality without the necessity of harmony or counterpoint, sometimes making demands upon the improvizations or – to continue the musical metaphor – toccata. Certainly, Bauman's sociology invokes some interesting improvizations and eclecticisms in his account of what he calls 'liquid modernity', providing insights into the locus of demands for improvement 'where fulfilment is always in the future' (2000: 28), but again – and perhaps significantly – he foregrounds the individual rather than language.

In drawing out a significant distinction between 'frightened individuals' who are forever confronted, as we have seen, by the various contradictions of systemic thinking revealed in this book and 'a dearth of solutions at their disposal', Bauman underlines the seemingly inexorable corrosion of citizenship in our unfolding liquid modern world (2000: 36, 38). In doing so he draws on the early nineteenth-century French political thinker and historian de Tocqueville, whose *Democracy in America* suggested to Bauman that 'setting people free may make them indifferent' (Bauman, 2000: 36). On this basis, Bauman notes how 'the individual is the citizen's worst enemy', the latter 'being inclined' to seek their 'welfare through the well-being of the city'. For him, 'the individual tends to be lukewarm, skeptical or wary about 'common cause', 'common good', 'good society' or 'just society' (Bauman, 2000: 36).

Moreover, Bauman also sees an 'abysmal' and 'growing gap between' what he calls 'the individual *de jure* and their chances to become an individual *de facto*' (2000: 39), providing a basis for his argument that 'true liberation' in this liquid modern world 'calls for more not less of the public sphere and public power' (2000: 51). But, what is not made explicit is the *polemos* incorporating the languages of both the natural world and of governmentality, the latter increasingly intervening and mediating the shaping of the growing fetus and newborn baby as an identity, as we witnessed earlier. From this perspective both the individual de jure and the individual de facto, in their identities, are always products of language.

In some ways it might be suggested that it is this play of difference in language that is a major source of anxiety for the individual. In the archaeology of this language, in seeking to uncover what lies hidden beneath, one helpful approach is suggested by etymology. Travelling back in time with the etymology of language, it is important to ask, de jure, what provides a basis for any law-like 'gathering together' (from the ancient Greek, *legein*) of language. Perhaps this is missed by Bauman because it takes us back into what he calls 'solid modernity' and his principle interest is with the characterization of 'liquid modernity'. Of specific concern here is the basis upon which 'individualization consists of transforming human identity from a given into a task' (Bauman, 2000: 31) – Giddens' project of the self (1991: 70–108). At issue is the hidden law-like gathering together of language, the 'upon which' that structures transformation (Heidegger, 1962: 371{324}).

Specifically, we are concerned with the task of becoming an individual who has seemingly endless capacity for learning throughout life. Here, taking us back into 'solid modernity', Bernstein's (2000) account of *Pedagogy, Symbolic Control and Identity* proves to be efficacious. He – like Bauman (2000) – does not appear to be conscious of the enframing or of its many implications. In moving into this particular discourse it is important to realize from the start that in Bernstein's language 'pedagogy' is not confined to the classroom or the lecture theatre; as a form of discourse it 'is founded on the principle of recontextualisation' (2000: 33). So, for example, Dasein that has been the focus of Heidegger's (1962) discourse has been numerously recontextualized over the years, not least as that 'invention', the 'individual', brought to our attention by MacIntyre (1984: 61).

For Bernstein, pedagogic discourse concerning the individual is always itself embedded within a regulating discourse (2000: 35). Rather than the play of temporality characteristic of Dasein, the individual is embedded in discourse regulating time, in accordance with chronometers, rather than the unfolding existence of Dasein. In place of pre-theoretical understandings of being-in-the-world in the context of ready-to-hand referential totalities, the individual is theorized as an object of economies of lifelong learning. It is surrounded by, but separated from, various other objects and subjects, providing a focus for the acquisition of skills and knowledge. In fact, rather than Heidegger's characterization of 'being-with' others being recognized as an essential and always already unfolding characteristic of Dasein, the individual in the pedagogic imagination is completely isolated in its relationship to assessment. What is not seen by either Bauman or Bernstein is that this invention, the individual continually unfolding in the enframing, reflects the violence of being set upon by traces of being that paradoxically drive us continually to make good the projections of managerialist discourse that are always of necessity incomplete.

Indeed, it is clear that 'regulating discourses', in designating what is considered to be 'thinkable' and 'unthinkable', have already specialized and separated any possible practices. In this way within the structures of higher education that are currently available, it becomes 'unthinkable' to consider the ontology of Dasein within discourses of formal education, despite the fact that Dasein has some pre-formal understandings of being. In the power practices of higher education, ontology is a matter deemed to be of interest only to specialist philosophers or theologians.

In fact, as forms of 'pedagogic device', discourses of lifelong learning, in beginning almost with the embryo and carrying with them the stamp of 'evaluation' as a measure of their own academic weight, are there solely for the purpose of providing a 'symbolic order of consciousness' for the individual, according to Bernstein (2000: 36). Such is the 'transformation' wrought in the enframing in lifelong learning where Dasein becomes an isolated individual who is alienated and estranged from its very self, being spoken from out of the language of a symbolic order mediating its consciousness. Here is the individual continually forged within the ever unfolding crucible of lifelong learning. Here, Marxist theory of the 'worker being alienated from the object' that is produced 'because it is owned and disposed of by another, the capitalist' is complemented and extended by the tendency of the enframing in constituting Dasein as objects in its economy. In the context of policy regarding 'education for citizenship', is it not both deeply ironic and completely contradictory to the principles enshrined in modern curricula that, in the extreme, Dasein may be constituted as alienated and always incomplete individuals in the enframing?

Moreover, in a pedagogized society, an individual is always rendered as deficient in terms of knowledge and skills because these are themselves both always highly context specific and in competition for the most extensive knowledge and highest forms of skills: the individual is rendered in its performativity as forever deficient in terms of learning. Learning throughout life becomes a way of assuaging the continual individual and collective anxieties constituted by performativity, by which, in this liquid modern world, 'fulfilment is always in the future' (Bauman, 2000: 28).

The Children's Fund

In practice, of course, the hard-edged logic in the enframing tends to be unconsciously dissimulated in Dasein's everyday interactions – interactions mediated in various ways by our pre-theoretical understandings of Dasein. The various projects designed to support the most disadvantaged young people in England through the Children's Fund provides a case in point.

The project involved 149 local authorities and reflected the core concerns of the New Labour Administration, when it first came into office in 1997, in identifying 'social exclusion' (Levitas, 2005), 'the improvement of circumstances and prospects of children and young people' (Williamson, 2005) and issues of 'crime and disorder' (Smith, 2003) as requiring action. The Children's Fund was established in 2001 and ran until 2008 (Broughton, 2005).

Here, the subtle, complex and mostly disguised aspects of the enframing are also apparent from consideration of the significance of lifelong learning for the expansion of governmentality. Like the individual in lifelong learning, communities involved with the Children's Fund were identified as deserving further action to address some of these issues. In response, three core themes emerged:

- 'participation', specifically, 'involvement with children and families'
- 'prevention', that is, what works and why
- 'partnership', focusing particularly on 'cross-sector and multi-agency partnership' involving professional agencies, 'children, young people, their families' and their communities

The very means of achieving the overarching telos of the Children's Fund projects was therefore multilayered and displayed the direct involvement of local groups in developing their own projects, each reflecting their own particular forms of the will-to-power in what had been valued.

What we should not lose sight of is that the agency of the various groups aided by Children's Fund projects did not foreground these themes; they were already part of the governmental strategy employed by the New Labour Administration. Moreover, the obvious rhetorical appeal in the themes had been greatly aided by the form of discourse structuring the various projects that were developed in practice. Each project in its own way had foregrounded the language of care, carrying both its psychological and ontological connotations.

According to a 'national evaluation of the Children's Fund', discourse emphasized the 'key individuals/champions' involved and the 'importance' of them 'listening' to 'young children, young people, parents and carers' (Edwards et al., 2006: ii, iv, 5). Moreover, in the performativity of the discourse, many professionals were invented anew as 'multi-agency' practitioners who would work across different departments and agencies in order to address some of the issues raised in the Children's Fund projects.

The projects directed considerable energy towards building trust in working with these various collectivities. For example, according to Edwards et al., 'a number of project workers emphasized that the level of trust and familiarity that children and young people developed with project workers over time had a positive influence on levels of participation that could be achieved in Children's Fund' (Edwards et al., 2006: 29). There were significant challenges involved. In experiential terms, these young people and their carers generally did not have a history of trusting authority figures (Edwards et al., 2006: 30). Trust and familiarity gained over time were seen as a way of 'embedding good practice and enabling the trust to take forward lessons learnt from the Fund in relation to children and young people's participation' (Edwards et al., 2006: 39).

The projects tended to be grounded in attempts to understand 'the active role that children and young people can play in shaping their environments' (Edwards et al., 2006: 4). According the evaluation, 'some stakeholders did not have a clear understanding of how participation activities would translate into the development of local approaches to tackling social exclusion' (Edwards et al., 2006: 13). Moreover, a number of stakeholders provided indications that they had a limited knowledge and understanding of the issues relating to children and young people's participation prior to the Children's Fund (Edwards et al., 2006: 13).

The levels of commitment that the projects generated is perhaps reflected in the tenor of the observations made by one of the Children's Fund's 'service providers' regarding the issue of understanding:

> I've got a goal in life for this project; it is to get children's participation embedded in all areas that has to be my ultimate goal. But on par with that it is about building the children's knowledge and understanding of their rights, their local communities and how they can affect them, and that means building confidence and self-esteem, which tends to happen along the way to be honest, but I think they are the main things . . . it's very much about providing them with a variety of experiences and opportunities that they just would not have. (Edwards et al., 2006: 18–19)

Indeed, the strong commitment engendered by these projects to engaging young children, young people and their carers is manifest in a number of reports.

The primary school project at Camden provides a good example of the importance of trust and commitment in helping to build partnership through the Children's Fund. The Audit Commission, AC, indicated that it had been 'delivered through a partnership consisting of "Coram Family", local statutory agencies and three schools' (2003: 16). The partnership, in fact, had developed 'methods for identifying early signs of difficulty in children and providing comprehensive support packages' (AC, 2003: 17). It had also provided the basis for the organization of additional activities in schools, designed to 'to improve children's well-being, including their mental and physical health, educational progress and social experiences, and also to strengthen home–school links through activities and services directed at parents' (AC, 2003: 17).

With the focus on children's and young people's well-being and their social experiences, it is easy to forget that these projects are part of the continued expansion of governmental apparatus grounded in the enframing. Certainly, Clarke et al.'s (2007) sociological study *Creating Citizen-Consumers* breaks the spell, but it falls short of considering the forces at work in the enframing. In the Children's Fund projects, those young people were also identified as 'citizens' (Edwards et al., 2006: i), and the report mentions that the children received training in citizenship (Edwards et al., 2006: 3; DfEE, 1999) and were, significantly, 'empowered' (Edwards et al., 2006: 11). Indeed, Clarke et al.'s study also brings their readers' attention to the same language, suggesting that being a citizen might be viewed as 'empowering', 'a means of challenging the paternalistic power of the professions and of ensuring that citizens might benefit from more flexible and responsive public service provision' (2007: 9). In fact, this group also uses the term *citizen–consumer*, but seems to hold back on any full explanation of the phrase.

In the case of the Children's Fund projects we should keep in mind the foregoing identifications with 'citizens' were made by researchers and governmental agencies. The projects formed part of a 'long-term' government 'strategy aimed at strengthening communities and families as places where children and young people can develop as healthy, responsible and engaged citizens' (Edwards et al., 2006: i). The ethic of the 'citizen', imputing an individual and collective concern for others, contains within this identification an aspiration and a force at work in moving collectivities into communities in accord with the legal and moral standpoint of 'children's rights' (Edwards et al., 2006: 15).

The language used by government agencies and researchers signaled not only human concerns for the well-being of people, but also for the people themselves. It provided a powerful vector for their own identities in becoming citizens. In the economy of those governmental projects, the performativity of 'citizen' and of 'citizenship' at once inserted themselves into the body of the objects involved in the projects, constituting them as subjects destined to be consumers of learning and other material products. The hard logic of governmental projects provides the grounds for bringing the body back and giving it direction within the standing reserve in the enframing. In our capitalist society, in the enframing the standing reserve is both the locus of an excess of energy of the body available for use and the locus of desire for consumption that can never be fully satiated.

The ground for capitalism in the enframing is provided by the principle of reason, connecting subjects and objects of our various economies and not primarily the temporality of Dasein. While the planning and participation in the Children's Fund projects was considered to be constituted within an 'inclusive environment', the world constituted in the economy of the enframing was based in this case on principles of participation, prevention and partnership. Counter to policy, but in accord with the principle of reason, it tends also to exclude the very poorest who do not possess the resources or the desires of those caught up in the standing reserve.

We can now see that the ancient city–citizen game, aligned with the educational practices of *paideia* as the seeds for 'aristocratic civism', which for Dean 'inculcated a desire to do good for the city', (2010: 93–5) has now taken a distinctly modern turn. The modern habitus of the citizen, inscribed in the enframing, is no longer a comportment confined to the elite; in the performativity of citizenship played out on the body in the standing reserve it now constitutes grounds for an ethic of consumerism. Unlike the ancient paideia that had been reserved for an elite of potential rulers, in reaching out to the body of society, modern pedagogies both individualize the body in accordance with the principle of assessment and indoctrinate the same body of individuals with a multiplicity of understandings of their own deficiencies as ideal citizens. Ontologically, indoctrination reaches down to Dasein's various understandings of its own being, always grounded in the possibility of 'being-with-others'. Clarke et al's (2007) citizen–consumer is therefore the product of modern pedagogized societies. As a subject, it is also an active agent in the standing reserve constituted in the enframing.

Lifelong learning

In making sense of the historicity of lifelong learning, we can see that MacIntyre's (1984) projection of understanding of ethics and morality in the late modern world in *After Virtue* becomes dominated by the illusion of some shared telos, whereas the foregoing deconstruction has brought to light the work of the will-to-power in its multiplicity of sometimes contradictory and often competing forms.

The very same will-to-power that Nietzsche saw in the clearest terms as the product of the valuing subject, became in Heidegger's (1977c) understanding the pivotal agent in the enframing, where being itself becomes reduced to a 'value'.

In Heidegger's thought, the metaphysical thinking enshrined in Nietzsche's doctrine is truly murderous. Values posited in the will-to-power are always open to being revalued and devalued by the knowing subject. For Heidegger, 'man has risen up into the I-ness of the *ego cogito*' of humanisms that over the past three and a half centuries have always placed human beings at the centre of things (1977b: 107).

In always being deficient as a product of history, being itself – what 'is' – is only ever a trace, a fragment. The modern subject, the individual, the citizen would seem to be forever destined to consume learning in its many different forms and other material forms of goods in order to make good such a lack. The metaphysics of lifelong learning, like any other form of metaphysics has no inherent telos, it is, as we have witnessed, the product of many different projections of the will-to-power in the enframing.

Heidegger's lament over the loss of understanding of our relationship with being, while providing the basis for an education in what is essential to Dasein, is always in danger of passing over the historicity of the subject. In examining historicity, Foucault's archaeologies attempt to make good the limitation, but in so doing take little direct account of being and of the enframing.

In some ways, therefore, what seems more productive for education and for learning throughout life is to return to the implications of Derrida's discourses concerned with our essential home: language. The consequences for education and for lifelong learning of Derrida's understandings of our complex and contingent relationships with language have yet to be thought. The scale of the challenge involved is perhaps given in the next chapter, where the concern is with our relationship with the language – this time, of numbers.

9 The Rhetoric of Numbers

At this chapter's writing, most schools, local authorities and, indeed, the government in England have come to use official quantitative metrics or systems of measurement as a basis for the monitoring and evaluation of student performance in public examinations. Such metrics also serve to evaluate the performance of these institutions themselves. It is the science of logic that grounds measures of professional work. In reflecting from a philosophical perspective on the professional labour involved, one might think there would be numerous issues arising from what at first may be assumed to be a radical disjunction between the unique lifeworlds where Dasein variously makes sense of its reality at the workplace and this science. In practice, no issues appear to have been raised in any of the literature that has critically examined quantitative metrics used in education.

Given the number and scale of operations involving systematic metrics, and given that questions concerning the ontology of Dasein have historically been almost exclusively confined to technical, specialist and – some would say – elitist discourses within philosophy and theology, this is perhaps hardly surprising. Indeed, at the level of the whole population involved, an assumed radical disjunction between the life-worlds of Dasein and the world of quantitative metrics is, perhaps, something of a surprise. That is, in being trained as a professional, one comes to know how to use and apply systems in measuring the quality and effectiveness of one's labours.

Moreover, although very few would argue with the contention that education is concerned primarily with nurturing and leading out Dasein, questions still remain concerning what the pervasive use of metrics means for children and students in being human themselves. Certainly, given the scale and scope of operations involving the media, the use of numeric data has also now become an integral part of young peoples' lives. As one leading teacher of English explained, 'The fact that data has come to be part of young peoples' experiences where numbers are not the language we speak, gives information a primacy and a power far beyond what it otherwise might assume'. In her words, 'Numbers have a mystique and a metaphysical power to them, and teachers have just come to accept them almost unquestioningly: teachers tend to be pragmatic and want to do the best for their students and numbers now take precedence' (Flint and Flint 2011c, in preparation).

In concrete terms and in the spirit of pragmatism, this final chapter opens by considering how things 'are' in education on the basis of a brief examination of the discourses of production and dissemination of quantitative analyses. It will show that the correspondence theory of truth, tending to be the preserve of many in our modern world – almost as though it were a necessity – is at work shaping specialist forms of discourse and practice, obfuscating and eliding any possible disjunctions and dislocations between the logic of numbers and the reality of human existence. It is these regimes of truth, we will show, that structure the discourses and practices of contemporary education.

Within these regimes, it is perhaps no surprise to find that the practical use of numerical data frequently represents itself as a way of engaging with the hard reality of things. This view, some contend, presupposes a direct correspondence between numbers and how things 'are'. In fact, the whole apparatus of statistics in education apparently is there to make good some of the limitations at work in the tacit inductivism of 'everyday' thinking. We posit that numbers get deployed to validate assertions that cannot be identical with the numbers used to clinch their truth.

The chapter takes a historical look at the authority of statistical data and its claims to demonstrate the reality of things in the field of education. It indicates how the internal logic of numerical data appears to offer a stringent account of things, while it is already dislocated from the reality it purports to represent. It indicates how a mathematical logic holds sway within its own circular movement, recognizing also that, outside this movement, the logic has no necessary purchase.

This chapter will analyse examples of statistics in education to disclose how advocates of numerical data seek a purity of knowledge in relation to a Platonic ideal of ghostly truth. The historical privileging of empiricism in the English cultural tradition will be examined as a 'natural' grounding for numerical, statistically validated modalities of knowledge. We consider an alternative view whereby empirical reality is always already compromised by the presence of a regime of truth. According to this view, numerical distractions – that is, statistics – may be a means for avoiding any confrontation with the complex and problematic issue of representation and its relation to being. The point of this discussion and deconstruction against indications drawn from the ontology of *Being and Time* (Heidegger, 1962) is to return us to the question of being in its relation to the field of education: as knowledge, as practice.

Finally, this chapter proposes an alternative way of engaging with the realities of education. In reflecting on the phenomenology of experience in education that has been articulated in the earlier chapters, a different order of knowing is suggested. This order takes into account the complex relations between varieties of key elements. These range from lived experience, governmental discourses and principles relating to the nature of state apparatuses and the objects and economies they seek to manage. Also included are regimes of knowledge, institutional structures and practices, professional education and – not least – possible modes of being and contemporary technologies of the self (Foucault, 1988b).

* * *

Can we ever escape the forces of history?

Gould's controversial and insightful account, *The Mismeasure of Man*, is a book that is sometimes used to inform work with postgraduate students in teaching quantitative research methods. As one reviewer of the book puts it, Gould's text opens a 'sustained' and 'informed attack on a narrowly focused . . . doctrine' of 'intelligence as a single entity', 'located within the brain', and the locus of quantification as one number for each individual' (1996: 24–5). At issue in this chapter is not so much the modus operandi of quantification per se, or the much cited problem of confusing correlation with causation, but rather our complex relationship as Dasein with quantitative metrics.

In this latter regard there is much common ground that continues to be deferred from Plato's discourses, where education was represented in philosophical terms. Indeed, for Gould, 'the spirit of Plato dies hard' (1996: 269). He claims:

> We have been unable to escape the philosophical tradition that what we can see and measure in the world is merely the superficial and imperfect representation of an underlying reality. Much of the fascination of statistics lies in our gut feeling – never trust a gut feeling – that abstract measures summarising large tables of data must express something more real and fundamental than the data themselves. (Gould, 1996: 269)

In the spirit of never trusting a gut feeling, this chapter further reflects on the question of whether the multiplicity of languages in the many specialist institutions where formal education is now being developed have ever escaped from what Derrida (1981: 120–71) understood as 'Plato's pharmacy' continuing to structure much of our modern language. The modus operandi of 'Plato's pharmacy' is based on a presupposition that there is a hidden reality behind our imperfect representations, so that the pharmacy may be understood as one particular dominant source for the on-going reproduction, repetition and reiteration of signs in the disseminative drift mediating and shaping much Western discourse. At issue are both the form and the development of the content of the metric systems now used in the name of education.

Metric systems used in the name of education

Certainly, any reference to Plato in discourses concerning the development of quantitative metrics is notable for its absence. On the surface, the forces at work that have prompted the now widespread utilization and application of quantitative metrics in educational systems have arisen largely from a requirement for more information by teachers. Teachers apparently needed this information back in the 1980s in order to raise the performance of sixth-form students in preparation for the competition they faced in gaining entry to higher education institutions. One of the first metric systems used in England that anticipated an apparent need and is now used by many secondary schools there and abroad was first developed at the University of Durham through the pioneering work of Fitz-Gibbon and her colleagues. This system will be used as an initial example.

In 1983, it grew from a project involving twelve schools in the northeast of England, focusing on developing the A Level Information System (ALIS) to what is now the major international Centre for Evaluation and Monitoring (CEM, 2010). Based at Durham University, the CEM now administers more than ten systematic metrics for schools through a number of complementary information systems. It is clear that from the original project there was a momentum to develop CEM: other monitoring systems soon followed, for example, 'YELLIS' – the Year 11 monitoring system – and 'MidYIS' – the 'middle years' information system.

Not surprisingly, over the years the development of these systems has reflected changes in both policy and the structures of examinations. In response to transformations in policy to a continuous system of formal education from the age of 4–16+ and the ever changing market for qualifications, following the introduction of the national curriculum, the CEM has continued to develop a number of additional monitoring systems for use in both primary and secondary education. Similarly, innovations and changes in examination systems in England are reflected in a number of refinements to the various monitoring systems being developed at the CEM. For example, the information and analysis made possible within the ALIS system now incorporates consideration of A-level examinations together with other post-16 qualifications, including the AS, advanced GNVQ[1], BTEC[2], AVCE[3], IB[4] Diploma and the YELLIS system. The latter now makes connections with both the GCSE[5] and the iGCSE[6]. The CEM now works with more than 9000 schools (CEM, 2010), including more than 1000 schools in 48 countries outside the United Kingdom (CEMInt, 2010) on grounds of systems providing baseline assessments of students' abilities that are claimed to be 'independent of any curriculum content'.

Indeed, in the marketplace of qualifications, developments have not been confined to CEM. At the post-16 level, the Advanced Level Performance System (ALPS, 2010) now enjoys a significant share of the post-16 market. In 2009, according to the ALPS website, 'over 1100 schools and colleges in over 80 Local Authorities received ALPS analyses'. In the same year, ALPS also claims to have 'provided top quality regional training attended by over 3000 senior teaching professionals'. In positioning itself in the market, ALPS foregrounds the fact that it is recognized by 'national bodies, including the Department for Education, DfE, the Office for Standards in Education (OfSTED) local authorities and the Sixth Form Colleges Forum as a leading value-added analysis and training system' that can be used by schools and colleges (ALPS, 2010).

The Fisher Family Trust (FFT, 2010), has now become a key provider of so called contextual value-added scores to schools throughout the country. It claims that a 'key focus' for this 'data analysis project' is the organization and administration of the 'more effective use of Performance Data' as a way of helping local authorities, schools and colleges throughout England and Wales (FFT, 2010).

Most secondary schools in England also use 'cognitive ability tests' administered by GL Assessment (2010) that have grown out of the work of the National Foundation for Educational Research (NFER). The

---

1   General National Vocational Qualification

2   British Technology and Education Council

3   Advanced Vocational Certificate of Education

4   International Baccalaureate

5   General Certificate of Secondary Education

6   International General Certificate of Secondary Education

latter has been part of the Granada Learning Group for the last decade. CAT[7] scores are presented as providing 'powerful' evidence that can be used in conjunction with teacher's assessments. CAT scores can then create the grounds for 'empty optimization imperatives' (Thomson, 2000: 306), for example, where such 'tools' are purported to 'unlock their pupils' learning potential' (UK Technology, 2010). 'Typically, CAT scores are now used as a 'baseline assessment' for young people in their first year of secondary education (year 7) alongside national data obtained from testing children at the end of Key Stage 2 of the national curriculum in their final year of primary education (year 6), currently under review. Given that the foregoing forms of testing are further complemented by government-instituted national curriculum assessments at the end of Key Stage 1 (6 years of age), it is hardly surprising that the groundswell of testing in England has attracted its critics. In fact, the former tests for all children at the end of Key Stage 3 of the national curriculum have now been replaced by the measurement of levels based upon teacher assessments (Directgov, 2010).

Assessment of Pupil Progress (APP, 2010) has emerged in England as a national system of teacher assessment of the progress made by students throughout Key Stage 3 (11–14 years of age), benchmarked against national standards. APP has been developed by the Qualifications and Curriculum Development Authority in partnership with the 'National Strategies' for improvement, opening professional development programmes for practitioners and managers (NatStrat, 2010). At the time of writing there was an expectation that all schools would have 'embedded' the APP approach to teacher assessment by 2011.

Interestingly, without any reference whatsoever to the metaphysics involved or indeed to any issues concerning the enframing, the Department for Education in England now administers the APP system, and there is an expectation within the organization of schooling that students will be required to raise their levels of performance. We will return to the issue of the metaphysics of these systems much later in this chapter.

At this point, in anticipation of a critical examination of these various systems of data analysis, we will also consider the 'Reporting and

---

7 Cognitive Ability Test

Analysis for Improvement through School Self Evaluation' or RAISEon-line system (OfSTEDRo-1, 2010c), connecting models of value added with the contexts of improving schools within particular communities. What follows is a brief explanation of the value-added scores and a more detailed exploration and deconstruction of quantitative metrics against indications drawn from Heidegger's (1962) *Being and Time*.

Analysis of the progress made by young children and students or the 'value added' by the system of education in place is based on measures of what is actually achieved in preliminary so-called baseline tests, usually taken up to two years prior to completion of a qualification, in comparison to statistically grounded projections of what they might have been expected to achieve in their final examinations. Measures of the expectation are obtained from mathematical models, based on the average level of student attainment, which is used to predict the likely level of attainment of students in a future examination. For example, the baseline assessment for ALIS is provided by GCSE results, the baseline for the YELLIS system is grounded in tests administered in year 10 and the mid-YIS system is founded on tests taken in year 7. The so-called value added measures the difference between the actual score of the student in a final examination and those predicted for the average from baseline tests: a 'positive' value-added score or 'residual' indicating that a student scores above the line on a graph predicted for the average and a negative residual indicating a performance at a level below the line.

It is our contention that, in the production of value-added scores for students, two interrelated events are concealed, with profound implications for the way the enframing unfolds over time in formal systems of education; the disguise constituted by the enframing is once again almost perfect. But, on reflection, is it possible to think about our relationship with the enframing in other ways?

Exploring other ways of thinking

At this stage it is important to recognize that we have been drawn already into a regime premised on an assumption of a correspondence theory of truth used by quantitative metrics. In other words, what is in our heads somehow corresponds directly to our sense of what is happening before our eyes. In schematic terms in the grammar of correspondence, any questions concerning the relationship between numeric data and the reality they purport to represent – indeed the very nature of truth itself – would always threaten these truths and so are in effect blocked by being moved away to other specialist discourses of philosophy dealing more directly with the truth of these questions. The repetition of discourses concerning the quantitative analysis of formal education therefore safeguards itself in a regime maintaining the integrity of truth as correspondence; of necessity, any questions otherwise threatening its veracity are precluded. In a number of leading books concerning how to do quantitative research, any reference to the nature of truth or questions concerning the issue of presenting again in numerical form prove impossible to find.

Clearly, the metrics and the ensuing quantitative analyses arise on the basis of students taking examinations. Let us imagine a student for the moment completely separated and removed from the obvious presence of an examination. At issue are any differences between statements made by an individual student in everyday conversation with their friends and the very same statements made in response to an examination question.

Looking at this individual student scenario, Heidegger does not generally use the terms *human being* or *individual*; rather, in his primary concern with the question of being, he uses Dasein to connote both an 'entity who has this particular being' and 'the being of humans' (Heidegger, 1962: 7, 58 {26–7; 84–5}). *Dasein* does not have a single English word equivalent, and so by convention, as we have seen already, it is not translated.

From a Heideggerian perspective, let us rejoin an individual student in conversation with friends, who, to borrow from Wittgenstein (2001{1953}), are located in one particular form of 'language game'. For Dasein, Heidegger would express this in terms being-with-someone-in-the-world. For the moment, let us imagine that Dasein is in a meditative mood. Any statements to a friend make sense in terms of Dasein's mood in a given situation. Mood here is not some additional subjective inner state that somehow mediates and possibly blocks action, but rather for Heidegger it 'is a way of being-in-the-world which itself discloses being-in-the-world' (Heidegger, 1962: 176{136}; Gorner, 2007: 74).

A whole range of meanings are possible for Dasein. As a temporal being Dasein is structured in the way it cares for things in its world, including this statement, in the movement of its unfolding relationship with its future and its past, which enables Dasein to make sense of these statements in the present. In this care structure, Dasein is for the most part open to falling and assuming the non-identity of an anonymous public group, 'they'. In these circumstances, what is signified by the original statements would be very different to points where Dasein is authentically being itself and fully understanding its own being. In short, for Dasein there are many possibilities that directly affect the interpretation and sense of any statements made. For Dasein, these possibilities make some sense in relation to these present statements; sense-making is pragmatic, almost without thinking in the ever unfolding play of temporality. It is play that structures the care shown by Dasein in regard to the particular statements made in conversation with a friend.

Let us now re-run the reflection, but this time with Dasein in a distinctly different 'language game', having fallen into being an individual who is in an examination and now makes identical statements to those made earlier, but this time in response to an examination question. The individual is now separated completely from everyone, unable to speak and numerically coded in accordance with procedures. As an anonymous individual, Dasein has been temporarily rendered unable to be authentic, therefore already reducing the possibilities open to the individual in making sense of the same statement. We should note here that the movement of temporality has not been extinguished; it has been simply redirected and reshaped. Moreover, the statement itself is now evaluated by Dasein and by others marking the examination against assessment criteria and therefore re-coded into a numerical or alphabetical mark connoting a ranking of performance. The possibilities of interpretation regarding the statement are now entirely circumscribed by the assessment criteria used. The statement and others made in the examination constitute the basis for an assessment of the performance of the numbered individual against the criteria used for purposes of assessment. In the economy of the examination, the assessed performance is coded in a way that it can be readily compared and analysed in relation to other separated numbered individuals.

We believe it is the meaning of being that shapes projections of understandings within each of the foregoing 'language games', without which there could be no language at all (Heidegger, 2000: 86). Differences

OMR sheet showing anonymous number of individual

between the mathematical and the demotic, in tending to remain concealed from view, in fact arise from the meaning of being. In order to make sense of the disjunction we perhaps need recourse to a short exegesis on the meaning of being. In Heidegger's register, this has a technical significance that is sometimes missed in readings of *Being and Time*.

In this pivotal work Heidegger draws out a so-called ontological difference between particular beings and being. In distinguishing the two terms, we can see that a particular being unfolds in its possibilities, so that conventionally and predictably the particular being on which I am now sitting is known as a chair, but as a particular being its various possibilities may include being a missile; an object on which to climb, lay down or sleep; a work of art; a place for hiding and so on. Moreover, in projecting possibilities of understanding there have been a number of references to 'being'. Being ordinarily connotes the presence of something, including, in this case, the chair. As Heidegger (2000) points out, our sense of the presence of something always works within a definite horizon where understanding is fulfilled. Within the horizon of being

All of the student names and numbers, the centre name and number, along with the name of the moderator are entirely fictional and are used to protect the anonymity of the individuals and the school involved.

(2000: 96) situating my own experience, ordinarily I do not even consider the possibility of my chair spontaneously igniting or dissolving in water, for example. In the generality of things, it is the horizon of my experience that tends to circumscribe and delimit what in every particular case, 'I' project as possibilities of understanding for a particular being.

On reflection, although on grounds of the 'principle of reason', the science of logic holds sway within its own circular movement between projections of particular understandings of objects and the horizon of the whole system, in this particular language game involving beings and being, the regime of quantitative metrics has no purchase whatsoever. (For the moment let us leave any questions concerning the mythology of circularity until later in this chapter.) Any understandings of truth as correspondence in each of the two contrasting language games are completely irreconcilable. Herein lies the basis for specialization. Both, however, are constituted on the basis of the meaning of being: in this technological age it is being that in remaining 'veiled and disguised' sets upon and orders the world of beings, in this case against the background structure of truth represented as correspondence (Heidegger, 1977b: 37). But, what does being mean?

Indeed, the small print of *Being and Time* makes a tripartite distinction wherein meaning is that constituting 'what is projected in understanding', in this case 'giving it an axis around which it can organize itself'. For Dasein, Heidegger (1962: 401{350}) showed formally that the meaning of being, so conceived, is temporality, that continual interplay of future and past that constitutes the present in the first place. 'Meaning signifies the "upon which" of a primary projection of understanding in terms of which an issue', in this case unfolding in the everyday world of Dasein, 'can be conceived in its possibility as that which it is' (Heidegger, 1962: 370–1{324}) . In other words, in the world of human beings completely unencumbered by examinations, the 'upon which' or that principle always already organizing all primary projections of understandings of beings in our language is temporality. In *Being and Time* temporality is uncovered in terms of a 'care structure', always already working, as we have seen, in our dealings with everything in our world (Flint, 2010a, b).

However, there is a complication arising from the language of the numeric quantification and the analysis of the results of examinations. In his more mature work, Heidegger shows that rather than 'temporality' in much of our dealings in this late modern world it is the 'principle of reason' that constitutes the 'upon which' that gives shape to projections of under-standings. In England, for example, we might say, in everyday discourse, 'I think that bird up in the sky over there is a red kite – I know they're quite rare round here. The reason I'm sure it is one, is because it has a distinct V in its tail and it has a very large wing span.' Often, we tend to project under-standings of what something is on grounds of the principle of reason; that is, the 'upon which' that shapes and orders our projections of understand-ings is that very principle. It is, as we have seen, the principle of reason that provides the grounds for the sciences of logic and statistics 'upon which' any quantification and its associated analyses are based. It is this principle that for Heidegger (1996) provides one prevailing modus operandi of the enframing. Rather than the free play of temporality, in the unfolding of an examination (and indeed a survey for research, for example) it is techno-logical enframing that is always already at work as the mode of revealing where things show up as resources that are optimally 'available for use'.

As we have seen already in formal systems of education the principle of assessment has come to dominate forms of educational organization. What counts as formal education is always determined on the basis of assessment; the principle of assessment is that 'upon which' that shapes and orders projections of understandings in the world of formal educa-tion in the enframing.

Reflecting back to being-with-others-in-the-world of Dasein, in the enframing, all of the possibilities explored earlier are rendered simply as sources of energy that are available for use in an economic system. Moreover, as we have witnessed repeatedly in this book, the individual is now simply rendered as an anonymous entity; the enframing consti-tutes the basis for Dasein's alienation. Also, the conditions put in place on the basis of the principle of assessment mean that rather than Dasein 'being-with', concretely it has been reduced to an isolated individual. Is it not ironic that regimes of testing identified earlier in the English sys-tem, developed in the name of education and highlighted in this book, simply provide the basis for alienating, ranking and separating indi-viduals from each other? In practice, they tend to be confounded by Dasein's care structure in 'being-with-others', unconsciously always already at work in the formal training of teachers (Flint, 2010a, b).

In considering the numbers coded on the basis of a quantitative assessment of an examination of the type considered above, there is always the risk that we utilize inductive logic in order to claim far more than is deserved for any patterns that may arise. Tacit inductivism in professional discussion arises when its premises probably support a conclusion. On the basis of the generally insufficiently questioned assumption that the premises are true, it is unlikely that the conclusion would be false. In these circumstances professionals often use statistics simply to provide measures of the probability that an outcome will be achieved. But, as a science of necessity it remains absolutely silent regarding 'the enframing'; necessity is here a condition of its integrity as a science.

Furthermore, once the transformation has arisen, and statements have been re-coded in a numeric system, the numbers used to code the original statements are re-presentations of the original. They are coded statements made on the basis of being-in-the-the world of Dasein; being structured by the temporality of care opens space for the unfolding possibilities of beings. The numbers used to clinch their truth, however, within a formal mathematical analysis, are structured by the principle of reason providing the grounds for a formal analytical process connecting subject with object. We therefore have a position where the numbers deployed to validate assertions can never be identical with the numbers used to clinch their truth, because the contexts for both operations are so radically different. The array of numbers disseminated in nearly all classrooms and schools in England have a power of their own, derived not from being grounded in the world of Dasein; they are simply rhetorical devices that are completely dislocated from being-in-the-world of Dasein. Currently, for example, at A-level the use of a Unified Mark Scale (UMS) could be seen as a case in point. The UMS is simply a scale providing the basis for a cohesive conversion of 'raw scores' from A-level (including applied A-level) and GCSE examinations (Store, 2010); they remain objects that Dasein is aware of in being-in-the-world. In Heidegger's (1962) terms they are simply present-at-hand objects that are known to exist but are not necessarily part of Dasein's world.

However, in the rhetorical practices of formal education, the principle of assessment says little about how the enframing unfolds and provides limited understanding of the underlying driving force for the enframing. The principle of assessment remains steadfastly silent in response to questions about how it has it come to dominate formal systems of education, that is, it has little to say about the drives the sustain the enframing and yet remain relatively unspoken in everyday practices, being having been confined until now only to specialist discourses of philosophy, educational philosophy and theology.

What is going on behind the rhetoric of numbers?

In returning to the issue of value-added scores, in direct relation to the enframing there was mention of a second process unfolding. We have already encountered a circular interrelationship between knowledge and truth in the earlier chapters (as Derrida reminded us earlier in this book, circles are always incomplete, always broken). That is, the endless search for truth, in being directed towards the production of new forms of knowledge on the basis of looking back at knowledge that has been already acquired within a specific field, is always caught up in a circle – Foucault's 'regime of truth' (2000: 132). Our desire for the morphology of a circle is almost insatiable, it would seem. It is there in our capacity to be able to search for truth imputing a modality of power that in Nietzsche's (1973) 'eternal return of the same' is uncovered as the 'will-to-power'. In Heidegger's (1977c) reductive but insightful reading of Nietzsche, however, it becomes the 'will-to-will'[8], seeking only its own 'empowering to power' through the endless acquisition of knowledge, for example. Here is the pivotal driving force for the enframing in the late modern world: the 'will-to-will', endlessly glossed in terms of improvement. Its significance for the issue of the rhetoric of numbers in education cannot be underestimated.

It is important to keep in mind that in Heidegger's reading of Nietzsche, the 'will' is the 'sphere of representation', that is, the sphere of projected understandings of beings and indeed 'the name of the being of beings as a whole' (Heidegger, 1968: 93, 95). In this sphere of representation there

---

8 The translator, William Lovitt, notes that in the German language, the second word, *Willen* (will) is a noun and the first a verb, *Wille* (will), in *Wille zum Willen* (Heidegger, 1978b: 78), which is impossible to show in the English translation of 'will-to-will'.

is also to be found a circular relationship between the acquisition of knowledge re-presented in terms of a numeric level and the search for truth because, formatively in looking back, knowing what has been achieved as a numeric grade can often prompt the search for whether a new higher grade can be achieved. This cyclical process may be repeated, and – like all circles – it does not have an end. The individual is caught up in an endless 'becoming' by a latent desire to overcome the impossible (Flint, 2010c: 10). Here, we speak advisedly of 'the individual' without any reference to human beings. In being rendered as an object and subject, the will as the sphere of representation constitutes its own locus of truth. The assessment of knowledge in terms of numeric grades simply adds to the truth of what is calculable in advance as objects.

It is important also to be mindful that the truth of what is calculable is not identical with the unfolding truth of an event before any re-coding in numeric form. The enframing, which shapes the projections of what is calculable, has yet to find a voice in the name of education. As such, in the context of formal systems of education, the enframing has tended to remain the sole province of specialized forms of educational philosophy (Blake et al., 2003).

However, significantly, in the enframing, the desire for truth as correctness aligned with the drive to overcome what is impossible are behind what Heidegger sees as the 'limitless quantification', absorbing all qualitative relations – until we come to treat quality as quantity. At issue in the enframing, expressed in the will-to-will of improvement, is the ontotheologically structured drive to order the world in accord with the principles of assessment and of reason. And, although the logics of quantification and of statistics have their own purity, providing, as they do, grounds for the projection of understanding exact possibilities, they can never overcome the many hidden lacunae in the reality of practice from which they are derived. The finality of quantitative measures and their associated statistical probabilities, however, tends to reinforce their status as exact, so that the moves towards quantification in the enframing are implicitly driven by attempts to reveal Plato's hidden reality behind the imperfect everyday world. For Heidegger (1977b), as one of the outcomes of the enframing, 'Bestand', standing reserve' (Heidegger, 1977b: 17), the beings unfolding in the everyday world of practice, are optimally ordered in a 'dangerous spiral of overcoming' (Thomson, 2000: 306).

In the coded space of the language of quantification there has been, until this point in time, no space at all to voice 'enframing' in the name of education. The reason is simple. In building a huge multi-lane motorway-like infrastructure of quantitative metrics grounding formal systems of education, it is not that anyone has lost sight of opening questions about the significant limitations of a correspondence theory of truth. Questions are simply pushed away with the sometimes disparaging view that they are matters for philosophers. In the hubris of the so-called real world of education, however, we all remain caught up in juridical structures of language: the law of a correspondence theory of truth inscribed in the discourses of metric systems. In fact, in the 'real world', all laws can be changed.

The significance of quantification within fields of formal education goes far beyond the pragmatism of readily available systems used to 'monitor the progress of students'. It goes far beyond earlier debates about the conflation of discourses of improvement with those of school effectiveness. It serves to level down 'what counts as being' to only that which is calculable in advance (Thomson, 2005: 149). The logic of enframing tends to reduce all entities to bivalent programmable information, digitized data, increasingly entering into a 'state of pure circulation' – 'as Baudrillard aptly expresses our paradoxical, endless destination' (Thomson, 2005: 149).

In our everyday world of formal education, the hard logic of this position and its consequences tend to be glossed over; news agencies now annually report seemingly endless tables of improving results and comparisons, that continue to sell the mythology of improvement as an rigorous empirically grounded science of practice. Culturally, human interest stories in the popular press have tended to open apparently endless debates about whether examination results mean that 'standards' of education are rising, and – in what is considered to be more serious coverage – there tend to be tacit assumptions that improvement as an exact science will arrive at the truth of the matter. Given enough time and research, the tacit assumption behind quantification and 'evidence based practice' is that the science of improvement will generate the truth –Plato's 'hidden reality' – regarding what is needed to produce the very highest quality system of education. It is our belief that this position is fundamentally flawed.

In fact, in *Being and Time*, Heidegger (1962: 149{113}) shows that for the most part in our everyday world our thoughts and actions tend to assume the standpoint of what 'one' does or what 'one' says or thinks in these situations. We agree that much newspaper coverage and, indeed, discourses of 'lifelong learning', speak directly to the anonymous standpoint of 'one' (Flint, 2010a). In speaking to the public, discourses tend towards a 'levelling down' of understandings in accordance with what is assumed may interest that anonymous entity, 'one'. What tends to remain lost in the fields of formal education is the extent to which the locus of truth in the enframing resides with the calculus of logic and the principle of reason (Heidegger 1996). These circumscribe and delimit the morphology of the space for one's being-in-the-world. The rich play of differences in the lifeworld of Dasein (Flint, 2011d) can so easily be reduced to that of the body – both individual and collective – and its various examination results. In its reduced form as a body, being-in-the-world of Dasein is now easily rendered as digitized information that can circulate in the economies of formal education systems around the globe and, indeed, in the economies of individual nations and their larger economic trading blocks, including Europe, Asia, America and so on. Moreover, in relation to the pure circulation of digitized data, the temporality of Dasein – forever driven by desires, solicitude, concerns, cares, thoughts and so on, as we have witnessed already in many different circumstances in this book, is rendered as a 'raw material' and a store of energy that is 'available for use' (Thomson, 2000: 306).

Until now the response from the academic community to issues regarding the adequacy of quantitative evidence obtained from schools, colleges and larger educational organizations has involved the refinement and development of quantitative analyses. It is, however, most significant, that the dissemination of outcomes to practitioners and organisations within formal systems of education has been met with an all-pervading silence regarding the issue of the enframing. Historically, outside specialist philosophical discourse, professionals are unlikely to have engaged with questions concerning the language and ontology of the enframing.

From a Heideggarian position, it is ironic that in cultural terms the very professionality of this particular community is constituted on grounds of what it sees as its critical engagement with the development of quantitative analyses used in formal systems of education, without any explicit consideration of the possibilities continually unfolding in Dasein's relationship with being.

Other forces of history at work in the English tradition

In contrast, this irony is unlikely ever to arise in the English tradition; quantitative analysis and the underlying science of logic is simply seen as a natural conflation of what empiricists in the twentieth century have regarded as 'necessary truths found(ed) in logic and mathematics and empirical truths, found elsewhere' (Hamlyn, 1967: 503). Here is the locus of the constitution of truth as correspondence found in metric systems used to evaluate education. In the English tradition the latter doctrine of empirical truths has its roots in the litany of the early modern philosophies of Bacon, Newton, Locke, Berkeley and Hume.

In an often wry characterization of *Englishness and the National Culture*, Easthope argues the case for an 'unacknowledged' continuity between seventeenth-century ideas concerning human nature and a 'cluster of assumptions' inscribed in modern English culture: 'reality is just there – look, I'm going to kick it; forget theory, all that matters is concrete judgements and particular analysis' (1999: 88). In deconstructing empiricism, Easthope draws on *Of Grammatology*, where Derrida challenges his readers with the incisive critical question: 'how can there be arguments for empiricism, and these arguments produced in the form of language'? (1976: 152). Despite the questioning that deserves to crush the very heart of empiricism, in the obituaries section of the Gaurdian newspaper Belsey has argued that for Easthope, the movement of empiricism 'has fended off every major intellectual development of the 20th century' (1999). It is the intractability regarding empiricism as the grounds for ever more powerful systems of quantitative evaluations used in the name of education that is our concern here.

The roots of empiricism go back to Bacon's method, identified in his 'Great Instauration', of amassing 'data', interpreting it 'judiciously, conduct(ing) experiments, and therefore learning the secrets of nature by planned and organized observation of its regularities'. In his now famous prefatorial remarks, published in 1620, five years after his death, Bacon reflected 'that the state of knowledge is not prosperous nor greatly advancing, and that a way must be opened for the human understanding entirely different from any hitherto known' (Bacon, 1996 [1854]). Bacon's method connoted nothing less than the reparative actions required in 'restoring man's lost mastery over nature' (Cranston, 1967: 237). It opened the door for the advancement of empiricism, the doctrine that holds that it is sensory experience rather than either reason or being human (what Heidegger saw as our relationship with beings) that is a source of knowledge.

Hamlyn detects the foundations of empiricism in the works of Epicurus and Aristotle in the ancient Greek world, and in the medieval philosophy of Aquinas, but suggests that it was Locke who 'set the tone for his successors' in the emerging world of modernity (Hamlyn, 1967: 499–501). Locke's book, *An Essay Concerning Human Understanding* opened what might be called a new way of ideas as 'remedies' for the 'imperfections' of 'words' (Locke, 1999 {1690}: 499), offered a biting critique of the rationalism advocated by Descartes and provided grounds for an assessment of the certainty of what he had distinguished as three types of knowledge – 'intuitive, demonstrative and sensitive' (Locke, 1999 {1690}: 520ff).

Locke's experimental method, derived, he claimed, from Newton (Locke, 1999 {1690}: 592) was directed towards building a true picture of the natural world from the smaller building blocks of empirically tested ideas. Truth, according to this doctrine, was somehow founded in sensory experience. This same approach was adopted by his successors, Berkeley and Hume. For Hamlyn, 'Berkeley had argued against those elements of Locke's philosophy' in presupposing that a 'physical reality' lies 'behind our ideas' (Hamlyn, 1967: 502). His aim was to 'produce a metaphysical view' of knowledge, showing 'the glory of God' (Hamlyn, 1967: 502).

Hume's philosophical project was directed towards weeding out inconsistencies and refining empiricism, being informed in the spirit and by practice of 'scepticism'. In his latter *Enquiry Concerning Human Understanding*, for example, he does much to clarify what he saw as 'observation treasured up in the course of experience', giving us the 'clue of human nature', and the basis for 'teach(ing) us to unravel all its intricacies' (Hume, 2008: 78). In this matter, mathematics occupies a pivotal position. For Hume, 'mathematics proceeds upon the supposition that certain laws are established by nature in her operations' (2008: 78). It is our contention that herein remain what are assumed to be the grounds for the large array of modern systems of quantitative evaluation used in formal education.

Although Hume understood Newtonian mechanics, he had also been constrained within 'Plato's pharmacy' throughout his work directed towards uncovering the truth of nature in the 'determinate' clarity afforded by the science of mathematics. In referring to Plato's pharmacy (Derrida, 1981) there is a sense that much of our modern world can be traced back to repetitions and reiterations of Plato's ways of understanding the world. Here was a science that for him could be used to overcome any 'superficial and imperfect representations of reality' (Gould, 1996: 269). Despite the fact that his 'enquiry' had taken no explicit account of our relationship with language or with being, it would seem that currently systems of formal education in the United Kingdom and elsewhere remain caught up in the same pharmacy Plato produced. In the world of young people, professional educators and analysts alike, there would seem to remain a relatively unquestioned and false assumption about the power of mathematics and of its grounding logic to provide a true picture of the world.

Returning to the present from this brief historical sojourn, it is apparent that the science of logic grounding statistics and quantitative analyses remains locked into this seventeenth-century view of the world. Moreover, in still being directed by the words of Plato towards the truth of the underlying reality concerning the improvement of education given in 'pure logic', the statistics and quantitative analyses would appear to assume the mantel of coming ever closer to revealing this reality.

However, from our earlier brief examination of Heidegger's understandings of being-with-others-in-the-world of Dasein, the development of quantitative analyses that follows – while in accord with the seventeenth-century worldview of Bacon and Newton – can be seen as nothing less than a complete distraction. The development of the quantitative analysis that follows is simply a diversion from the pivotal task of making sense of our relationship with being, with language, and with the complex issues of representation in language.

Yet another diversion in the name of quantitative analysis

When viewed through a Heideggerian lens, those 'statistical adjustments' provide indications of the temporal care structure always already at work in the world of Dasein, care in this case structured and intentionally directed towards taking account of a number of defined and measurable characteristics of young people who are the subject of measurements and statistical analyses. However, rather than conceiving of these various 'characteristics' as ways of being, in statistical analysis these young people are quite unconsciously reconstituted as 'concatenations of forces in service to the human will' (Thomson, 2000: 306), here in the form of representations made by statisticians entirely in accordance with their own training and the logic of statistical inquiry.

In the pragmatism of everyday school practices, there is little time to reflect on these matters and little discursive space. Many schools in the United Kingdom now use the FFT framework as the driving force in their evaluation and monitoring of student progress. In fact, FFT and the new government system, Reporting and Analysis for Improvement through School Self Evaluation, both draw on CVA modelling in order to structure numeric analyses of the performance of schools.

Within the paradigm of quantitative analysis, Ray (2006: 15) highlights the importance of agencies administering the baseline testing being independent of the government in order to obtain high quality numeric data: both the Qualification and Curriculum Authority (QCA) and the National Assessment Agency (NAA) administer testing for CVA data, rather than the central government agencies of the former DCSF (now the DfE). In fact, the critiques Downy and Kelly (2008) and Ray (2006) developed appear to make good some of the limitations of inductive thinking based on numeric data. Both critiques appeared to be predicated on assumptions that, given greater sophistication and thought regarding the modelling, it was possible to move to a position where the numbers placed in the models constituted a direct correspondence with how things are. There would appear to be a lawlike structure within language itself that disposes whole professional communities to the pursuit of truth, understood by these groups in terms of a direct correspondence with what is represented as the reality of schools.

In the hidden silence constituted by these discourses of quantitative analysis speak the voices of Plato, Bacon, Newton, Hume and others. The silence in which these voices speak is inscribed in the actions taken in the name of the language of improving education as statutary structures of apparatuses of state. The individual can do nothing but 'stand before the law' in structures where it is directed into a space constituted on grounds of the theology of a pure calculus of logic. The ontological grounds for this theology are the actions taken by Dasein. Herein lies the basis for the organization of improvement. In the language of improvement and in the privileging of numbers and quantification is the theological assumption of the science of logic as the locus of truth and therefore of the highest being. However, within discourses that examine critically the nature of quantification, a juridical structure concerning truth as correspondence makes it almost impossible to be reflexive about these metrics. Remarkably, this law-like structure silences any questions concerning the relationship of beings with the underlying calculus of logic grounded in the principle of reason as the enframing. Enframing, it has been shown, is further delimited and directed in its intentionality by the nihilism of the 'will-to-will' on grounds of the ontological foundation for current dominant formal systems of education, and in the actions taken in accordance with the theology of improving organizations.

Although metaphysics is at work in projecting understandings of forms of action and organization, its voice, too, has been silenced in this particular tradition. The law-like structures always already at work in the language bequeathed by Plato and the so-called Enlightenment thinkers tend to preclude this possibility.

For example, Downy and Kelly (2008) – in pointing to issues regarding the oversimplification in the nature of school performance, the non-linearity in data and the fact that CVA is not a fixed constant but a continually developing model – appear to suggest that the numerical analyses are coming ever closer to engaging with how things are. Further weight that this indeed is their underlying ontotheological standpoint is only added by their concern that CVA provides a 'relative' rather than 'absolute measure of performance', being itself is predicated on the assumption that there is indeed an absolute reality in this ideology (in practice being is only ever a trace, a fragment, the 'cinders' left after an event).

Likewise, Ray's (2006) approach to the critique of quantitative analysis would appear to be similarly premised on assumptions concerning moves through quantitative analysis towards an engagement with a hard reality. For example, in questioning value added data he asks, 'Can the media be encouraged' to present data 'accurately'? (2006: 54). He also raised a number of 'more specific issues', including the question of 'when and how should confidence intervals be given' and whether 'schools should be measured as significant in relation to the national average' (2006: 54). If questions remain as to whether the numeric analysis for either Ray (2006) or Downy and Kelly (2008) does, in fact, move us towards a hard reality, then the former government agency, the DCSF, leaves us in no doubt about their position on this matter. In their presentation, 'Data in School: A Guide for the Bewildered' based on the experiences of St Peters High School (2010) teachers spoke of test results and attendance figures from schools constituting 'hard data', that is, data no longer open to interpretation.

The imputation here of the hard reality of things seems to presuppose a direct correspondence between numbers and how things are. It indicates that in their reliance on metrics modern governments have yet to emerge from highly questionable seventeenth-century thinking. It raises the question of whether other ways of thinking are possible. More critically, does the foregoing argument not open critical reflections on what is now an almost overwhelming diversion constituted by our metric systems?

Critical reflections on metric systems used to evaluate formal systems of education

At one level, the statement that hard data is no longer open to interpretation from the former government agency, the Department for Children, Families and Schools (DCSF) in England reflects just how completely professional educational communities have become encultured into the language of quantitative analysis. But this is much more than simply a matter of learning the rules of a particular language game, in this case involving numbers and quantitative analyses that many people have significant difficulties with, and play accordingly. In these circumstances, Dasein would otherwise always be disposed to other possibilities and our formal systems would break down.

Foucault's (1977) account of 'panopticism' provides an explanation of what sustains professional communities who draw on the technical language of statistics in order to monitor educational progress. The architecture of the panopticon, a product of Bentham's (1962{1843}) imagination (Foucault, 1977: 200–09), is included as the self-directed subjects its prisoners, who are prevented from seeing each other by the absence of any adjoining windows in each of their cells and as subjects and objects of surveillance are always intensely aware of their own visibility. In practice the panopticon constitutes an abstract architecture: a disciplinary structure of coded space for socializing the docile body – of a specified population or of individuals – which, as its self-directed subjects, are always made intimately aware of the objects of surveillance that define its targets for action. In Foucault's conception, the panopticism at work in prisons, hospitals, schools, the work place and so on is the basis for a 'disciplinary society'. Clearly, in this late modern world, given the emergence of what the sociologist Bauman (2000: 129) calls 'synopticism' – the continual monitoring of the behaviours of each other – the former systems of social control through panopticism are manifestly fallible. Yet, in a visit to any school in England the dominance of quantitative monitoring systems is apparent everywhere. Clearly, synopticism and panopticism, in their various manifestations, do not provide any explanation of our seemingly insatiable and illusory circular drive for truth in education as an apparent mirror of reality, the so-called fact of the 'hard data' available.

Data, of course, creates its own particular conundrum. At best, from its etymology *data* only ever expresses what is given in language (and by implication leaves in silence what is not given). Of necessity, therefore, any drive for absolute truth regarding a social phenomenon is impossible because of the remainder that is never given in data. Therefore, unconsciously or otherwise, Dasein tends to be forever driven in its intentionality to overcome impossibility. But the drive is only there in relation to research data. The everydayness of professional life is sometimes characterized by the absence of any research. There is, however, a more all-pervasive source of impossibility within all forms of language, namely, being itself. For example, if I say that 'I ran to catch a bus' then the identities of the pronoun, 'I', the verb – to run – and the noun – the bus – are expressions of being; being unfolds and comes to presence in every verb and noun in our language. But the plenitude and totality of what comes to presence in each case is an illusion, borne out of the mythological circular economy of an apparent origin. My action of running may well be a repetition of what others have done before. Considering this alongside the purity of memory, Derrida breaks the sanctuary of the metaphoric circle:

> I would say that what I suffer from inconsolably always has the form, not only of loss, which is often! – but of the loss of memory: that what I am living cannot be kept, thus repeated, and – how to put it? – decipherable, as if an appeal for a witness had no witness, in some way, not even the witness that I could be for what I have lived. This is for me the very experience of death, of catastrophe' (1995b: 207).

What Derrida has called the 'catastrophe' of memory renders impossible the identity of what is thought to be known. Being is only ever a trace, it being always impossible to fully recollect and recreate a particular presence identified by being, the is; Derrida refers to the 'cinders' that remain. Essentially, it is the fallibility of memory and the traces of being left behind that continually emerge as the major locus of desire for the will-to-power and the will-to-will that are endlessly represented in the rhetorical language of improvement (Flint, 2010c).

When viewed through a Heideggarian lens, the foregoing critical engagement with statistics and the modelling of systems of education can be seen as not only a complete distraction, but paradoxically, through its development and the continual striving for improvement, as the very driving force for its own sustained overcoming of the impossible. The full scope of the paradox is perhaps better gauged from an examination of the school effectiveness literature, similarly providing in its own way a critical engagement with questions concerning the nature of effectiveness and the measurement of how effective schools are in raising standards of education. Here, statistics, the quantitative modelling of systems of education and the underlying science of logic are not only distractions from real questions concerning our education of Dasein (rather than individuals), they actually provide the locus and the driving force for the will-to-will as the enframing re-presented and disguised in the rhetoric of improvement.

It would seem that the endless appeal to the science of logic and systematic educational metrics reflects attempts to arrive at the truth of how to enact and organize an ever improving system. On this reading, to paraphrase Marx, one is reminded of his paradoxical injunction, 'Man makes his own history, not of his own making', though many education services indeed remain caught up in 'Plato's pharmacy'. The reason for this has much to do with metaphysics, continuing in its work in the fields of school improvement and effectiveness, but virtually never recognized and, until now, never opened to question within the field of improvement. As Thomson's (2000; 2005) insightful and controversial readings of Heidegger make transparent, over the past two millennia since Plato, metaphysics has variously invented a number of systems for grounding beings in being: for example, in the action taken to improve schools. Here, as we have seen in this entire book, is the ontological grounding for improvement. At the same time, metaphysics has also projected understandings of the highest being, in this case the ever improving organization of the education service as ultimately determined by the science of logic. Herein lies what amounts to a tacit theological dimension of the education service. As long as we remain within its own regime of truth, of course, logic would appear to provide the basis of that very same truth.

However, there are a number of points where the metaphysics of this particular ontotheological home constituted in the language of improvement becomes impossible. Let us just remind ourselves of the case. The so-called hard reality within this particular home for the education service, in accordance with the principle of reason, is constituted on the basis of the calculable actions of the individual within a multiplicity of specified forms of organization, themselves directed towards the truth in accordance with the theology of ever improving systems. However, the addressees of the logic are not 'you' or 'me' or any other human beings, in fact, but the invention of objects (or sub-jects) we call 'individuals' that provide a perfect fit with the calculus. As Dasein, we simply find ways of adapting and working to develop these systems. This has the effect of adding further layers of organization, where the underlying metaphysics and the logic of the system become ever more deeply buried. It opens questions once more on the thorny issue of whether we can ever escape the forces of history. Indeed, is it at all possible to ever rethink the structures of the enfram-ing when our thinking has not only become delimited, but we are for-ever in danger of being reduced to 'cyborgs' in the name of formal systems of education?

Are there other ways of thinking for all those in education?

In this chapter, and indeed in this whole book, we have sought to uncover points where the applied calculus of logic not only becomes impossible as a basis for understanding and predicting human behaviour but will, of necessity, remain impossible. In our earlier comparison of being-in-the-world of Dasein talking with friends and being in an examination, we showed that logic can never address the unfolding stories of Dasein. Like-wise, in representing what is given, there is a built-in impossibility of the analysis of data used for research ever giving a complete understanding of social behaviours. In another sense the training of professionals in the education service addresses itself to the individual, the anonymous 'one' who provides models of professional behaviours. It nevertheless remains impossible to foretell just how being-in-the-world of Dasein mediates professional models. In similar vein, the logic of the examination system and formal modalities of assessment is to produce the anonymous indi-vidual, 'one' as a 'learner', another object and subject in the economy of education that is characterized increasingly in terms of the ongoing calcu-lus of 'learning'. All of these various instances of what is found to be impos-sible for the science of logic in fact tend to be dissimulated by practices mediated by everyday discourses and human interactions.

Moreover, within the metaphysical boundaries of an ontotheological home, constituted in the enframing where formal education emerges on the basis of logic, the invocation of the 'will-to-will' has a continual storehouse of impossibilities to overcome. It is this storehouse that, as we have seen, feeds the very doctrine of improvement. Is it ironic in a secular society that the voice of this litany should still remain strong in its unconscious appeal to the very same metaphysics in the latest APP system put in place by two successive governments in England? Paradoxically, however, the very elements of social phenomena remain beyond the possibilities of the logic and of quantitative metrics, and are rendered in the enframing as 'standing reserve' – resources that are available for use 'merely to be optimally ordered and efficiently disposed of in a dangerous spiral of constant overcoming' (Thomson, 2000: 306). At this point in our history, if the foregoing deconstruction is correct, this (these) 'spiral(s) of overcoming' is (are) currently built into formal systems of education. But this is not a necessity that we have to endure.

The coded structure of truth as correspondence inscribed in the language of quantitative analysis, where the enframing finds its grounds, along with our reliance upon the principle of assessment for the metric systems used in formal education are not any more inviolable than any other forms of law. Paradoxically, however, it 'is' the 'hard reality' of contemporary formal systems of education so many people now have a part in, that the 'they' – Heidegger (1962: 164–6{127–8}) uses the expression 'das Man' to identify actions that are largely determined by what 'one' does in such circumstances, with no one being themselves the 'they' – are ever in danger of driving us away from our very humanity.

In coming to the end of the book, it is the vital relationship with being that this book attempts to give voice to in the name of education. In all of the chapters we have attempted to show that this is no longer simply a matter that philosophers can push to one side. Many European philosophers, particularly, have been fully aware of these issues for more than 50 years, but until recently they have tended to be ignored within the dominant Anglo-American tradition of analytical philosophy and therefore have had limited influence. Here, instead of being sidelined by the language games that variously continue to sweep great populations of people along, we have attempted to open ways of questioning and thinking derived from philosophy in discourses of formal education.

Each chapter has deconstructed a picture of the 'real world' of education where in the extreme there is always the danger that our complex relationship with being, constituted in the enframing, is leaving us alienated from ourselves and endlessly having to adapt to the hard logic. In so doing, each chapter has also opened ways of thinking that if fully enacted would make obvious just how much of a distraction our various fetishes really are, for both the products and for other surface effects of the enframing revealed in this book. One of the subtexts of our argument, of course, is to become more reflexive, not just about the language games that variously position us, but in the ways that, in the multiplicity of games played in the name of education, being is increasingly setting upon us.

In working with the enframing, we want to place particular emphasis upon a quite different order of knowing, foregrounding the phenomenology and ontology of experience that has been articulated in the earlier chapters. Experientially, this order foregrounds our own historicism as reflexive temporal beings. In taking language as our home, it is founded on our complex relationship with being. In other words, in its various pedagogic forms, an order of knowing in the name of education recognizes at last its own power in recontextualizing Dasein in our increasingly pedagogized societies. In the hard reality of the everyday world, it is education and not philosophy that has the power to constitute our essential and enduring home in language (Flint, 2010c).

In this social order, the enframing in the language of education and its hidden ruling structures does not have to remain caught up in a highly questionable seventeenth-century worldview that appears to remain, somehow, further legitimated by particular readings of Plato that are also not beyond question. Laws can always be changed.

We began this book by considering, as practitioners, the ways the enframing in education has come to variously position people within discourses and their associated practices. We have also shown many examples of its means–ends rationality shaping discourses and colonizing practices that we have come to understand as a particular kind of revealing, where everything comes to be seen as calculable objects and subjects. We have seen how this works by the enframing inscribing itself in our very language as educational edicts constituted in regimes of truth.

Equally, our writings have attempted from the outset to uncover some fragments of Dasein's relationship with being. In the coded space of the words in this book there is a place where a new order of knowing has unfolded. It is a knowing that in foregrounding lived experience takes account of the complex relations between multiplicities of key elements. It is a way of knowing that is concerned with approaching and uncovering beings in their relationship with being. Perhaps foremost among these is the way in which the anonymous 'one' comes to reproduce governmental discourses and principles inscribed in the nature of the state apparatuses of education and the economies of objects 'they' seek to manage. It is an order of knowing that alerts us to the very regimes of knowledge and practices that bear directly on professional education. It opens questioning and thinking that encourages us to be reflexive about the ways professional discourse can so easily bind us tightly up within technologies of the self.

Fifteen Theses on Education 10

1. The rise of the schooled society signifies a change in the relations between the state and the population. The school is at the centre of this transformation. The transformation is still in the process of being worked through.

2. The school constitutes an essential instrument of contemporary governance. This is its primary function and supervenes all other ostensible functions. This function has both pastoral and disciplinary dimensions.

3. Schooling may be seen as a developing technology of population management. It constitutes a sophisticated 'apparatus', in the Foucauldian sense, for a range of functions, including a police function, a pastoral function, a socialization function, a social reproduction function and an educative function. It seems unlikely that the educative function could be liberated from the other functions.

4. Technologies of schooling shape, order and define identities in accord with the will-to-improvement with its underlying principle of assessment. The metaphysics of schooling has strongly influenced the language of identity.

5. The language of schooling now provides a dominant symbolic order enfolding the identity and development of the individual and the citizen. This language has extended beyond the limit of the school, being decentred in the dispersed institutional 'space' produced by governmentality. Schooling is not confined by school walls.

6. Successive attempts to redefine and refunction schooling in the direction of equality have not realized their goals. Schooling continues to distribute rewards unevenly in relation to social class cultural factors, including habitual uses of language and orientations to meaning.

7. The end of the nineteenth century saw a transformation in childhood. Increasingly, children came within the ambit of the law and of an array of institutions, ideas and practices. Childhood is now further saturated with specifications for development, norms for control and systematic regulation of conduct and identity. Much of this government occurs through institutions of education and is designed to promote the self-regulating citizen of the well-regulated future.

8. Age stratification is a far-reaching, powerful and questionable phenomenon that is an essential component of education in modernity. Its naturalized status indicates that it remains largely 'unthought'. Age stratification is vital to the norm-related culture of development that many consider inimical to creative development.

9. The curriculum specifies norms of knowledge and orientations to meaning. Many of the norms of knowledge and meaning are arbitrary and historically received ideas rather than essential, vital forces. The curriculum addresses its populations differently according to their class-cultural orientation and identity. The curriculum demands recognition for its own specific and contingent forms of knowledge and meaning. In doing so, it excludes other forms of knowledge and orientations to meaning.

10. Education has become the dominant principle of being in our society. We are encouraged to think of ourselves and to conduct ourselves essentially as subjects of education. We are unfinished entities, works in progress, and only education can both remediate our lack and provide meaning for our pathway. Education is projected as the solution to grand problems beyond the self: to social divisions and conflicts. We do not have to think like this.

11. Educational research has been dominated by the ethic of improvement. In line with a general drive towards 'impact', this tendency favours narrowly focussed and intellectually limited empirical research within the perceived order of development. There is no a priori reason why educational research should be dominated by a drive towards impact. Anxieties about the decentring of educational research are predicated on a longing for a mythical past of cohesion, of engagement in a 'common pursuit' that is neither realizable nor desirable.

12. In its calculus, the language of numbers promotes a platonic ideal of ghostly truth and privileges an empiricism that is always in danger of forgetting its metaphysical grounding. Statistics as a form of language provides a home to the alienated self of educational improvement. Ironically, mathematical ways of examining and evaluating individuals, institutions and systems in the field of education are unsullied by the specificities of experience.

13. Lifelong learning has become a mechanism for a new, 'personalized' managerialism dedicated to promoting self-development as a metaphysical principal. One main function of the rise of lifelong learning has been the extension through life of the technologies of the self that are enacted through schooling.

14. The current enframing in the education of teachers provides little in its formal structures to challenge hegemonic discourses and practices. Nevertheless, the possibilities of being otherwise remain as strong as ever: the practices of ITE constitute a possible locus of inspiration for the iteration of fresh orientations and discourses.

15. 'Technological enframing' in discourses and practices of improvement is not some unavoidable fate, a truth visited upon us by the gods that we simply have to endure. While it is a powerful force in our contemporary world, it is nevertheless subject to a deconstructive resistance that can take many forms, with many possible effects.

References

Advanced Level Performance System, ALPS (2010) www.alps-va.co.uk/About-Alps, accessed 25 August. 2010

Agamben, G. (1993) *The Coming Community*, Minneapolis and London: University of Minnesota Press.

Aglietta, M. (1979) *A Theory of Capitalist Regulation: The US Experience*, London: New Left Books.

Ahmad, A. (1992) *In Theory*. London: Verso.

Alexander, R. (2006a) *Education as Dialogue: Moral and Pedagogical*, Cambridge: Dialogos.

Alexander, R. (2006b) *Towards Dialogic Teaching: Rethinking Classroom* (4th Edition), Cambridge: Dialogos.

Allen, M. (2008) *Cleansing the City*, Athens: Ohio University Press.

Allen, R. and Vignoles, A. (2007) 'What should an index of school segregation measure?', *Oxford Review of Education*, 33(5): 643–6.

Althusser, L. (1977) *Lenin and Philosophy and Other Essays*, London: New Left Books.

Althusser, L. (1984) *Essays On Ideology*, London: Verso.

Alweiss, L. (2003) *The World Unclaimed: A Challenge to Heidegger's Critique of Husserl*, Athens: Ohio University Press.

Anderson, B. (1983) *Imagined Communities: Reflections on the Origin and Spread of Nationalism*, London: Verso.

Anderson, P. (1992) *English Questions*, London: Verso.

Anyon, J. (2008) *Theory and Educational Research*, London: Routledge.

Apple, M. (1996) *Cultural Politics and Education*, Buckingham: Open University Press.

Arendt, H. (1993) *Between Past and Future*, New York: Penguin Books.

Aries, P. (1962) *Centuries of Childhood: A Social History of Family Life*, London: Jonathan Cape.

Aronowitz, S. and Giroux, H. A. (1986) *The Conservative, Liberal and Radical Debate over Schooling*. London: Routledge and Kegan Paul.

Ashton, D. (2002) 'Redirecting the research agenda', in Reeve, F., Cartwright, M. and Edwards, R. (eds) *Supporting Lifelong Learning: Volume 2 – Organising Learning*, London and New York: RoutledgeFalmer, 21–33.

Aspin, D. N. and Chapman, J. D. (2000) 'Lifelong learning: concepts and conceptions', *International Journal of Lifelong Education*, 19(1): 2–19.

Assessment of Pupil Progress, APP (2010) http://curriculum.qcda.gov.uk/key-stages-3-and-4/assessment/Assessing-pupils-progress/Where-are-the-materials-available-from/index.aspx, accessed 1 December. 2010

Association of Teachers and Lecturers, ATL (2008) *Inspection of initial teacher education, 2008–2011: Response from the Association of Teachers and Lecturers,* London: ATL, www.atl.org.uk/Images/Inspection%20of%20initial%20teacher%20education%20response.pdf, accessed 2 August, 2010.

Audit Commission (2003) *Services for Disabled Children: A Review of Services for Disabled Children and their Families,* London: Audit Commission.

Austin, J. L. (1975{1962}) *How to Do Things with Words: The William James Lectures Delivered at Harvard University in 1975* (2nd edn), Urmston, J. L. and Sbisa, M., (eds) Oxford and New York: Oxford University Press.

Bacon, F. (1996 [1854]) Francis Bacon (1561–1626) *The Great Instauration,* Philadelphia: The Works, available at: http://history.hanover.edu/courses/excerpts/111bac.html, accessed on 30 September, 2010.

Bagley, C. (2006) 'School choice and competition: a public market in education revisited', *Oxford Review of Education,* 32(3): 347–62.

Ball, S. (1999) 'Performativity and fragmentation in "postmodern schooling"', in Carter, J. (ed.) *Postmodernity and the Fragmentation of Welfare,* London: Routledge.

Ball, S. (1981) *Beachside Comprehensive,* Cambridge: Cambridge University Press.

Ball, S. J. and Bowe, R. (1992) 'Subject Departments and the "implementation" of National Curriculum Policy', *Journal of Curriculum Studies,* 24(2): 97–115.

Baldick, C. (1983) *The Social Mission of English Criticism 1848–1932,* Oxford: Basil Blackwell.

Bandura, A. (1986) *Social Foundations of Thought and Action,* Englewood Cliffs, NJ: Prentice-Hall.

Bandura, A. (1997) *Self-Efficacy: The Exercise of Control,* New York: W. H. Freeman.

Barber, M. (1997) 'Reengineering the political/educational system', *School Leadership and Management,* 17(2): 187–99.

Barnett, K., McCormick, J. and Conners, R. (2001) 'Transformational leadership in schools – panacea, placebo or problem?', *Journal of Educational Administration,* 39(1): 24–46.

Barnett, R. (2002) 'Learning to work and working to learn', in Reeve, F., Cartwright, M. and Edwards, R. (eds) *Supporting Lifelong Learning: Volume 2 – Organising Learning,* London and New York: RoutledgeFalmer, 1–20.

Barnett, R. (2003) *Beyond All Reason: Living with Ideology in the University,* Buckingham, Philadelphia: Open University Press.Bartlett, J. (2007) *Meeting the challenges of school leadership in secondary educational establishments* Education International: Birmingham, England, 15–16 May, available at: http://download.ei-ie.org/docs/IRISDocuments/Education/School%20Leadership/2007%20May%2015-16%20Meeting%20the%20challenges%20of%20school%20leadership%20in%20secondary%20educational%20establishment/2008-00160-01-E.doc, accessed 10 August 2010

Barthes, R. (2000 {1972}) *Mythologies,* trans. A. Lavers, New York: Random House.

Bass, B. M. (1985) *Leadership and Performance beyond Expectation,* New York: Free Press.

Bass, B. M. (1990) 'From transactional to transformational leadership: learning to share the vision', *Organizational Dynamics,* (Winter): 19–31.

Bates, E. Marchman, V., Thal, D., Fenson, L., Dale, P., Reznick, S., Reilly, J. and Hartung, J. (1994) 'Developmental and stylistic variation in the composition of early Vocabulary', *Journal of Child Language*, 21, 85–124.

Bates, E., Dale, P. and Thal, D. (1995) 'Individual differences and their implications for theories of language development' in Fletcher, P. and MacWhinney, B. (eds), *The Cross-Linguistic Study of Sentence Processing*, 225–56, New York: Cambridge University Press.

Batsleer, J., Davies, T., O'Rourke, R. and Weedon, C. (1985) *Rewriting English: Cultural Politics of Gender and Class*, London: Methuen.

Bauman, Z. (1991) *Modernity and the Holocaust*, Cambridge: Polity Press.

Bauman, Z. (2000) *Liquid Modernity*, Cambridge: Polity Press.

Bauman, Z. (2004) *Identity*, Cambridge: Polity Press.

Baxter, J. E. (2008) 'The Archaeology of Childhood', *Annual Review of Anthropology*, 37: 159–75.

Becker, H. S. (1952) 'Social-Class Variations in the Teacher-Pupil Relationship', *Journal of Educational Sociology* 25 (8): 451–65.

Bédarida, F. (1979) *A Social History of England 1851–1990*, London: Methuen.

Bell, A. (1808) *The Madras School*, London: Murray.

Belsey, C. (1999) 'Antony Easthope: Cultural critic undaunted by words, wisdom and waiters', *The Guardian*, 17 December.

Bennis, W. and Nanus, B. (1985) *Leaders: The Strategies for Taking Charge*, New York: Harper & Row.

Bentham, J. (1962{1843}) The *Works of Jeremy Bentham*, Bowring, J. (ed.), Edinburgh: William Tate, available at http://oll.libertyfund.org/index.php?option=com_staticxt&staticfile=show.php%3Ftitle=2234&Itemid=27, accessed 20 November 2010.

Bentley, T. (1999) 'Labour's learning revolution', *The Economist*, 9 October: 42.

Bernstein, B. (1971) *Class, Codes and Control: Theoretical Studies Towards a Sociology of Language*, London: Routledge and Kegan Paul.

Bernstein, B. (ed.) (1973) *Class, Codes and Control: Vol. 2*, London: Routledge and Kegan Paul.

Bernstein, B. (1996) *Pedagogy, Symbolic Control and Identity* (1st edn), Lanham, MD: Rowman & Littlefield Publishers.

Bernstein, B. (2000) *Pedagogy, Symbolic Control and Identity* (2nd edn), Lanham, MD: Rowman & Littlefield Publishers.

Bettelheim, B. (1967) *The Empty Fortress. Infantile Autism and the Birth of the Self*, New York: Free Press.

Biggs, J. (2002) *The 2002 Vernon-Wall Lecture: The Changing Role of Psychology in Educational Practice*, London: British Psychological Society.

Blake, W. (1971 {1794}) *Songs of Innocence and Experience*, Toronto: Dover.

Blake, N., Smeyers, P., Smith, R. and Standish, P. (2003) *The Blackwell Guide to the Philosophy of Education*, Oxford: Blackwell Publishing.

Blanden, J., Gregg, P. and Machin, S. (2005) *Intergenerational Mobility in Europe and North America: Report for the Sutton Trust*, London: Centre for Economic Performance.

Bluebond-Langner, M. (1980) *The Private Worlds of Dying Children*, Princeton: Princeton University Press.

Boix Mansilla, V. and Gardner, H. (1994) 'Teaching for Understanding Within and Across the Disciplines', *Educational Leadership*, 51(5): 14–18.

Booth, W., Colomb, G. and Williams, J. (1995) *The Craft of Research*, Chicago: University of Chicago Press.

Boud, D. and Lee, A. (2009) *Changing Practices of Doctoral Education*, London and New York: Routledge.

Bourdieu, P. (1990) *In Other Words*, Cambridge: Polity Press.

Bourdieu, P. (1991) *Language and Symbolic Power*, Cambridge: Polity Press.

Bourdieu, P. and Passeron, J. (1977) *Reproduction in Education, Society and Culture*, London: Sage Publications.

Bowles, S. and Gintis, H. (1976) *Schooling in Capitalist America: Educational Reform and the Contradictions of Economic Life*, London: Routledge and Kegan Paul.

Bray, T. (2009) 'An Archaeological Perspective on the Andean Concept of Camaquen: Thinking Through Late Pre-Columbian Ofrendas and Huacas', *Cambridge Archaeological Journal*, 19(3): 357–66.

British Broadcasting Commission [BBC] (2010) 'News, education and family – Q & A: Academies and Free Schools', www.bbc.co.uk/news/10161371, accessed 21 August 2010.

Bromcom (2002) www.bromcom.com/.

Broughton, K. (2005) 'Research into Practice: The National Evaluation of the Children's Fund', *Practice*, 17(2): 135–9.

Bruner, J. (1990), *Acts of Meaning*, Cambridge, MA: Harvard University Press.

Burden, R. and Williams, M. (1998) *Thinking Through the Curriculum*, London: Routledge.

Burns, J. M. (1978) *Leadership*, New York: Harper & Row.

Burridge, E. and Ribbins, P. (1994) 'Promoting Improvement in Schools: Aspects of Quality in Birmingham', in Ribbins, P. and Burridge, E. (eds) *Improving Education: Promoting Quality in Schools*, London and New York: Cassell.

Bush, T. (2007) *Theories of Educational Leadership and Management* (3rd edn), London: Sage Publications.

Butler, J. (1993) *Bodies that Matter: On the Discursive Limits of Sex,* New York: Routledge.

Butler, J. (1997) *Excitable Speech*, London: Routledge.

Butler, J. (2004) *Precarious Life: The Power of Mourning and Violence*, London and New York: Verso Books.

Caldwell, B. J. (1997) 'A Gestalt for the Reengineering of School Education for the Knowledge Society', *School Leadership & Management*, 17(2): 203–15.

Caputo, J. (1987) *Radical Hermeneutics: Repetition, Deconstruction, and the Hermeneutic Project*, Bloomington and Indianapolis: Indiana University Press.

Carr, W. (2007) 'Educational Research as a Practical Science', *International Journal of Research and Method in Education*, 30(3): 271–8.

Casey, E. S. (1998) *The Fate of Place: A Philosophical History*, Berkeley and Los Angeles: University of California Press.

Castells, M. (1998) *The Rise of the Network Society: Information Age: Economy, Society, and Culture volume 1: The Information Age: Economy, Society* (2nd edn), West Sussex: John Wiley & Sons, Ltd.

Cicourel, A. V. and Kitsuse, J. I. (1971) 'The social organization of the high school and deviant adolescent careers' *in Cosin*, B. R., Dale, I. R., Esland, G. M. and Swift, D. F. (eds) London: Routledge and Kegan Paul.

Cognitive Ability Test (CAT) (2011) 'Cognitive Ability Tests', available at: www.satsguide.co.uk/help__other_exams_and_subjects/cats__cognitive_abilities_tests.htm, accessed 10 June 2010.

Centre for Evaluation and Monitoring (International) [CEMInt] (2010) *CEM Connect International*, Issue 2, June 2009, available at www.pipsproject.org/documents/newsletters/international/CEM%20Connect%20International%20Issue%2002.pdf.

Centre for Evaluation and Monitoring [CEM] (2010) www.cemcentre.org/, accessed 25 August 2010.

Ceruti, C. (2004) 'Human Bodies as Objects of Dedication at Inca Mountain Shrines (North-Western Argentina)', *World Archaeology*, 36 (1):103–22.

Clark, E. (1993) *The Lexicon in Acquisition*, Cambridge: Cambridge University Press.

Clarke, J. and Newman, J. (1997) *The Managerial State*, London, Thousand Oakes, CA and New Dehli: Sage Publications.

Clarke, J., Newman, J., Smith, N. and Vidler, E. (2007) *Creating Citizen–Consumers: Changing Publics and Changing Public Services*, London: Sage Publications.

Claxton, G. (2006) 'Expanding the capacity to learn: A new end for education?', Opening Keynote Address, British Educational Research Association Annual Conference, Warwick University, 6 September.

Clendinnen, I. (1991) *Aztecs: An Interpretation*, Cambridge University Press: Cambridge.

Cochran-Smith, M. and Lytle, S. L. (2001) 'Beyond certainty: Taking an inquiry stance on practice', in Lieberman, A. and Miller, L. (eds) *Teachers Caught in the Action: Professional Development that Matters*, New York: Teachers College Press, 45–58.

Cody, D. (2010) 'Child Labour', *The Victorian Web*, www.victorianweb.org/ history/hist8.html.

Coffield, F. (1999) 'Breaking the Consensus: Lifelong Learning as Social Control', Inaugural Lecture presented at the University of Newcastle, 2 February.

Coffield, F. (2008) 'Just suppose teaching and learning became the first priority', London: Learning and Skill Network, available at: http://tlp.excellencegateway.org.uk/ecpd/ecpd_modules/downloads/coffield_if_only.pdf, accessed 20 November, 2010.

Coffield, F., Edward, S., Finlay, I., Hodgson, A., Spours, K. and Steer, R. (2008) *Improving Learning, Skills and Inclusion: The impact of policy on post-compulsory education*, London and New York: Routledge, available at: http://arrts.gtcni.org.uk/gtcni/bitstream/2428/49240/1/Coffie ld%252Bet%252Bal%252BImproving%252BLearning%252BSkills%252Band%252BInclusion-toc-ch1.pdf, accessed 20 August, 2010.

Cohen, S. (2002) *Folk Devils and Moral Panics*, London: Routledge.

Copeland, I. (1999) *The Making of the Backward Pupil in Education in England 1870–1914*, London: Woburn Press.

Cotton, T. and Mann, J. (2003) *Improving Primary Schools: Improving Communities*, Stoke-on-Trent, UK and Sterling Virginia: Trentham Books.

Coveney, P. (1967) *The Image of Childhood*, Harmondsworth: Penguin.

Cox, B. (1994) *The Battle for the English Curriculum*, London: Hodder and Stoughton.

Cranston, M. (1967) 'Bacon, Francis', in Edwards, P. (Editor in Chief) *The Encyclopedia of Philosophy, Volume 1*, New York: Macmillan Publishing Co. and The Free Press, 235–40.

Creemers, B. P. M. and Kyriakides, L. (2011) *Improving Quality in Education: Dynamic Approaches to School Improvement*, Abingdon, Oxon: Routledge.

Crespi, F. (1992) *Social Action and Power*, Oxford: Blackwell.

Critchley, S. (1997) 'What is Continental Philosophy?', *International Journal of Philosophical Studies*, 5(3): 347–63.

Croxford, L. (2010) 'Tensions between the Equity and Efficiency of Schooling: The Case of Scotland', *Education Inquiry*, 1(1): 5–20.

Cuban, L. (1988) *The Managerial Imperative and the Practice of Leadership in Schools*, Albany, NY: State University of New York Press.

Cunningham, H. (2006) *The Invention of Childhood*, London: BBC Books.

Dale, P. (1991) 'The validity of a parent report measure of vocabulary and syntax at 24 months' in *Journal of Speech and Hearing Sciences*, 34, 565–71.

Dalin, P. with Rolff, H-G., in cooperation with Kleekamp, B. (1993) *Changing the School Culture*, London and New York: Cassell.

Davies, B. (2008) 'Passionate Leadership in Action', in Davies, B. and Brighouse, T. (eds) *Passionate Leadership in Education*, London: Sage.

Davies, B. and Ellison, L. (2003) *The New Strategic Direction and Development of the School: Key Frameworks for School Improvement Planning*, London: RoutlegeFalmer.

Dean, M. (2010) *Governmentality: Power and Rule in Modern Society* (2nd edn), London: Sage Publications.

Delpit, L. (1995) *Other People's Children: Cultural Conflict in the Classroom*, New York: The New Press.

Deming, W. E. (1986) *Out of the Crisis*, Cambridge: MIT Press.

Department for Children, Schools and Families [DCSF] (2005) 'Birth to Three Matters', www.dcsf.gov.uk/everychildmatters/publications/0/1478/, accessed 15 August 2010.

Department for Children, Schools and Families [DCSF] (2008) 'The Early Years Foundation Stage Principles', www.education.gov.uk/publications/standard/publicationDetail/Page1/DCSF-00261-2008#downloadableparts, accessed 10 September 2010.

Department for Education [DfE] (1992) *Initial Teacher Training (Secondary Phase)* (Circular 9/92), London: DfE.

Department for Education [DfE] (1993) *The Initial Training of Primary School Teachers: New criteria for courses* (Circular 14/93), London: DfE.

Department for Education [DfE] (2011) www.education.gov.uk/, accessed 10 November 2011.

Department for Education And Employment [DfEE] (1997) *Teaching: High Status, High Standards* (Circular 10/97), London: DfEE.

Department for Education and Employment [DfEE](1998a) *Requirements for Courses of Initial Teacher Training* (Circular 4/98), London: DfEE.

Department for Education and Employment [DfEE] (1998b) *The Learning Age: A renaissance for a new Britain*, www.lifelonglearning.co.uk/greenpaper/, accessed 28 August 2010.

Department for Education and Employment [DfEE] (1999) *The National Curriculum for England: Citizenship, Key Stages 3–4*, London: HMSO.

Department for Education and Science [DfES] (2003a) *Every Child Matters*, London: HMSO, CM5860.

Department for Education and Skills [DfES] (2003b) 'Personal Development Planning', www.ics.heacademy.ac.uk/resources/pdp.php, accessed 25 August 2010.

Department of Education and Science [DES] (1984) *Initial Teacher Training: Approval of courses* (Circular 3/84), London: DES.

Department of Education and Science [DES] (1989) *Initial Teacher Training: Approval of courses* (Circular 24/89), London: DES.

Derrida, J. (1972) *Positions*, trans. Bass, A., Chicago: University of Chicago Press.

Derrrida, J. (1973) *Speech and Phenomena and Other Essays on Husserl's Theory of Signs*, trans. Allison, D., Evanston, IL: Northwestern University Press.

Derrida, J. (1974) *Of Grammatology*, trans. Spivak, G., Baltimore: Johns Hopkins University Press.

Derrida, J. (1976) *Of Grammatology*, trans. Spivak, G., Baltimore: Johns Hopkins University Press.

Derrida, J. (1978) *Writing and Difference*, London: Routledge & Kegan Paul.

Derrida, J. (1981) 'Plato's Pharmacy', in Derrida, J., *Dissemination*, trans. Johnson, B., London: Athlone Press.

Derrida, J. (1982) 'Différance', in *Margins of Philosophy*, trans. Bass, A., Chicago: University of Chicago Press.

Derrida, J. (1987) *Positions*, London: Athlone.

Derrida, J. (1988) 'Signature, Event, Context', trans. Weber, S. and Mehlman, J., in *Limited Inc.*, Evanston, IL: Northwestern University Press.

Derrida, J. (1989a {1978}) *Edmund Husserl's Origin of Geometry: An Introduction*, trans. Leavey, J. P., Lincoln: University of Nebraska Press.

Derrida, J. (1989b) *Of Spirit*, Chicago: University of Chicago Press.

Derrida, J. (1991) *Given Time. I. Counterfeit Money*, trans. Kamuf, P., Chicago: Northwestern University Press.

Derrida, J. (1995a) *The Gift of Death*, Chicago: University of Chicago Press.

Derrida, J. (1995b) *Points . . . Interviews, 1974–1994*, Weber, E. (ed.), trans. Kamuf, P. et al., Stanford: Stanford University Press.

Derrida, J., (2000) *Of Hospitality*, Stanford: Stanford University Press.

Derrida, J. (2001) *On Cosmopolitanism and Forgiveness*, London: Routledge.

Derrida, J. (2004) 'Living On', in Bloom, H., Man, P. D., Derrida, J., Hartman, G. and Miller, J. H. (eds) *Deconstruction and Criticism*, London and New York: Continuum.

Derrida, J. and Ferraris, M. (2002) *A Taste for the Secret*, trans. Donis, G., Cambridge: Polity Press.

Directgov (2010), 'Understanding the National Curriculum', www.direct.gov.uk/en/Parents/ Schoolslearninganddevelopment/ExamsTestsAndTheCurriculum/DG_4016665, accessed 1 December 2010.

Donald, J. (1992) *Sentimental Education*, London: Verso.

Donnachie, I. and Hewitt, G. (1999) *Historic New Lanark*, Edinburgh: Edinburgh University Press.

Dooley, M. and Kavanagh, L. (2007) *The Philosophy of Derrida*, Stocksfield, Northumberland: Acumen.

Doré, G. and Jerrold, B. (2006) *London: A Pilgrimage*, London: Anthem Press.

Downy, C. and Kelly, A. (2008) 'Utilising value-added progress data in the context of Every Child Matters', paper presented at the International Congress for School Effectiveness and Improvement, Auckland, New Zealand, 6–8 January.

Dreyfus, H. (1991) *Being-in-the-World*, Cambridge, MA: MIT Press.

Dreyfus, H. L. and Rabinow, P. (1982) *Michel Foucault: Beyond Structuralism and Hermeneutics*, Chicago: University of Chicago Press.

Dreyfus, H. L. and Wrathall, M. A. (2007a) 'Martin Heidegger: An Introduction to His Thought, Work and Life', in Dreyfus, H. L. and Wrathall, M. A. (eds) *A Companion to Heidegger*, Oxford: Blackwell Publishing.

Dreyfus, H. L. and Wrathall, M. A. (2007b) *A Companion to Heidegger*, Oxford: Blackwell Publishing.

Dromi, E. (1987) *Early Lexical Development*, Cambridge: Cambridge University Press.

Doyle, B. (1989) *English and Englishness*, London, Routledge.

Eagleton, T. (2000) *The Idea of Culture*, Oxford: Blackwell.

Easthope, A. (1999) *Englishness and National Culture*, London and New York: Routledge.

Every Child Matters [ECM], www.everychildmatters.gov.uk/aims/.

Education.gov (2011) Department for Education website, www.education.gov.uk/, accessed 10 January 2011.

Edwards, A., Barnes, M., Allan, E., Apostolov, A., Barnes, M., Beirens, H., Benjamin, S., Blackledge, S., Broughton, K., Coad, J., Day-Ashley, L., Evans, R., Fielding, T., Fox, C., Germain, R., Hek, R., Hughes, N., Loveless, L., Mccabe, A., Mccutcheon, M., Morris, K., Mason, P., Peim, N., Popova, A., Plumridge, G., Smith, P., Spicer, N., Warren, S., Wiseman, P. and Yamashita, H. (2006) *Prevention and Early Intervention in the Social Inclusion of Children and Young People: National Evaluation of the Children's Fund*, London: DfES, Research Report RR603.

Edwards, R. and Usher, R. (eds) (2004) *Space, Curriculum and Learning*, Charlotte, NC: Information Age Press.

Engeström, Y. (2003) 'Activity Theory and Individual and Social Transformation', in *Perspectives on Activity Theory*, Engeström, Y., Miettinen, R. and Punamahi, R.-L. (eds), Cambridge: Cambridge University Press, 19–38.

Eraut, M. (1997) 'Perspectives on defining "The Learning Society"', paper presented for the ESRC Learning Society Programme, Brighton: Institute of Education, University of Sussex.

Education and Social Research Council, ESRC (2011) www.esrc.ac.uk/about-esrc/information/research-ethics.aspx.

Europe (2010) European Lifelong Learning: Europe Unit, www.europeunit.ac.uk/eu_policy__education/lifelong_learning.cfm, accessed 27 August 2010.

Fanon, F. (1967) *The Wretched of the Earth*, Harmondsworth: Penguin.

Fielding, M. (2001) *Taking Education Really Seriously: Four Years 'Hard' Labour*, New York: RoutledgeFalmer.

Fielding, M. (2008) 'Beyond Student Voice to Democratic Community: An exploratory paper', presented at 'New Developments in Student Voice: Shaping schools for the future', a conference held at Birkbeck College, University of London, 12 June, www.scribd.com/doc/13414578/Michael-Fielding-Beyond-Student-Voice-to-Democratic-Community-Esmee-Fairbairn-Paper-12-June-08, accessed 28 August 2010.

Fink, B. (1995) *The Lacanian Subject: Between Language and Jouissance*, Princeton: Princeton University Press.

Fink, B. (2002) *Reading Seminar XX: Lacan's Major Work on Love, Knowledge, and Feminine Sexuality*, Barnard, S. (ed.), New York: State University of New York Press.

Fisher Family Trust [FFT] (2010) www.fischertrust.org/downloads/dap/Training/Making_best_useof_FFT_estimates.pdf, accessed 1 December 2010.

Flint, K. J. (2009) 'A Derridean reading of the zone of proximal development: the monster in the play of *différance*', *Educational Review*, 61(2): 211–27.

Flint, K. J. (2010a) 'Being-in-the-world of practice: further exploration of our relationship with technology', in Gibb, P. T. (ed.) *Philosophical Contribution to Work Based Studies*, Springer: notification of contract from the editor – December.

Flint, K. J. (2010b) 'Deconstructing tacit knowledge: exploring the temporal play of being within professional practice', paper presented at The International Conference on Professional Vocational and Workplace Learning held at the University of Middlesex, Cyprus, 24–28 June.

Flint, K. J. (2010c) 'They are Playing with our Futures: A Heideggarian Reading of Late Modern Systems of Education', paper presented at the University of Huddersfield, 25 November.

Flint, K. J. (2011a) 'Deconstructing workplace "know how" and "tacit knowledge": exploring the temporal play of being within professional practice', *Higher Education, Skills and Work-Based Learning*, 1(2): 128–46, Emerald Group Publishing.

Flint, K. J. (2011b) 'Play, Improvement and the School to Come: A Derridean reading of our relationship with the Other', paper presented to *Educational Philosophy and Theory*, September.

Foucault, M. (1970) *The Order of Things: An Archeaology of the Human Sciences*, trans. Sheridan, A. M., New York: Pantheon.

Foucault, M. (1977) *Discipline and Punish: The Birth of a Prison*, trans. Lane, A., London: Penguin Press.

Foucault, M. (1980a) *Power/Knowledge: Selected Interviews and Other Writings 1972–77*, Gordon, C. (ed.), New York: Pantheon Press.

Foucault, M. (1980b) 'The Confession of the Flesh', in *Power/Knowledge Selected Interviews and Other Writings 1972–1977*, Brighton: Harvester, 194–228.

Foucault, M. (1984) 'Truth and Power', in Faubion, J. D., (ed.) *Essential Works of Michel Foucault: Volume Three – Power*, trans. Hurley, R. and others, New York: The New Press, 111–33.

Foucault, M. (1988a) *Politics, Philosophy, Culture*, London: Routledge.

Foucault, M. (1988b) *Technologies of the Self*, Boston: University of Massachusetts Press.

Foucault, M. (1991) 'Governmentality', in Burchell, G., Gordon, C. and Miller, P. (eds) *The Foucault Effect: Studies in Governmentality*, London: Harvester Wheatsheaf, 87–104.

Foucault, M. (1994a) 'Governmentality', in Faubion, J. D. (ed.) *Power: Essential Works of Michel Foucault, 1954–1984, Volume 3*, trans. Hurley, R. and others, New York: New York Press.

Foucault, M. (1994b) 'Truth and Juridical Forms', in Faubion, J. D. (ed.) *Power: Essential Works of Michel Foucault, 1954–1984, Volume 3*, trans. Hurley, R. and others, New York: New York Press.

Foucault, M. (1994c) 'Truth and Power', in Faubion, J. D. (ed.) *Power: Essential Works of Michel Foucault, 1954–1984, Volume 3*, trans. Hurley, R. and others, New York: New York Press.

Foucault, M. (1998) *The History of Sexuality Vol.1: The Will to Knowledge*, London: Penguin.

Foucault, M. (2007) *Security, Territory, Population*, New York: Palgrave.

Foucault, M. (2008) *The Birth of Biopolitics*, London: Palgrave.

Friedman, L. (2010) 'Do Academy Schools Really Work?', *Prospect*, 168, www.prospectmagazine.co.uk/2010/02/in-a-league-of-their-own/, accessed 21 August 2010.

Fullan, M. (1993) *Change Forces*, London: The Falmer Press.

Fullan, M. (1999) *Change Forces: The Sequel*, London: The Falmer Press.

Fullan, M. (2001) *The New Meaning of Educational Change*, New York: Teachers College Press.

Fullan, M. (2003a) *Change Forces with a Vengeance*, London and New York: Routledge, Taylor & Francis Group.

Fullan, M. (2003b) *The Moral Imperative for School Leadership*, Thousand Oaks, CA: Sage Publications.

Fullan, M. (2005) *Leadership and Sustainability*, Thousand Oaks, CA: Sage Publications.

Fullan, M. (2007) *The New Meaning of Educational Change* (4th edn), London and New York: Routledge, Taylor & Francis Group.

Fullan, M. and Hargreaves, A. (1998) *What's Worth Fighting For Out There*, New York: Teachers College Press.

Fullan, M. with Stieglebauer, S. (1991) *The New Meaning of Educational Change*, London: Cassell.

Furlong, J. (2002) 'Ideology and reform in teacher education in England: Some reflections on Cochrain-Smith and Fines', *Educational Researcher*, 31(6): 23–5.

Furlong, J., Barton, L., Miles, S., Whiting, C. and Whitty, G. (2000) *Teacher Education in Transition*, Buckingham and Philadelphia: Open University Press.

Gadamer, H-G. (1984) 'The Hermeneutics of Suspicion', in Shapiro, G. and Sica, A. (eds) *Hermeneutics: Questions and Prospects,* Amhurst: University of Massachusetts Press, 63.

Gadamer, H-G. (1989) *Truth and Method,* London: Continuum.

Gadamer, H-G. (1994) *Heidegger's Ways,* Albany: State University of New York Press.

Gadamer, H-G. (2004) *Truth and Method,* trans. Weinsheimer, J. and Marshall, D. G., London and New York: Continuum.

Gardner, J. W. (1990) *On leadership,* New York: Free Press.

Gibbons, M., Limoges, C., Nowotny, H., Schwarzman, S., Scott, P. and Trow, M. (1994) *The New Production of Knowledge: The dynamics of science and research in contemporary societies,* London: Sage Publications.

Giddens, A. (1976) *New Rules of Sociological Method,* London: Hutchinson, 75.

Giddens, A. (1984) *The Constitution of Society: Outline of the Theory of Structuration,* Cambridge: Polity Press.

Giddens, A. (1990) *The Consequences of Modernity,* Stanford, California: Stanford University Press.

Giddens, A. (1991) *Modernity and Self-Identity: Self and Society in the Late Modern Age,* Cambridge: Polity Press.

Gillborn, D. (1990) '*Race', Ethnicity and Education: Teaching and Learning in Multi-Ethnic Schools,* London: RoutledgeFalmer.

Gillborn, D. (2005a) 'Forget what you think you know about race and education: new approaches to racism in policy and practice', keynote address British Educational Research Association Graduate Student Conference, University of Glamorgan, 14 September.

Gillborn, D. (2005b) 'It takes a nation of millions (and a particular kind of education system) to hold us back', in Richardson, B. (ed.) *Tell It Like It Is: How Our Schools are Failing Black Children,* London: Bookmarks, 88–96.

Gillborn, D. (2008a) *Racism and Education: Coincidence or Conspiracy,* London and New York: Routledge, Taylor & Francis Group.

Gillborn, D. (2008b) 'Coincidence or Conspiracy? Whiteness, policy and persistence of the Black/White achievement gap', *Educational Review,* 60 (3): 229–48.

Gillborn, D. and Mirza, H. (2000) *Educational Inequality: Mapping Race, Class and Gender,* London: OfSTED.

Gillborn, D. with Youdell, D. (2000) *Rationing Education: Policy, Practice, Reform and Equity,* Buckingham, UK: Open University Press.

Gladman, F. J. (1886) *School Work Control and Teaching Organisation and Principles of Education,* London: Jarrold.

GL Assessment (2010) www.glassessment.co.uk/downloads/CAToverview6.pdf, accessed 15 October 2010.

Gorard, S. (2001) *Quantitative Methods in Educational Research: The Role of Numbers Made Easy,* London and New York: Continuum.

Gorard, S. (2006) 'Value-added is of little value', *Journal of Educational Policy,* 21(2): 233–41.

Gorard, S. (2007) 'What does an index of school segregation measure? A commentary on Allen and Vignoles', *Oxford Review of Education,* 33(5): 669–77.

Gorard, S. (2008) 'Research impact is not always a good thing: a re-consideration of rates of "social mobility" in Britain', *British Journal of Sociology of Education*, 29(3): 317–24.

Gorard, G. and Smith, E. (2006) 'Beyond the "Learning Society": What have We Learnt from Widening Participation Research?', *International Journal of Lifelong Education*, 25(6): 575–94.

Gorard, S. Behaviour and Discipline in Schools – Education Committee, www.publications. parliament.uk/pa/cm201011/cmselect/cmeduc/516/516vw06.htm

Gorner, P. (2007) *Heidegger's Being and Time: An Introduction*, Cambridge: Cambridge University Press.

Gould, S. J. (1996) *The Mismeasure of Man*, New York and London: W. W. Norton & Company.

Grace, G. (1990) 'Labour and education: the crises and settlements of education policy', in Holland, M. and Boston, J. (eds) *The Fourth Labour Government*, Auckland: Oxford University Press.

Grace, G. (1995) *School Leadership: Beyond Education Management – An Essay in Policy Scholarship*, London: The Falmer Press.

Grenfell, M. (1996) 'Bourdieu and Initial Teacher Education – A Post-Structuralist Approach', *British Educational Research Journal*, 22(3): 287–303.

Grenfell, M. and James, D. (1998) *Bourdieu and Education: Acts of Practical Theory*, London: Falmer Press.

Griffiths, J. (2003) *NFER the First Fifty Years 1946–1996*, Slough: NFER.

Griffiths, M. (1998) *Educational Research and Social Justice*, Buckingham: Open University Press.

Gutmann, A. (1999) *Democratic Education* (with a new preface and epilogue), Princeton: Princeton University Press.

Halliday, M. A. K. (1979) *Language as Social Semiotic*, London, Edward Arnold.

Halsey, A. H. (ed.) (1961) *Ability and Educational Opportunity*, Paris: Organization for Economic Cooperation and Development.

Halsey, A. H., Heath, A. F. and Ridge, J. M. (1980) *Origins and Destinations*, Oxford: Clarendon.

Hamlyn, D. W. (1967) 'Empiricism', in Edwards, P. (Editor in Chief) *The Encyclopedia of Philosophy, Volume 1*, New York: Macmillan Publishing Co. and The Free Press, 499–505.

Hammer, M. and Champy, J. (1993) *Reengineering the Corporation*, New York: Harper Collins.

Hammersley, M. (2007) 'The Issue of Quality in Qualitative Research', *International Journal of Research and Method in Education*, 30(3): 207–305.

Haraway, D. (2003) 'A Cyborg Manifesto: Science, Technology, and Socialist-Feminism in the Late Twentieth Century', in Scharff, R. C. and Dusek, V. (eds) *The Philosophy of Technology – The Technological Condition: An Anthology*, Oxford: Blackwell Publishing, 429–50.

Hargreaves, A. (1994) *Changing Teachers, Changing Times: Teachers Work and Culture in the Postmodern Age*, London: Cassell.

Hargreaves, A. (1995) 'Development of desire: A postmodern perspective', in Guskin, T. R. and Huberman, M. (eds) *Professional Development in Education: New Paradigms and Practices*, New York: New Teachers Press.

Hargreaves, D. (2000) 'Teaching as a research based profession: possibilities and prospects', Teacher Training Agency Annual Lecture 1996, in Moon, B., Butcher, J. and Bird, E. (2000) *Leading Professional Development in Education*, London: RoutledgeFalmer, 200–10.

Hargreaves, A. (2003) *Teaching in the Knowledge Society: Education in the Age of Insecurity*, Maidenhead, Berkshire: Open University.

Hargreaves, A and Fink, D. (2006) *Sustainable Leadership*, San Francisco: Jossey-Bass.

Hargreaves, A. and Shirley, D. (2009) *The Fourth Way: The Inspiring Future for Educational Change*, Thousand Oakes, CA: Sage Publications.

Hargreaves, D., Hestor, S. and Mellor, F. (1975) *Deviance in Classrooms*, London: Routledge and Kegan Paul.

Harris, A. (2002) 'Distributed leadership in schools: leading or misleading?', paper presented at the Educational Leadership, Management and Administration Society, Birmingham, September.

Harris, A. (2003) 'Teacher leadership as distributed leadership: heresy, fantasy or possibility?', *School Leadership and Management*, 23(3): 313–24.

Harvey, D. (1991) *The Condition of Postmodernity*, Oxford: Basil Blackwell.

Hegel, G. W. F. (1977) *Phenomenology of Spirit*, Oxford: Oxford University Press.

Heidegger, M. (1962) *Being and Time*, trans. Macquarie, J. and Robinson, E., Oxford: Blackwell Publishing.

Heidegger, M. (1968) *What is Called Thinking*, New York: Harper & Row.

Heidegger, M. (1977a) 'The Age of the Word Picture', in *The Question Concerning Technology and Other Essays*, trans. Lovitt, W., New York: Harper & Row, 115–54.

Heidegger, M. (1977b) *The Question Concerning Technology and Other Essays*, trans. Lovitt, W., London: Harper & Row.

Heidegger, M. (1977c) 'The Word of Nietzsche', in *The Question Concerning Technology and Other Essays*, trans. Lovitt, W., New York: Harper & Row, 53–112.

Heidegger, M. (1977d) 'Science and Reflection', in *The Question Concerning Technology and Other Essays*, trans. Lovitt, M., London: Harper & Row.

Heidegger, M. (1977e) 'Science if the Theory of the Real', in *The Question Concerning Technology and Other Essays*, trans. Lovitt, W., New York & London: Harper & Row, 155–82.

Heidegger, M. (1982) 'Valuation and the Will to Power' in Krell, D. F. (ed.) *Nietzsche – Volume IV: Nihilism*, trans. Capuzzi, F. A., New York: Harper & Row.

Heidegger, M. (1991) *The Principle of Reason*, trans. Lilly, R., Bloomington and Indianopolis: Indiana University Press.

Heidegger, M. (1993a) 'The Origin of the Work of Art', in *Martin Heidegger: Basic Writings*, London: Routledge, 139–212.

Heidegger, M. (1993b) 'The Question Concerning Technology', in *Martin Heidegger: Basic Writings*, London: Routledge.

Heidegger, M. (1993c) 'What is metaphysics?', in *Martin Heidegger: Basic Writings*, London: Routledge, 93–110.

Heidegger, M. (1998) *Pathmarks*, McNeill, W. (ed.), Cambridge: Cambridge University Press.

Heidegger, M. (2000) *Introduction to Meta*physics, trans. Fried, G. and Polt, R., New Haven and London: Yale University Press.

Heidegger, M. (2002) *The Essence of Truth: On Plato's Cave Allegory and the Theaetetus*, trans. Sadler, T., London: Continuum.

Hendrick, H. (ed.) (2005) *Child Welfare and Social Policy*, Bristol: Policy Press.

Hirst, P. H. (1975) *Knowledge and the Curriculum*, London: Routledge and Kegan Paul.

Hirst, P. H. and Peters, R. S. (1970) *The Logic of Education*, London: Routledge and Kegan Paul.

Holbroad, M. (2009) 'Ontology, Ethnography, Archaeology', *Cambridge Archaeological Journal*, 19(3): 431–41.

Hopkins, D. (1997) 'Powerful Learning, Powerful Teaching, Powerful Schools', Revised Inaugural Lecture presented at the Jubilee Campus, University of Nottingham, 17 February: 135–58.

Hopkins, D. (2001) *School Improvement for Real*, London and New York: RoutledgeFalmer.

Hopkins, D. (ed.) (2005) *The Practice and Theory of School Improvement: International Handbook of Educational Change*, Dordrecht, Netherlands: Springer.

Hopkins, D., Ainscow, M. and West, M. (1994) *School Improvement in an Era of Change*, London and New York: Cassell.

Hopkins, D. and Reynolds, D. (2001) 'The Past, Present and Future of School Improvement: Towards the Third Age', *British Educational Research Journal*, 27(4): 459–75.

Horn, P. (1989) *The Victorian and Edwardian Schoolchild*, Gloucester: Alan Sutton.

Horn, P. (1994) *Children's Work and Welfare, 1780–1890*, Cambridge: Cambridge University Press.

House Of Commons, Education and Skills Committee [HCESC] (2003) *Secondary Education: Pupil Achievement* (Seventh Report of Session 2002–03), report, together with formal minutes, oral and written evidence, ordered by the House of Commons, HC513, 17 September, www.publications.parliament.uk/pa/cm200203/cmselect/cmeduski/513/513.pdf, accessed 20 August 2010.

Hoyle, E. and Wallace, M. (2005) *Educational Leadership: Ambiguity, Professionals & Managerialism*, London: Sage Publications.

Hughes, J., Jewson, N. and Unwin, L. (2007) *Communities of Practice: Critical Perspectives*, London: Routledge.

Hunt, T. (2004) *Building Jerusalem*, London: Weidenfeld & Nicolson.

Hunter, I. (1988) *Culture and Government*, London: Macmillan.

Hunter, I. (1994) *Rethinking the School*, Sydney: Allen & Unwin.

Inwood, M. (1999) *A Heidegger Dictionary*, Oxford: Blackwell Publishing.

Irigaray, L. (2002) *The Way of Love*, trans. Bostic, H. and Pluhá ek, S., London and New York: Continuum.

Irigaray, L. (2007) *Je, Tu, Nous: Towards a Culture of Difference*, trans. Martin, A., Abingdon, Oxon: Routledge.

Irigaray, L. (ed.) with Green, M. (2008) *Teaching*, London and New York: Continuum.

Institute of Government (2010) 'Big Society Public Services – education, a new relationship between schools and government?', www.instituteforgovernment.org.uk/our-events/53/big-society-public-services-education-a-new-relationship-between-schools-and-government, accessed 10 September 2010.

Jackson, N., Lintonbon, J. and Staples, B. (2010) *Saltaire: The Making of a Model Town*, Reading: Spire Books.

Jones, D. (1990) 'The genealogy of the urban schoolteacher', in Ball, S. (ed.) *Foucault and Education: Disciplines and Knowledge*, London: Routledge.

Jones, D. K. (1977) *The Making of the Education System,*. London: Routledge and Kegan Paul.

Joyce, B., Calhoun, E. and Hopkins, D. (1999) *The New Structure of School Improvement: Inquiring Schools and Achieving Students*, Buckingham and Philadelphia: Open University Press.

Joyce, B., Calhoun, E. and Hopkins, D. (2009) *Models of Learning: Tools for Teaching with a Foreword by Estelle Morris*, Maidenhead and Berkshire: Open University Press.

Juran, T. M. (1979) *Quality Control Handbook*, New York: McGraw Hill.

Kanigel, R. (1997) *The One Best Way: Frederick Winslow Taylor and the Enigma of Efficiency*, New York: Viking.

Kant, I. (2000) *The Critique of the Power of Judgment*, Cambridge: Cambridge University Press.

Kay-Shuttleworth, J. (1862) *Four Periods of Public Education*, London: Longman.

Kay-Shuttleworth, J. (2007) '*Public Education as reviewed in 1832–1839–1846 and 1862*', London: Spottiswood & Co., archives digitized by Microsoft from the University of California Libraries.

Keddie, N. (1973) '*Classroom knowledge*' in Young (ed.) *Tinker, Tailor - The Myth of Cultural Deprivation*, Harmondsworth: Penguin.

Kirkham C., Harris S., and Grzybowski S. (2005) 'Evidence-based prenatal care: part 1. General prenatal care and counseling issues', *American Family Physician*, 71: 1307–16, 1321–2, www.scribd.com/doc/42835755/Evidence-Based-Prenatal-Care-Part-I, accessed 23 August 2010.

Koehn, M. (2002) 'Childbirth Education Outcomes: An Integrative Review of the Literature', *Journal of Perinatal Education*, 11(3): 10–19.

Labov, W. (1972) *Language in the Inner City: Studies in the Black English Vernacular*, Philadelphia: University of Pennsylvania Press.

Lacan, J. (1968) *Speech and Language in Psychoanalysis,*. Baltimore: Johns Hopkins University Press.

Lacan, J. (2006a). *Ecrits*. New York: Norton.

Lacan, B. (2006b) 'The Subversion in the Subject and the Dialectic of Desire in the Freudian Unconscious', in Lacan, B. *Écrits*, trans. Fink, B. in collaboration with Fink, H. and Grigg, R., New York and London: W. W. Norton & Company.

Lane, H. (1979) *The Wild Boy of Aveyron*, St Albans: Paladin.

Learning and Skills Improvement Service [LSIS] (2009) *A New Improvement Strategy for the Learning and Skills Sector*, London: LSIS, LSIS153, www.lsis.org.uk/Documents/Publications/NewNIS.pdf, accessed 20 January 2011.

Lefevre, H. (1991) *The Production of Space*, Oxford: Blackwell.

Leithwood, K., Mascall, B. and Strauss, T. (2008) *Distributed Leadership According to the Evidence*, New York: Routledge.

Lifelong Learning, UK [LLUK] (2010) 'A Sector Skills Agreement for the Lifelong Learning Sector, Stage 1: Skills Needs Assessment – England', www.lluk.org/documents/070430_lluk_ssa_stage1_england_report.pdf, accessed 21 August 2010.

Locke, J. (1996) *Some Thoughts Concerning Education & Of the Conduct of the Understanding*, Indianapolis: Hackett.

Locke, J. (1999) *An Essay Concerning Human Understanding*, Pennsylvania: The Pennsylvania State University, available at: http://experiment.iitalia.com/librarysplit2/John%20Locke%20-%20An%20Essay%20Concerning%20Human%20Understanding.pdf, accessed on 1 September 2011.

Louis, K. S. and Miles, M. B. (1990) *Improving the Urban High School: What Works and Why*, New York: Teachers College Press.

Lowe, R. and Seaborne, M. (1977) *The English School: Its Architecture and Organization*, vol. 2, London: Routledge and Kegan Paul.

Lyotard, J-F. (1984) *The Postmodern Condition: A Report on Knowledge*, trans. Bennington, G. and Massumi, B., foreword by Jameson, F., King's Lynn, Norfolk: Biddles.

Lyotard, J-F. (1986) *The Postmodern Condition*, Manchester: Manchester University Press.

Lyotard, J-F. (1991) *The Inhuman: Reflections on Time*, Cambridge: Polity Press.

MacIntyre, A. (1984) *After Virtue: A Study in Moral Theory* (2nd edn), Notre Dame: University of Notre Dame Press.

MacIntyre, A. (2007) *After Virtue: A Study in Moral Theory* (3rd edn), Notre Dame: University of Notre Dame Press.

Maclure, M. (2003) *Discourse in Educational and Social Research*, Buckingham and Philadelphia: Open University Press.

Maclure, M. (2006a) 'The bone in the throat: some uncertain thoughts on baroque method', *International Journal of Qualitative Studies in Education*, 19(6): 729–45.

Maclure, M. (2006b) 'A Demented Form of the Familiar': Postmodernism and Educational Research, *Journal of Philosophy of Education*, 40(2): 223–39.

Mann, J. F. (1979) *Education*, London: Pitman.

Mann, R. D. (1959) 'A review of the relationship between personality and performance in small groups', *Psychological Bulletin* 66(4): 241–70.

Market (2010) www.marketdataenterprises.com, accessed 25 August 2010.

Mayhew, H. (1861) *London Labour and the London Poor*, London: Griffin, Bohn and Company.

Mccann, P. (1996) 'James Kay-Shuttleworth: Journey of an Outsider', *Historical Studies in Education*, 1: 122–125, Spring.

Miller, J. H. (2004) 'The Critic as Host', in Bloom, H., Man, P. D., Derrida, J., Hartman, G. and Miller, J. H. (eds) *Deconstruction and Criticism*, London and New York: Continuum.

Mintzberg, H. (2004) *Managers not MBAs*, San Francisco: Berret-Koehler.

Montessori, M. (1972) *The Secret of Childhood*, New York: Ballantine.

Montessori, M. (1988) *Montessori Method*, London: Random House Publishers.

Moon, J. (1999) *Reflection in Learning and Professional Development: Theory and Practice*, London: Kogan Page.

Muijs, D. and Reynolds, D. (2005) *Effective Teaching: Evidence and Practice* (2nd edn), London: Sage Publications.

Nancy, J-L. (1983) *La Communauté Désoeuvrée*, Paris: Christian Bourgois.

National Strategies [NatStrat] (2010) http://nationalstrategies.standards.dcsf.gov.uk/, accessed 1 December.

National Foundation for Education Research, NFER (2010) www.nfer.ac.uk/nfer/about-nfer/.

Nowotny, H., Scott, P. and Gibbons, M. (2001) *Re-Thinking Science: Knowledge and the Public in an Age of Uncertainty*, Cambridge: Polity.

Number 10 (2010) www.number10.gov.uk/wp-content/uploads/dfe-srps.pdf, accessed 20 August 2010.

O'Donoghue, T. and Whitehead, C. (2008) *Teacher Education in the English Speaking World: Past, Present and Future*, Charlotte, NC: Information Age Publishing, Inc.

O'Donoghue, T. and Whitehead, C. (eds) (2008) *Teacher Education in the English Speaking World: Past, Present, and Future*, Charlotte, NC: Information Age Publishing.

Office for Standards in Education [OfSTED] (2010a) www.ofsted.gov.uk/, accessed 19 August 2010.

Office for Standards in Education [OfSTED] (2010b) www.ofsted.gov.uk/Ofsted-home/Forms-and-guidance/Browse-all-by/Education-and-skills/Schools, accessed 20 August 2010.

Office for Standards in Education, RAISEonline [OfSTEDRo-l] (2010c) www.ofsted.gov.uk/schools/dataandinformationsystems.cfm, accessed 1 December 2010.

Office for Standards in Education [OfSTED] (2010d) www.ofsted.gov.uk/, accessed 12 August 2010.

Owen, R. (1824) *An Outline of the System of Education at New Lanark*, Glasgow: Glasgow University Press.

Oxford English Dictionary [OED] (2011) www.oed.com/, accessed 2 September 2011.

Parkhurst, H. (1922) *Education On The Dalton Plan*, New York: E. P. Dutton & Company.

Peim, N. (1993) *Critical Theory and the English Teacher*, London: Routledge.

Peim, N. (2001) 'The History of the Present: Towards a Contemporary Phenomenology of the School', *History of Education*, 30: 2, 177–90.

Peim, N. (2003) Changing English? Rethinking the Politics of English Teaching (Sheffield: NATE).

Peim, N. A. and Flint, K. J. (2009) 'Testing Times: Questions concerning assessment for school improvement', *Educational Philosophy and Theory*, 41(3): 342–61.

Peters, T. and Waterman Jr, R. H. (2004) *In Search of Excellence: Lessons from America's Best Run Companies*, London: Profile Books (first published in 1982).

Pierides, D. (2006) 'Teacher education and its policies in Australia: Making space for a new Urban Education project', *Pennsylvania Graduate School of Education, GSE, Perspectives on Urban Education*, 4(1): 1–8.

Pring, R. (2000a) 'Editorial Conclusion: a philosophical perspective', *Oxford Review of Education,* Vol. 26, Nos. 3&4, 2000.

Pring, R. (2000) 'The False Dualisms of Educational Research', *Journal of Philosophy of Education,* 34: 2, 247–60.

Qualifications and Curriculum Development Agency, QCDA (2010) www.qcda.gov.uk/, accessed 12 August 2010.

Radford, A, (1990) *Syntactic Theory and the Acquisition of English Syntax,* Oxford: Blackwell, 240–1.

Ray, A. (2006) *School Value-Added Measures in England: A Paper for the OECD Project on the Development of Value-Added Models in Education Systems,* London: Department for Education and Skills.

Reeve, F., Cartwright, M. and Edwards, R. (eds) (2002) *Supporting Lifelong Learning: Volume 2 – Organising Learning,* London and New York: RoutledgeFalmer.

Reiff, P. (1975) *To My Fellow Teachers,* New York: Delta Books.

'Report of the Commission of Inquiry into the Employment of Women and Children in Agriculture' (2010 {1867}): 1867–8.

'Reports from Commissioners Inquiring into Children's Employment' (2010): 1842–3.

Ricouer, P. (1977) *Freud and Philosophy,* New Haven: Yale University Press.

Rist, R. (1970) 'Student social class and teacher expectations: The self-fulfilling prophecy in ghetto education'. *Harvard Educational Review* 40.

Rose, N. (1990) *Governing the Soul: Technologies of Human Subjectivity,* London: Routledge.

Rose, N. (1999) *Powers of Freedom. Reframing Political Thought,* Cambridge: Cambridge University Press.

Rosenthal, R. and Jacobson, L. (1968) *Pygmalion in the Classroom,* New York: Holt, Rinehart and Winston.

Rouse, J. (2005), 'Heidegger's philosophy of science' in Dreyfus, H. L. and Wrathall, M. A. (eds), *A Companion to Heidegger,* Blackwell Oxford: Blackwell Publishing: 173–90.

Russell, B. (1998) *The Impact of Science on Society,* London: Routledge.

Said, E. (1978) *Orientalism,* Harmondsworth: Penguin.

Schön, D. A. (1983) *The Reflective Practitioner: How Professionals Think in Action,* New York: Basic Books.

Schön, D. A. (1990) *Educating the Reflective Practitioner: Toward a New Design for Teaching and Learning in the Professions,* San Francisco: Jossey-Bass.

School System (2010) www.number10.gov.uk/wp-content/uploads/dfe-srps.pdf, accessed 20 August 2010.

Scott, D. and Usher, R. (1996) *Understanding Educational Research,* London: Routledge.

Senge, P. (1990) *The Fifth Discipline,* New York: Doubleday.

Senge, P., Cambron-McCabe, N., Lucas, T., Smith, B., Dutton, J. and Kleiner, A. (2000) *Schools that Learn,* New York: Doubleday.

Sillar, B. (1994) 'Playing with God: Cultural Perceptions of Children, Play and Miniatures in the Andes', *Archaeological Review from Cambridge* 13(2): 47–63.

Silver, H. (1973) *Equal Opportunity in Education: A Reader in Social Class and Educational Opportunity,* London: Methuen.

Smitherman, G. (2000) *Talkin' That Talk: Language, Culture and Education in African America*, London: Routledge.

Snook, I. (1999) 'Teacher Education: Preparation for a Learned Profession?', paper presented at Conference AARE/NZARE, Melbourne, 29 November–2 December, www.aare.edu.au/99pap/sno99148.htm, accessed 10 August 2010.

Spillane, J. P. (2006) *Distributed Leadership*, San Francisco: Jossey-Bass.

Spivak, G. (1990) *The Post-Colonial Critic*, London: Routledge.

Steedman, C. (1995) *Strange Dislocations: Childhood and the Idea of Human Interiority 1780–1930*, London: Virago.

Stern, C. and Stern, W. (1928) *Die Kindersprache: eine psychologische und sprachtheoretische Unteruchung*, Leipzig: Barth.

Stogdill, R. M. (1948) 'Personal factors associated with leadership: a survey of the literature', *Journal of Psychology*, 25: 35–71.

Stow, D. (1850) *The Training System, the Moral Training School, and the Normal Seminary*. London: Longman Brown Green.

St Peters High (2010) www.st-petershigh-Stoke.Sch.uk/

Stronach, I. (2000) 'The tyranny of transparency', *British Educational Research Journal*, 26(3): 309–21.

Stronach, I. (2006) 'On promoting rigour in educational research: the example of the RAE', *Journal of Educational Policy*, 22(3): 343–52.

Sultana, R. G. (2005) 'The Initial Education of High School Teachers: A critical review of major issues and trends', *Studying Teacher Education*, 1(2): 225–43.

Sure Start, www.surestart.gov.uk/surestartservices/settings/introduction, accessed in 2008.

Taylor, C. (1989) *Sources of the Self. The Making of Modern Identity*, Cambrdige: Cambridge University Press.

Teacher Development Agency, TDA (2010a) www.tda.gov.uk, accessed 10 November 2010.

Teacher Development Agency, TDA (2010b) 'Professional Standards for Teachers', www.tda.gov.uk/teacher/developing-career/professional-standards-guidance/professional-standards.aspx?_cs=1745074864&keywords=qualified+teacher+status, accessed 10 August 2010.

Teachernet (2010) www.teachernet.gov.uk/management/atoz/l/lifelonglearning/, accessed 29 August 2010.

Tennant, M. (1997) *Psychology and Adult Learning* (2nd edn), London: Routledge.

Thomas, G. (2007) *Education and Theory*, Maidenhead: Open University Press.

Thompson, F. M. L. (1990) *The Cambridge Social History of Britain 1750–1950*, Cambridge: Cambridge University Press.

Thomson, I. (2000) 'Ontotheology? Understanding Heidegger's *Destruktion* of Metaphysics', *International Journal of Philosophical Studies*, 8(3): 297–327.

Thomson, I. (2005) *Heidegger on Ontotheology: Technology and the Politics of Education*, Cambridge: Cambridge University Press.

Trifonas, P. P. (2001) *Umberto Eco and Football – Postmodern Encounters*, Grange Road, Duxford, Cambridge: Icon Books Ltd.

University of South Australia, UniSA (2011) www.unisa.edu.au/resdegrees/programs/profdoct.asp, accessed June 2011.

Villegas-Reimers, E. (2003) *Teacher Professional Development: An International Review of the Literature*, Paris: UNESCO, International Institute for Educational Planning.

Viswanathan, G. (1989) *Masks of Conquest: Literary Study and British Rule in India*, New York: Columbia University Press.

Walden University (2011) 'Walden University PhD in Special Education': opening web page, available at: http://www.universities.com/Distance_Learning/Walden_University_PhD_in_Education_Special_Education.html, accessed January 2011.

Walvin, J. (1982) *A Child's World. A Social History of English Childhood, 1800–1914*, London: Heinemann.

Watts, J. (ed.) (1977) *The Countesthorpe Experience: The First Five Years*, London: George Allen & Unwin.

Weber, M. (1947) *The Theory of Social and Economic Organisation*, trans. Henderson, A. M. and Parsons, T., Glencoe: The Free Press.

Weber, M. (1958) *The Protestant Ethic and the Spirit of Capitalism,*. New York: Charles Scribner's Sons.

Wenger, E. (1998) *Communities of Practice: Learning, Meaning and Identity*, Cambridge: Cambridge University Press.

West, M., Ainscow, M. and Hopkins, D. (1997) 'Tracking the Moving School: challenging assumptions, increasing understanding of how school improvement is brought about', paper presented at *The European Education Research Association Annual Conference*, Frankfurt.

West, M., Jackson, D., Harris, A. and Hopkins, D. (2002) 'Learning through leadership, leadership through learning' in Riley, K. A. and Louis, K. S. (eds), *Leadership for Change and School Reform: International Perspectives*, London: RoutledgeFalmer.

Whelan, F. (2009) *Lessons Learned: How Good Policies Produce Better Schools*, London: Fenton Whelan.

Williams, R. (1983) *Keywords*, London: Fontana.

Willis, P. (1979) *Learning to Labour*, Aldershot: Gator.

Wittgenstein, L. (1953/2001) *Philosophical Investigations*, Oxford: Blackwell Publishing.

Wittgenstein, L. (1970) *Lectures and Conversations on Aesthetics, Psychology and Religious Belief*, Oxford: Blackwell.

Wittgenstein, L. (1994) *Tractatus Logico-Philosophicus*, London: Routledge.

Woods, P. A., Bagley, C. and Glatter, R. (1998) *School Choice and Competition: Markets in the Public Interest?*, London: Routledge.

Wordsworth, W. (1996) *The Prelude*, Harmondsworth: Penguin.

Wordsworth, W. (2000) *The Major Works*, Gill, S. (ed.), Oxford: Oxford University Press.

Wordsworth, W. and Coleridge, S. T. (1798) *Lyrical Ballads*, London: J. & A. Arch.

Wright, P. (1996) *Managerial Leadership*, London: Routledge.

Yeats, W. B. (2000) *The Collected Poems*, London: Wordsworth Editions.

Young, M. (1971) *Knowledge and Control*, London: Collier-Macmillan.

Zahavi, D. (2001) *Husserl and Transcendental Intersubjectivity*, Athens: Ohio University Press.

Zeichner, K. (2008) 'The United States', in O'Donoghue, T. and Whitehead, C. (eds) *Teacher Education in the English Speaking World: Past, Present, and Future*, Charlotte, NC: Information Age Publishing.

Index